Teachin

Publishe
Director

Teaching
the Engl
new and
are refor
and the
ities of
experien

Titles in

Gail Ash
TEACHI

Charles
TEACHI

Robert
TEACHI

Michael
TEACHI
Approa

David H
TEACHI

Andrew
TEACHI

Anna P
TEACH

Forthco

Gina W
TEACH

Teachin
Series Standing Order ISBN 978–1–4039–4441–2 Hardback
978–1–4039–4442–9 Paperback
(*outside North America only*)

You can receive future titles in this series as they are published by placing a standing order. Please contact your bookseller or, in case of difficulty, write to us at the address below with your name and address, the title of the series and the ISBN quoted above.

Customer Services Department, Macmillan Distribution Ltd, Houndmills, Basingstoke, Hampshire RG21 6XS, England

---

Also by David Higgins

FRANKENSTEIN: Character Studies

ROMANTIC GENIUS AND THE LITERARY MAGAZINE

STUDYING ENGLISH LITERATURE *(co-edited with Ashley Chantler)*

Also by Sharon Ruston

LITERATURE AND SCIENCE *(editor)*

ROMANTICISM

SHELLEY AND VITALITY

THE INFLUENCE AND ANXIETY OF THE BRITISH ROMANTICS: Spectres of Romanticism *(editor)*

Teaching Romanticism

Edited by

David Higgins
Lecturer in English Literature, University of Leeds

and

Sharon Ruston
Professor in Nineteenth-Century Literature and Culture, University of Salford

palgrave
macmillan

First published 2010 by
PALGRAVE MACMILLAN

Palgrave Macmillan in the UK is an imprint of Macmillan Publishers Limited, registered in England, company number 785998, of Houndmills, Basingstoke, Hampshire RG21 6XS.

Palgrave Macmillan in the US is a division of St Martin's Press LLC, 175 Fifth Avenue, New York, NY 10010.

Palgrave Macmillan is the global academic imprint of the above companies and has companies and representatives throughout the world.

Palgrave® and Macmillan® are registered trademarks in the United States, the United Kingdom, Europe and other countries.

ISBN-13: 978–0–230–22484–1 hardback
ISBN-13: 978–0–230–22485–8 paperback

This book is printed on paper suitable for recycling and made from fully managed and sustained forest sources. Logging, pulping and manufacturing processes are expected to conform to the environmental regulations of the country of origin.

A catalogue record for this book is available from the British Library.

A catalog record for this book is available from the Library of Congress.

10 9 8 7 6 5 4 3 2 1
19 18 17 16 15 14 13 12 11 10

Printed and bound in Great Britain by
CPI Antony Rowe, Chippenham and Eastbourne

Contents

List of Figures and Tables

Figures

Tables

Acknowledgements

The editors are very grateful to Ben Knights for his support with this project, to Gavin Edwards for excellent advice on the book at proposal stage, and to Paula Kennedy of Palgrave Macmillan for commissioning the book. David Higgins would like to thank friends and colleagues at the Universities of Chester and Leeds, especially Derek Alsop and Ashley Chantler, for their support and advice. Sharon Ruston would like to thank all colleagues, past and present, in the English programme at Keele University, but particularly Anna Barton, with whom she redesigned the Romanticisms module and who has helped make teaching it so much fun.

Series Preface

One of many exciting achievements of the early years of the English Subject Centre was the agreement with Palgrave Macmillan to initiate the series "Teaching the New English." The intention of the then Director, Professor Philip Martin, was to create a series of short and accessible books which would take widely-taught curriculum fields (or, as in the case of learning technologies, approaches to the whole curriculum) and articulate the connections between scholarly knowledge and the demands of teaching.

Since its inception, "English" has been committed to what we know by the portmanteau phrase "learning and teaching." Yet, by and large, university teachers of English – in Britain at all events – find it hard to make their tacit pedagogic knowledge conscious, or to raise it to a level where it might be critiqued, shared, or developed. In the experience of the English Subject Centre, colleagues find it relatively easy to talk about curriculum and resources, but far harder to talk about the success or failure of seminars, how to vary forms of assessment, or to make imaginative use of Virtual Learning Environments. Too often this reticence means falling back on received assumptions about student learning, about teaching, or about forms of assessment. At the same time, colleagues are often suspicious of the insights and methods arising from generic educational research. The challenge for the English group of disciplines is therefore to articulate ways in which our own subject knowledge and ways of talking might themselves refresh debates about pedagogy. The implicit invitation of this series is to take fields of knowledge and survey them through a pedagogic lens. Research and scholarship, and teaching and learning are part of the same process, not two separate domains.

"Teachers," people used to say, "are born not made." There may, after all, be some tenuous truth in this: there may be generosities of spirit (or, alternatively, drives for didactic control) laid down in earliest childhood. But why should we assume that even "born" teachers (or novelists, or nurses, or veterinary surgeons) do not need to learn the skills of their trade? Amateurishness about teaching has far more to do with university claims to status, than with evidence about how people learn. There is a craft to shaping and promoting learning. This series of books is dedicated to the development of the craft of teaching within English Studies.

Ben Knights
Teaching the New English *Series Editor*
Director, English Subject Centre
Higher Education Academy

The English Subject Centre

Founded in 2000, the English Subject Centre (which is based at Royal Holloway, University of London) is part of the subject network of the Higher Education Academy. Its purpose is to develop learning and teaching across the English disciplines in UK Higher Education. To this end it engages in research and publication (web and print), hosts events and conferences, sponsors projects, and engages in day-to-day dialogue with its subject communities.

http://www.english.heacademy.ac.uk

Notes on the Contributors

Stephen C. Behrendt is George Holmes Distinguished University Professor of English at the University of Nebraska, where he teaches widely in eighteenth- and nineteenth-century British literature, art and culture, and most particularly in Romanticism. His most recent book is *British Women Poets and the Romantic Writing Community* (2009). In addition to publishing on pedagogy and media, he is also a poet whose most recent collection of poems is *History* (2005).

Sally Bushell is Senior Lecturer and Co-Director of The Wordsworth Centre in the Department of English and Creative Writing, Lancaster University. She is co-editor of the Cornell edition of *The Excursion* (2007) and author of *Re-reading The Excursion* (2002) and *Text as Process: Creative Composition in Wordsworth, Tennyson and Dickinson* (2009).

Brycchan Carey is Reader in English Literature at Kingston University, London. He is the author of *British Abolitionism and the Rhetoric of Sensibility: Writing, Sentiment, and Slavery, 1760–1807* (2005) and editor (with Peter Kitson) of *Slavery and the Cultures of Abolition: Essays Marking the British Abolition Act of 1807* (2007) and (with Markman Ellis and Sara Salih) of *Discourses of Slavery and Abolition: Britain and its Colonies, 1760–1838* (2004). He is currently completing a book on the origins and development of Quaker antislavery rhetoric in the seventeenth and eighteenth centuries.

Sue Chaplin is Senior Lecturer in English at Leeds Metropolitan University where she teaches Romanticism, eighteenth-century literature and Gothic fiction. She is the author of *Speaking of Dread: Law, Sensibility and the Sublime in Eighteenth-Century Women's Fiction* (2004), *The Gothic and the Rule of Law* (2007) and a number of articles in the fields of Romanticism, Gothic Studies and critical legal theory. She is co-editor of the Romanticism division of the online journal *Literature Compass* and Executive Officer of the International Gothic Association.

Steve Clark is currently Visiting Professor at the Graduate School of Humanities and Sociology, University of Tokyo, and co-editor (with Masashi Suzuki), of *The Reception of Blake in the Orient* (2006). His most recent publication is *Liberating Medicine 1720–1835* (co-edited with Tristanne Connolly, 2009).

Thomas C. Crochunis is Assistant Professor of English specializing in secondary English education and drama at Shippensburg University in Pennsylvania. He has published work in *Romanticism on the Net, Gothic Studies, European Romantic Review, Victorian Studies,* and various edited volumes. He is co-editor (with Michael Eberle-Sinatra) of the *British Women Playwrights around 1800* web project and the forthcoming *Broadview Anthology of British Women Playwrights, 1777–1843,* and has helped to organize a number of the Romantic-era drama and theatre history pre-conference workshops that have been held in conjunction with the North American Society for the Study of Romanticism annual conference.

John Goodridge is Professor of English at Nottingham Trent University. He is the author of *Rural Life in Eighteenth Century English Poetry* (1994) and a forthcoming study of John Clare's poetry. His many editing projects include a selection of Bloomfield, Dyer's *Fleece,* John Philips's *Cyder,* two volumes of essays on Clare and (as general editor and volume editor for 1860–1900) the six-volume Pickering and Chatto labouring-class poets project. He is a Fellow of the English Association and a Vice-President of the John Clare Society.

David Higgins is Lecturer in English Literature at the University of Leeds. He is the author of *Romantic Genius and the Literary Magazine* (2005) and *Frankenstein: Character Studies* (2008), and editor (with Ashley Chantler) of *Studying English Literature* (2009). His current research focuses on Romantic autobiography and national identity.

Harriet Kramer Linkin is a Professor of English Literature at New Mexico State University. She has published widely on Romantic-era writers and is the editor of the first scholarly edition of *The Collected Poems and Journals of Mary Tighe* (2005) as well as co-editor (with Stephen C. Behrendt) of two collections on Romantic women poets: *Romanticism and Women Poets: Opening the Doors of Reception* (1999) and *Approaches to Teaching Women Poets of the British Romantic Period* (1997).

Murray Pittock is Bradley Professor of English Literature at the University of Glasgow, and formerly held chairs at the universities of Manchester and Strathclyde. Among his recent books are research editions of James Hogg's *Jacobite Relics* (2002–3, two volumes) and monographs on *James Boswell* (2007) and *Scottish and Irish Romanticism* (2008).

Sharon Ruston is Professor of Nineteenth-Century Literature and Culture at the University of Salford. She has published *Shelley and Vitality* (2005) and *Romanticism* (2007), edited "Literature and Science", the 2008 volume of *Essays and Studies*, and written a number of journal articles on Romantic-period literature and science. She is currently Vice-President of the British Association for Romantic Studies.

Masashi Suzuki is Professor of English at Kyoto University and Ex-president of the Japan Association of English Romanticism. His publications include *Visionary Poetics: a Study of William Blake* (1994), and *The Reception of Blake in the Orient* (co-edited with Steve Clark, 2006).

Sophie Thomas is Associate Professor of English at Ryerson University in Toronto. She has published on a wide range of Romantic topics, including her recent book *Romanticism and Visuality: Fragments, History, Spectacle* (2008), and is currently working on a project involving ruins, fragmentary objects and collections in the Romantic period.

Sarah Wootton is Senior Lecturer in English Studies at Durham University. She is the author of *Consuming Keats: Nineteenth-Century Representations in Art and Literature* (2006) and co-editor (with Mark Sandy) of a special issue of *Romanticism and Victorianism on the Net* (no. 51, 2008). Her second book, entitled *The Rise of the Byronic Hero in Fiction and on Film*, is under contract with Palgrave Macmillan. She is also a co-director and founder of the Romantic Dialogues and Legacies Research Group at Durham University.

Chronology

1770 Hogg born; William Wordsworth born; Chatterton dies; Goldsmith, *The Deserted Village*

1771 Scott born; Dorothy Wordsworth born; Beattie, *The Minstrel*; Mackenzie, *The Man of Feeling*

1772 Coleridge born; Tighe born; Jones, *Poems, Chiefly Translations from Asiatick Languages*

1773 Barbauld (née Aiken), *Poems*; Wheatley, *Poems on Various Subjects*

1774 Southey born; Goethe, *Die Lieden des jungen Werthers*

1775 American War of Independence begins; Austen born; Lamb born

1776 American Declaration of Independence; Smith, *Wealth of Nations*

1777 Owenson (Lady Morgan) born; Chatterton, *Poems*; Sheridan's *School for Scandal* first performed

1778 France enters alliance with America; Hazlitt born; Rousseau dies; Voltaire dies; Burney, *Evelina*

1779 Moore born; Cowper and Newton, *Olney Hymns*

1780 Gordon Riots

1781 Rousseau, *Confessions*; Schiller, *Die Räuber*

1782 Cowper, *Poems*; Rousseau, *Les rèveries du promeneur solitaire*

1783 Treaty of Paris ends American War of Independence; Pitt the Younger becomes PM; Blake, *Poetical Sketches*

1784 Leigh Hunt born; Johnson dies; Smith, *Elegiac Sonnets*

1785 Peacock born; De Quincey born; Cowper, *The Task*; Yearsley, *Poems, on Several Occasions*

1786 Beckford, *Vathek*; Burns, *Poems*; Clarkson, *An Essay on the Slavery and Commerce of the Human Species*

1787 Impeachment of Warren Hastings; Committee for the Abolition of the Slave-Trade formed

1788 Byron born; More, *Slavery: a Poem*; Yearsley, *Poem on the Inhumanity of the Slave Trade*

1789 Storming of the Bastille; Declaration of the Rights of Man; Blake, *Songs of Innocence*; Equiano, *The Interesting Narrative*

1790 Baillie, *Poems*; Blake, *The Marriage of Heaven and Hell*; Burke, *Reflections on the Revolution in France*; Kant, *Critique of Judgement*; Radcliffe, *A Sicilian Romance*; Wollstonecraft, *Vindication of the Rights of Men*; Williams, *Letters Written in France*

1791 Birmingham riots in which Joseph Priestley's house and laboratory are destroyed; Louis XVI's flight to Varennes; slave rebellion in Saint-Domingue (Haiti); Erasmus Darwin, *The Botanic Garden*; Inchbald, *A Simple Story*; More, *Cheap Repository Tracts*; Paine, *Rights of Man*; Robinson, *Poems*

1792 Abolition of French monarchy; "September Massacres" in Paris; London Corresponding Society established; P. B. Shelley born; Gilpin, *Essays on Picturesque Beauty*; Wollstonecraft, *Vindication of the Rights of Woman*

1793 Louis XVI executed in France; war between France and Britain; The Terror; Clare born; Hemans (née Browne) born; Blake, *Vision of the Daughters of Albion*; Godwin, *Enquiry into Political Justice*; Smith, *The Old Manor House*

1794 Habeas Corpus suspended; Treason Trials; Robespierre executed; Blake, *Europe, Songs of Innocence and of Experience*, and *Urizen*; Godwin, *Caleb Williams*; Radcliffe, *Mysteries of Udolpho*

1795 Seditious Meetings Act and the Treasonable Practices Act passed; Keats born; Edgeworth, *Letters for Literary Ladies*; Lewis, *The Monk*

1796 French invasion threat; Edward Jenner gives first smallpox vaccination; Burns dies; Bage, *Hermsprong*; Samuel Taylor Coleridge, *Poems on Various Subjects*; Robinson, *Sappho and Phaon*; Seward, *Llangollen Vale, with Other Poems*; Wollstonecraft, *A Short Residence*

1797 Naval mutinies at Spithead and Nore are suppressed; Burke dies; Wollstonecraft dies; Mary Shelley (née Godwin) born; *The Anti-Jacobin Review*; Radcliffe, *The Italian*

1798 Irish rebellion; Battle of the Nile; Baillie, *Plays on the Passions*; Coleridge, *Fears in Solitude*; Inchbald, *Lover's Vows*; Malthus, *Essay on the Principle of Population*; Wordsworth and Coleridge, *Lyrical Ballads*

1799 Napoleon becomes First Consul; Wordsworth completes two-part *Prelude*; Park, *Travels*; Seward, *Original Sonnets*

1800 Act of Union with Ireland; Volta invents the electrical battery; Cowper dies; Robinson dies; Bloomfield, *Farmer's Boy*; Edgeworth, *Castle Rackrent*; Robinson, *Lyrical Tales*

1801 George III refuses to pass bill allowing Catholic emancipation and Pitt resigns; Toussaint L'Ouverture liberates black slaves in Saint-Domingue (Haiti); Chateaubriand, *Atala*; Hogg, *Scottish Pastorals*; Robinson, *Memoirs*; Southey, *Thalaba*

1802 Peace of Amiens; Landon born; *Edinburgh Review*; *Weekly Political Register*; Bloomfield, *Rural Tales*; Chateaubriand, *René*

1803 War with France resumes; execution of Emmet after failed Irish rebellion; Erasmus Darwin, *The Temple of Nature*

1804 Pitt forms coalition government; Napoleon becomes Emperor; Blake, *Milton*

1805 Battles of Austerlitz, Trafalgar, and Ulm; Godwin, *Fleetwood*; Hazlitt, *Essay on the Principles of Human Action*; Scott, *The Lay of the Last Minstrel*

1806 Grenville becomes Prime Minister; Smith dies; Yearsley dies; Barrett-Browning (née Barrett) born; J. S. Mill born; Owenson (Lady Morgan), *The Wild Irish Girl*; Robinson, *Poetical Works*

1807 Slave trade abolished; Grenville resigns over Catholic emancipation and Portland becomes PM; De Staël, *Corinne*; Charles and Mary Lamb, *Tales from Shakespeare*; Smith, *Beachy Head and Other Poems*; Wordsworth, *Poems, in Two Volumes*

1808 Peninsular War and Convention of Cintra; *The Examiner*; Goethe, *Faust*; Hemans, *England and Spain*; Scott, *Marmion*

1809 Portland resigns and Perceval becomes PM; Paine dies; Seward dies; Tennyson born; Charles Darwin born; *Quarterly Review*; Byron, *English Bards and Scotch Reviewers*; Coleridge, *The Friend*

1810 Tighe dies; Scott, *The Lady of the Lake*; Seward, *Poetical Works*; Southey, *Curse of Kehama*

1811 Prince of Wales becomes Regent; Luddite disturbances; Austen, *Sense and Sensibility*; Hunt, *The Feast of the Poets*; Owenson (Lady Morgan), *The Missionary*

1812 Perceval assassinated; Liverpool becomes PM; Napoleon invades Russia; Browning born; Dickens born; Barbauld, *Eighteen Hundred and Eleven*; Byron, *Childe Harold's Pilgrimage* (I–II); Hemans, *Domestic Affections*

1813 Luddite leaders tried; Hunt imprisoned for libelling the Prince Regent; Southey becomes Poet Laureate; Austen, *Pride and Prejudice*; Byron, *The Giaour* and *The Bride of Abydos*; Coleridge, *Remorse*; P. B. Shelley, *Queen Mab*

1814 Paris falls to allies; Napoleon abdicates and is exiled to Elba; Bourbons restored; Congress of Vienna; Austen, *Mansfield Park*; Byron, *The Corsair* and *Lara*; Scott, *Waverley*; Wordsworth, *The Excursion*

1815 Napoleon escapes and returns to rule for the "Hundred Days"; Battle of Waterloo; Napoleon surrenders and is exiled to St Helena; "Holy Alliance"; Corn Law passed; Byron, *Hebrew Melodies*; Scott, *Guy Mannering*; Wordsworth, *Poems* and *The White Doe of Rylstone*

1816 Economic problems and popular unrest; Spa Fields riot; Austen, *Emma*; Byron *Childe Harold's Pilgrimage* (III); Cobbett, *Political Register*;

Coleridge, *Christabel* and *The Statesman's Manual*; Hoffman, *Nachtstücke*; Hunt, *The Story of Rimini*; Scott, *The Antiquary*; P. B. Shelley, *Alastor*; Wilson, *City of the Plague*

1817 Habeas Corpus suspended; Seditious Meetings bill; Austen dies; De Staël dies; *Blackwood's Edinburgh Magazine*; Byron, *Manfred*; Coleridge, *Biographia Literaria* and *Sibylline Leaves*; Hazlitt, *Characters of Shakespeare's Plays* and *The Round Table*; Hemans, *Modern Greece*; Keats, *Poems*; Mill, *History of British India*; Moore *Lalla Rookh*

1818 Burdett's reform bill defeated; Emily Brontë born; Austen, *Northanger Abbey* and *Persuasion*; Byron, *Childe Harold's Pilgrimage* (IV); Hazlitt, *Lectures on the English Poets*; Hunt, *Foliage*; Keats, *Endymion*; Scot, *Rob Roy* and *Heart of Midlothian*; Mary Shelley, *Frankenstein*; P. B. Shelley, *The Revolt of Islam*

1819 "Peterloo massacre"; "Six Acts"; Ruskin born; Eliot born; Byron, *Don Juan* (I–II); Crabbe, *Tales of the Hall*; Hazlitt, *Political Essays*; Hemans, *Tales and Historic Scenes in Verse*; Scott, *Bride of Lammermoor*; P. B. Shelley, *Rosalind and Helen*; Wordsworth, *Peter Bell*

1820 Revolution in Spain; George III dies and George IV accedes; Queen Caroline trial; Cato Street conspiracy; *London Magazine*; Clare, *Poems*; Keats, *Lamia, etc.*; Maturin, *Melmoth the Wanderer*; Scott, *Ivanhoe*; P. B. Shelley, *The Cenci* and *Prometheus Unbound*

1821 Greek War of Independence begins; Napoleon dies; Keats dies; John Scott dies; Byron, *Cain, Don Juan* (III–V), *Marino Faliero*, and *Sardanapalus*; Clare, *The Village Minstrel*; De Quincey, *Confessions of an Opium Eater*; Egan, *Life in London*; Hazlitt, *Table Talk*; P. B. Shelley, *Adonais*

1822 Lord Castlereagh commits suicide; P. B. Shelley dies; *The Liberal*; Byron, *The Vision of Judgment*; Hemans, *Welsh Melodies*; P. B. Shelley, *Hellas*; Stendhal, *De l'amour*

1823 Radcliffe dies; Byron, *Don Juan* (VI–XIV); Hazlitt, *Liber Amoris*; Hemans, *The Siege of Valencia*; Lamb, *Essays of Elia*

1824 Combinations Act repealed; National Gallery founded; Byron dies; Byron, *Don Juan* (XV–XVI); Hogg, *Confessions of a Justified Sinner*; Landon, *The Improvisatrice*; P. B. Shelley, *Posthumous Poems*; Wedderburn, *The Horrors of Slavery*

1825 First steam locomotive railway opens; Barbauld dies; Coleridge, *Aids to Reflection*; Hazlitt, *The Spirit of the Age*; Pushkin, *Boris Godunov* and *Eugene Onegin*

1826 Hazlitt, *The Plain Speaker*; Mary Shelley, *The Last Man*

1827 Blake dies; Clare, *The Shepherd's Calendar*; Disraeli, *Vivian Grey*; Scott, *Life of Napoleon*

1828 Repeal of Test and Corporation Acts; Wellington PM; Bulwer, *Pelham*; Hazlitt, *Life of Napoleon*; Hemans, *Records of Women*; Hunt, *Lord Byron and Some of His Contemporaries*

1829 Catholic Emancipation; Metropolitan Police Act; Greek War of Independence ends; Coleridge, *On the Constitution of Church and State*; Landor, *Imaginary Conversations*

1830 Wellington leaves office; Grey PM; July Revolution in France; George IV dies; Hazlitt dies; *Fraser's Magazine*; Cobbett, *Rural Rides*; Moore, *Life of Byron*; Stendhal, *Le rouge et le noir*; Tennyson, *Poems*

Introduction

David Higgins and Sharon Ruston

The title of this book raises an immediate problem. Do we, in fact, teach Romanticism at all? After all, criticism of the last three decades has tended to be suspicious of the notion of Romanticism as a coherent force that somehow binds together the literature and/or culture of the late eighteenth- and early nineteenth centuries. Furthermore, earlier scholarly constructions of Romanticism have been subject to sustained critique, principally for valorizing the masculine sublime at the expense of the other forms of consciousness and writing. Would it not be more accurate to have entitled this book "Teaching Literature of the Romantic Period", or even "Teaching Literature from *c.*1780 to *c.*1830"? Perhaps, and yet Romanticism, even when it is being interrogated, still has a certain power in critical parlance, in teaching literature of the period, and, indeed, in the academic literary marketplace. It is a term that the discipline may find troubling, indefinable, and potentially exclusionary, and yet, perhaps for those very reasons, it simply will not go away. We have therefore decided, after some consideration, to use "Romanticism" in the title of the book and in various parts of the text, with the proviso that we are well aware that the term is highly problematic. In fact, whenever "Romanticism" is used, it should be understood as being placed into question; a project taken on explicitly by several chapters of this book. The reader who is troubled by the monolithic implications of "Romanticism" may, therefore, wish to read it as "Romanticism?", "~~Romanticism~~", or "Romanticisms." For, above all, the essays in this book reveal the rich variety of the literature of the period.

The initial impetus for *Teaching Romanticism* came in 2006 when, supported by the English Subject Centre, a questionnaire designed to find out how Romanticism was taught was filled out by academic staff in over fifty Higher Education institutions across the UK.[1] This questionnaire revealed a number of interesting things: Romanticism is still clearly an integral part of English degrees, most often taught in level two as a survey module, with further more specialized modules taught at level three and postgraduate level. It seems that the literature of the late eighteenth- and early nineteenth-century has not to date become subsumed into longer period courses, such as "literature of the long nineteenth century." Indeed, despite the fact that it covers such a short time period and that its historical borders can be and have been contested, it is still usually given as much room on the curriculum as longer period modules, such as the Renaissance. It is equally clear from the questionnaire results, though, that Romanticism is being questioned and interrogated on these modules (the term itself, "as a concept," came second highest in the list of themes covered). This book is intended to examine the diverse and exciting ways in which Romanticism is being taught today – what texts are being presented to students, how modules are being delivered and assessed – and to suggest new and fruitful connections between teaching and research.

It is obvious that the range of texts taught has expanded substantially over the last thirty years. However, it is also obvious that the undergraduate teaching of Romanticism often does not fully reflect the important recovery of female, black, labouring-class and other previously neglected writers that has so impacted upon research into the Romantic era. This gap between teaching and research is addressed by the first part of this book ("The Changing Canon"), which contains essays written by those who are teaching a new kind of Romanticism, or placing canonical Romantic texts into different teaching contexts. These chapters also address the role of publishers in deciding what we teach, examining the availability of primary texts and the use of anthologies. The second part of the book ("Approaches to Teaching Romanticism") considers different forms of pedagogical practice, such as teaching in specific locations, using new technologies, or helping students to engage with theory. Contributors reflect on their own experiences, presenting case studies of particular modules and teaching sessions, and thus firmly ground theoretical discussions within a practical framework. This collection of essays, therefore, represents current practice in the classroom, as well as considering the state of Romantic studies and suggesting ways in which research might be incorporated into university teaching.

According to the 2006 survey, the overwhelming majority of UK academics use Duncan Wu's *Romanticism: an Anthology* (2005); but, whichever anthology was used, 80 per cent of respondents felt that the anthology was not sufficient for their needs on the course and/or that they needed to supplement the anthology with additional resources.

When asked whether all the texts that tutors wished to teach were currently in print, forty-four respondents replied that they were and twenty-nine that there were texts they had trouble obtaining. The list of these (available on the BARS website) makes for interesting reading, revealing simultaneously the (restrictive) influence of canon formation on publishing (and vice versa) and the wide range of material being taught on these modules. Some texts are those that would have been in favour in years past, such as Walter Scott's novels and Peacock's *Nightmare Abbey* (which is now in print, Peacock 2007), whereas others clearly reflect the research that has concerned itself with less canonical writers.

The survey shows that, in UK undergraduate courses at least, the "big six" poets (Blake, Wordsworth, Coleridge, Byron, Shelley and Keats) are very much present in our classrooms; most often tutors dedicate one seminar or lecture to the work of each of these authors. Fifty-seven per cent of respondents answered that no plays are taught. While Jane Austen and Mary Shelley most often have one seminar or lecture dedicated to teaching their work, few other female writers achieved this level of engagement. That said, many writers who have been marginalized in the teaching (and research) of this period in the past are mentioned briefly or a short extract of their work is considered at some point in the module. However, the list of those most often not taught is long and contains female writers, black writers and, also, male writers who were once very firmly part of the Romantic canon such as Scott and Southey. Anecdotal evidence suggests that the situation in the United States and Canada may well be similar.

A primary aim of this book is to put these findings into context, to investigate them further, and give examples from real-life pedagogy that suggest new ways of approaching the question of which texts to teach. Many of the essays in this book are written by academics who work on writers, genres or regions that have been "recovered" in our research but not always, according to the survey, in undergraduate teaching: Scottish, Irish and Welsh Romanticism (Pittock), drama (Crochunis), labouring-class poets (Goodridge), female and queer writers (Ruston), black writers (Carey), and European writers (Higgins). Each author suggests ways in which students can be encouraged to engage with this material, whether as part of a survey Romanticism module, or as a more specialized module.

The question of whether to use an anthology to aid teaching is one that persists in these essays, and has been a controversial topic recently with the advent of a number of competing titles. Clearly no single anthology can possibly cater to the needs of all tutors, each with their own research interests and opinions on what should be included. The argument remains, though, that these texts are canon-forming, or at least, canon-reflecting, and as such are influential on our teaching and the dissemination of the subject to wider audiences. In a recent review of two new anthologies, Simon Kövesi declares that "the male canon is back" (Kövesi 2008: 42). He argues that the "confining lens of the Big Six" in both anthologies marks a return to mid-twentieth century versions of the period's literature, asking whether these "two books signal a sudden reduction of the diversity of Romanticisms" (42, 43). The 2006 survey suggested that, in many institutions, the canon has not really changed for undergraduate teaching, or not as much as we might have thought it would. One reason for this may be the institutional inertia that is partly a result of the difficulties that young academics entering the discipline have in gaining permanent employment. There is often a substantial time lag between finishing a doctorate and being in a position to make a significant impact on the undergraduate curriculum. Thinking in broader terms, though, the choices that we all have to make about which texts to teach are overdetermined and raise questions that the discipline still has yet fully to explore. To what extent should the content of a Romanticism module be determined by what texts were most widely read during the period? Or by what events or discourses seem the most significant? How much should it be determined by the desire to reflect social diversity, both then and now, and allow hitherto marginalized voices to be heard? And what about questions of aesthetic value? As John Goodridge reminds us at the end of his chapter on labouring-class poets, some texts "may be more worth reading (and worth reading more of) than others." But how do we judge this as critics, especially given that our responses to Romantic-period texts may themselves be conditioned by a "Romantic" aesthetic that valorizes certain sorts of writings over others? One could imagine a survey Romanticism module that, on good historicist grounds, excluded (for example) Blake, Coleridge, Keats, Percy Shelley and William Wordsworth, and yet this might be a module that many academics would not want to teach.

Harriet Kramer Linkin's essay in the second part of this book shows that the changes to the "research canon" have impacted strongly on the kinds of courses being taught at postgraduate level, in the UK, the US and Canada. There we can see the real and tangible effects of the recovery work and reconfiguration of Romanticism that has taken place over the past thirty years. However, there is also a sense from the other essays in this book that some undergraduate students, at least, are getting the opportunity to experience a more diverse Romanticism than the one traditionally taught. Stephen Behrendt, for example, reveals that he is working without an anthology; instead his students are creating their own carefully edited and annotated texts of books and poems that would not otherwise be easily available for critical attention. In a truly inspirational way, Behrendt's students are doing the recovery work for themselves, and the excitement that we all feel as researchers is clearly something they enjoy too. In a time of anxiety about falling standards, it is salutary to be asked to reflect on what undergraduates of varying abilities *can* achieve, rather than to complain about their failings.

Diversity is also reflected in David Duff's forthcoming new anthology for Oxford University Press, which takes an innovative approach to Romantic literature: it will be organized around the idea of archipelagic or "Four Nations" Romanticism, thus revealing "the different national traditions within British Romanticism, and the relations between them." Murray Pittock's chapter in this book on Scottish, Irish and Welsh Romanticism reflects on the extent to which Romantic studies has tended neglect this issue; Duff's anthology answers Pittock's demand that "Romanticism must be more open to nation, language and dialogue to appeal to the student body of today and the researchers of the future."

One problem that rears its head in many of the chapters in this book is that of nomenclature. Kövesi refers to the shift that took place in critical thought: "to the interrogation of Romanticism as an ideology and its gradual replacement with a detailed sense of a Romantic literary *period* rather than a restrictive, exclusive *-ism*" (42). Susan Chaplin's chapter offers a sustained and thorough example of how this difficulty is in fact an important aspect of teaching this literature. The module she describes in "Theorizing Romanticism" is built upon the idea that we should not accept unthinkingly a concept that has been produced with hindsight and "is at the very least a slippery notion." Similarly, the module on European Romanticism described in David Higgins's chapter asks students to consider Romanticism as the result of an ongoing process of cultural construction that began in the period itself. There remains, as Linkin's essay notes, the "still vexing issue of conflating the historical period with an ideology or aesthetic." Also, it seems that there is no agreement about which dates should form that historical period: in the 2006 survey twenty-seven respondents chose the option 1775–1830 to describe the period they taught, ten chose 1780–1820, but most chose 'Other' here (thirty-nine respondents) and there was no real pattern to the dates used instead. A sensible attempt to circumvent these problems by a new name, the "Romantic Century" (1750–1850), has had limited success. We began this introduction by considering the problem of the titles of this book. Some university teachers of the texts discussed in this book might not want to think of themselves as "Romanticists," or as teaching something called "Romanticism," even if that something is being contested. "Romanticism" may seem to some as rather an unhelpful way of thinking about (literary) history, a term that threatens to occlude more interesting and diverse approaches to the late eighteenth and early nineteenth centuries. A counter argument to this understandable position is that, like it or not, the history of this concept is ineluctably intertwined with the history of literary criticism, that it still strongly affects the texts we teach and the approaches that we take to them, and that therefore it is better addressed explicitly rather than swept under the pedagogical carpet.

The essays in this book intersect with each other in a number of important ways. Some have explicit political agendas (Goodridge, Carey, Ruston, Pittock); others remind us to be aware of the range of formal and theoretical approaches we use in our teaching (Wootton, Chaplin); the potential usefulness of other disciplines to our teaching of literature, or to genuinely interdisciplinary ways of teaching (Bushell, Thomas); the benefits of examining a particular genre or form (Crochunis, Goodridge); the importance of context (institutional, regional, national) in affecting how teaching takes place (Bushell, Behrendt, Linkin, Clark and Suzuki); and the possibilities posed by comparative literary studies, whether transnational, national, postcolonial or regional (Carey, Higgins, Pittock). While remaining receptive to the broader context of Romantic studies, all the essays place the reader within a real pedagogical setting, and show him or her how colleagues are teaching today. Sally Bushell's essay illustrates how teaching can go beyond the book, into the hills and dales in which texts were written; Sarah Wootton's reminds us again of the text itself, and what close attention to the words on the page can achieve, particularly in association with a consideration of the text's historical context. Stephen Behrendt's essay shows how students' ICT skills can be harnessed to help them engage with literary texts; Sue Chaplin examines how a carefully conceived module can enable students to address complex theoretical issues; and John Goodridge considers how biography can be used to deepen students' understanding of labouring-class poetry.

Harriet Kramer Linkin provides an important survey of the state of Romantic postgraduate studies that also picks out the most exciting programmes currently available. Steve Clark and Masashi Suzuki reflect broadly on the history and current state of British Romantic studies in Japan, but also give concrete examples of how Romanticism might be taught at Japanese universities. Similarly, Thomas Crochunis considers how questions surrounding research into Romantic theatre can be engaged with in classroom practice. Several chapters offer detailed module outlines, such as Sophie Thomas's account of teaching "Romanticism and Visual Culture" at MA level, which suggests at the same time important ways in which such a module might lead to refiguring of what Romanticism means. David Higgins and Brycchan Carey both present modules that help students to engage with Romanticism as a transnational phenomenon. Sharon Ruston's chapter on "Romanticism and Gender" and Murray Pittock's chapter on "Scottish, Irish and Welsh Romanticism" show that the work that happens in the classroom does not simply address students' (and tutors') understanding of literary texts, but encourages reflection on their own identities.

This book can be used in a number of different ways, and offers a range of resources for both new and experienced university teachers of Romanticism. The first part, in particular, provides an overview of the state of Romantic studies and addresses some of the key issues that affect which texts we choose to teach. The second part offers all kinds of practical suggestions for university teachers, ranging from the use of anthologies, to different types of assessment, to classroom activities, to entire course outlines. The detailed chronology and lists of further reading will also provide academics with information and signposts that will help to support their teaching. More than anything, though, this book speaks to the vibrancy and diversity of Romantic studies and considers the various ways that this might be communicated to our students. It shows that, whatever the problems and challenges of Higher Education in the twenty-first century, the university classroom can still be a place of intellectual excitement, experimentation and transformation.

Note

1. A summary and report of the survey results can be found online ("Survey Results" 2006).

Works cited

Kövesi, Simon (2008) "Review of Uttara Natarajan (ed.), *The Romantic Poets: a Guide to Criticism* and Michael O'Neill and Charles Mahoney (eds. *), Romantic Poetry: an Annotated Anthology,*" *BARS: Bulletin and Review*, 33: 42–3.

Peacock, Thomas Love (2007) *Nightmare Abbey*, ed. Lisa Vargo (Ontario: Broadview Press).
"Survey Results: Teaching Romanticism Questionnaire" (2006) *BARS Website* http://www.bars.ac.uk/teaching/survey/surveyresults.php.
Wu, Duncan, ed. (2005) *Romanticism: an Anthology*, 3rd edn. (Oxford: Blackwell).

Part I
The Changing Canon

1
Labouring-Class Poetry

John Goodridge

> I am seeking to rescue the poor stockinger, the Luddite cropper, the "obsolete" hand-loom weaver, the "utopian" artisan, and even the deluded follower of Joanna Southcott, from the enormous condescension of posterity.
>
> (Thompson 1968: 13)

The study of labouring-class poetry began for me with the excitement of discovery, first via an association copy of Chatterton's Rowley Poems inherited from a great-grandfather (see Goodridge 2004), then as a belatedly precocious mature student, happy to discover my own new poets from the past with a little help from my patient lecturers. Taking my cue from E. P. Thompson (as above), I began to focus on the "rescue" of what Brian Maidment in his 1987 anthology would term "self-taught" poets. Seeming support for this endeavour came with the founding of the John Clare Society in 1981 and the growing richness of Clare scholarship and, perhaps most of all, from Roger Lonsdale's two landmark anthologies of eighteenth-century poetry (1984 and 1989). I was struck not only by the exceptionally rich content of these two volumes – food for decades of reading and teaching – but also by the revolutionary implications of Lonsdale's concise, scholarly introduction to his *New Oxford Book of Eighteenth Century Verse* (1984). Beginning with the sober statement that we seem to know eighteenth-century poetry pretty well, Lonsdale swiftly unpicked the then familiar consensus, showing us how little the corpus of eighteenth-century poetry had been sifted, and how scholarship had returned again and again to the same "familiar material" and the "most respectable and predictable genres, which are guaranteed to offer few or no surprises." The situation was "explicable only if we recognize the hypnotically influential way in which the eighteenth century succeeded in anthologizing itself." The multi-volume anthologies on which almost all scholarly work had been based emerged at a "precise historical moment," the period of reaction following the French Revolution, so "it need be no surprise that moderation, decorum, restraint and propriety were the criteria controlling admission" to the canonical anthologies. Consequently "the eccentric, the vulgar, the extravagant, the disturbing, the subversive," and entire groupings including women and labouring-class poets, were simply excluded (Lonsdale 1984: xxxvi). The contents of Lonsdale's anthology, its companion, and others published since, amply demonstrate that all these groupings and types of writers existed in significant numbers and wrote many poems worth reviving.

Teaching labouring-class poetry and other forgotten areas of eighteenth-century and Romantic poetry was thus first opened as a serious possibility, and given its first potential guides and course readers. Lonsdale offered persuasive proof of both a historically explicable neglect, and a body of neglected work worthy of scholarship. It remained only to find a place for such material in the curriculum, and a *modus operandi* for teaching it. I offer here some account of the potentials and pitfalls I discovered in opening up such a programme of teaching within an English and a Humanities degree.

An early problem was the inherent bias within English Studies, a legacy of its own early struggles for academic respectability, towards exclusive focus on the great writers. Nowhere was this more apparent than in Romantic Studies which, notwithstanding useful early work on women poets, was still very much dominated in the early 1990s by the big six poets, vividly reimagined by David Worrall in the comically anachronistic image of the "S.S. 'Romanticism'... a be-funnelled Cunarder, six smoke stacks bellowing sparks and smoke and the deck awash with thoroughly albatrossed mariners" (Worrall 1992: 5). Yet coming to my first university lectureship at that time, I found what seemed to me a surprising appetite in the institution for letting my outcasts into the curriculum. John Clare in particular seemed to press all the right ecological, regional, aspirational and student cohort identity buttons. And not only Clare, whose poetry was becoming more widely valued elsewhere too: many other neglected writers and categories of writing and their recovery were made welcome in the burgeoning scholarship and consequently research-enhanced teaching that followed the institution's metamorphosis from a polytechnic to a university in the early 1990s. I was able rapidly to establish teaching modules on "John Clare and the self-taught tradition" and "Eighteenth-century women poets," while topics like the "labour" poems of Stephen Duck and Mary

Collier (*The Thresher's Labour*, 1730; *The Woman's Labour*, 1739) found a place in other modules and eventually even sneaked into the first year survey course, tucked between *Hamlet*, Blake and *Mary Barton*. A new level two module on "Radical Recoveries" broadens the scope to drama and the novel.

There were a few signs of anxiety (though none from the students). A Shakespearian colleague made gentle fun of me for teaching "Donald Duck and Margaret Collywobble" rather than proper poetry like *Paradise Lost*. Another, a Victorianist, urged me to stretch my students with some of the great eighteenth-century novels I may have been neglecting in favour of Donald and Margaret. My own slight unease at the untroubled way I had got first-year students reading Duck and Collier prompted me to ask a visiting scholar – a pioneer of Collier scholarship – whether we should worry about having created a generation of students who were happy reading Mary Collier but might not read (for example) Alexander Pope. Her wise answer was that they if did not read Pope then they would not understand *The Woman's Labour*. How would they find out where Collier honed her couplet art, or found the resources to lob at Duck such a rhetorically studied jibe as: "Those mighty Troubles which perplex your Mind, / (Thistles before, and Females come behind)" (Collier 1989: ll. 123–4)? Nor would they understand why it might seem subversive for a washerwoman to write about her life in a high Popean style.

Beyond the general question of whether the largely non-canonical body of labouring-class poetry can find a place in English courses (and clearly it can, under the right conditions), there are theoretical issues to resolve in teaching this material, as well as questions of resources and scholarship. In a careful review of the second *Labouring-Class Poets* series (Goodridge et al. 2006) Brian Maidment points out that the current revival of scholarship in this field revisits an "unfinished historiographical and pedagogic debate" about "the extent to which working men and women were able to find their own literary voice and articulate the particularity of their own experience." This important debate is "considerably complicated," says Maidment, "by its scholarly origins." As he explains:

> The first anthologies of such writing derived not from Britain but from Communist and Socialist Europe (Kovalev in Russia and Ashraf in East Germany), and were meant as teaching anthologies which defined working-class poetry as a form of industrial writing that proceeded directly from the industrial and urban experience of the oppressed factory workers and dispossessed artisans in Manchester, Leeds, and the industrialising valleys of the North of England. Such

> anthologies were led by notions of "authenticity" (that is, the extent to which the writer had remained uncorrupted by the besetting dangers of social deference, literary ambition, and intellectual vanity) and "opposition" (the extent to which the writing challenged the socio-political hegemonising forces of dominant ideologies). Thus writers with known political affiliations, especially committed Chartists, were foregrounded, and the more "literary" issues of form and voice and their relationship to social experience were largely ignored. (Maidment 2007: 182)

In other words these writers have already been coopted, for specific political purposes, and extensively so. Maidment dates this "historiological and pedagogical debate" to "the last thirty years," but we can also find earlier appropriations and politically partisan readings of working-class writing. The Kovalev anthology was published in 1956 (Ashraf's work was published in the 1970s), but the idealization and narrow definition of such writings is present in the propaganda of the Stalin era, and is behind the scepticism expressed towards this tradition at that time by Orwell (1968) and Trotsky (1970), inter alia. Indeed a great deal of debate about *peasant poetry* and *proletarian culture* took place throughout the twentieth century, and may be tracked back even further (not just via Marx and Engels) through the Victorian and Romantic periods to the eighteenth century. But the rise of the Soviet Union, and its early cultural shift from radical experimentalism to an official art in which worker and peasant were portrayed heroically had an enormous impact, in the West as well as the East, on how working-class culture would be understood.

In a teaching context, such a dramatically interventionist reception history of working-class writing might be seen as a boon, offering much food for student debate and discussion (which of course it can be). But for scholars in search of historical truth it has been more problematic, seeming like a closing down of potential source materials and critical approaches, even a tainting of the evidence. Thus the very term "working-class writing" has increasingly felt too politically loaded and limiting to describe this large, heterogeneous body of work. Maidment's pioneering study/anthology of working-class poetry, *The Poorhouse Fugitives* (1987), uses the term "self-taught," consciously moving the emphasis from the political to the educational sphere – and perhaps also attempting to bury once and for all the (wildly inaccurate) term "uneducated." The editorial group I work with in the field introduced the rather neutral term "labouring-class," to broaden the corpus of writings beyond the industrial/political emphasis of "working-class," while keeping still within a recognizable tradition. Reception theory teaches us that each reader brings their own agenda and weight of expectations to a text, but the recent study of labouring-class poetry has placed great emphasis on taking these texts as far as possible on their own terms, both to avoid Thompson's "enormous condescension" and to open up what is clearly a much richer seam than was mined by the Kovalev–Ashraf approach.

Thus in teaching labouring-class poetry of the Romantic period one needs to be intently aware, not only of its historical neglect – the shadow of the big six – but of the body of expectations we bring to the topic. For example, if we read something like Robert Bloomfield's *The Farmer's Boy* (1800), our first instinct might be to judge its realism and authenticity as a first-hand (and from below) account of life as a farm boy (Bloomfield 2007). This is broadly reasonable, and will often form the first line of approach in student work. But teaching the text more carefully will expose fallacies in such an approach. The poem was actually written, not by a "farmer's boy," but a self-educated adult shoemaker working in a London sweatshop, reading plentifully and daydreaming of his rural adolescence in Suffolk, when he had worked on his uncle's farm for a year or two. Bloomfield self-consciously builds a literary persona ("Giles") on whom to hang this rural vision, and adapts pre-existing literary structures, principally the four-part shape of Thomson's *Seasons*, and the couplet art of Goldsmith, Crabbe and others. We cannot assume, as tends to happen with such poems, that it is (a) autobiographical, (b) honest, (c) true, and (d) unmediated.

Students should not, for example, assume that the poem is necessarily uncorrupted by idealizing pastoral traditions. But on the other hand, they should question the equally steamrolling view that the poem is just a comforting pastoral fantasy. The presence of cold, hardship, pain and death – not just the controlled melancholy of "et in arcadia ego," but (for instance) an unflinching description of the slaughter of first-born lambs, in "Summer" – warns us that pastoralism cannot explain it any more fully than the *authentic* fallacy. Suspicion of the poem's success in the marketplace (20,000 copies sold in early editions), may prompt comparison to, say, the second edition of *Lyrical Ballads*, published the same year, whose proportionately low sales (like those of Keats's poems) might be taken as evidence of another, more spartan sort of literary authenticity.

The biographical dimension of labouring-class poetry is important in appraising these sorts of issues, and in teaching labouring-class poetry of the Romantic period I try and sensitize students to the tricky issue of how far to hang critical meaning on biographical data. It is important to get this right, because the life-stories of these writers are often the hook that catches most student interest. In critical and pedagogical terms this can be a good or a bad thing. I learned of its ability to draw students in when I began leading field trips to John Clare's Helpston and Stamford. Inspired by Clare Society walks run by Noël Staples, Rodney Lines and others, I took students to many of the resonant places in Clare's life, from his Helpston cottage (now under development as a centre for environmental and ecological education), to the Hole in the Wall pub in Stamford where he drank late with his fellow Burghley Park gardeners, and the Stamford branch of W. H. Smith's that was formerly the shop where he bought books, ran up debts and once, distressingly, insulted his key patron, Lord Exeter, by failing to recognize him. Invariably, student engagement leaped upwards following these trips, but the interest was more biographical than literary, and in Clare's case this too often meant a preoccupation with his late-period "madness," often a critical dead end in Clare studies.

But biographical awareness can have a more positive role in studying labouring-class poetry, if used to understand the poetry better (or in being itself part of the poetry's meaning). The voices of labouring-class poets can emerge in distorted ways, either half-strangled by the noose of patronly and public expectation, or bursting out in frustrated or compensatory over-confidence. Getting to grips with the life stories can put us in tune with such presentational issues. James Woodhouse's poems, for example, eloquently illustrate some of the difficulties of self-presentation. Woodhouse, one of the five principal poets canonized in Robert Southey's extended essay on the "Uneducated Poets" (1831) was a shoemaker with an appetite for landscape. *Poems on Several Occasions. By James Woodhouse, Journeyman Shoemaker* (1766), is the "corrected" second edition of a volume first published by Robert Dodsley two years earlier. Its author was by now a minor literary celebrity and had met figures like Dr Johnson (who later dismissed the young shoemaker's celebrity to Boswell as "all vanity and childishness," Boswell 1953: 443).

The book's title page, grandly laid-out in the eighteenth-century manner, boasts "several additional pieces never before published" and a prefixed "List of his Generous Benefactors on the former Publication, And the Subscribers to the present Edition." Copies are rare, but one can look through a page-image file of the volume on the online ECCO database and get the full visual effect of what met its first readers.

Turning the title page, we meet a large-print dedication (for the comfort of present readers, I shall not reproduce here the many full-word capitalizations): "To the Right Honourable George, Lord Lyttelton, Baron of Frankley," in "humble acknowledgment of his condescension, humanity and beneficence towards the Author." It would be "presumption" to enlarge on Lyttelton's virtues, but you can bet Woodhouse is going to do so anyway, claiming they are "every day exerted in the highest, and most extensive sphere," whilst his genius "not only adorns the present, but will illuminate future ages." One thinks of Raymond Williams's sardonic verdict on similar emanations from Bloomfield: "The creeping humility is an acquired taste" (Williams 1973: 134).

But Robert Bloomfield, as the new electronic edition of his voluminous correspondence (2009) amply shows, was capable of resisting the overawing power of patronly beneficence, albeit with stress and difficulty. Woodhouse seems caught by its mesmerizing gaze. The next page begins a humble "Author's Apology"; after that comes an "Advertisement to the First Edition," which begins with thanks to Mr Shenstone's "benevolence" in having permitted "the lowest of his neighbours" (glossed as "poor Crispin, our author") to frequent his estate, The Leasowes, and ends with a list of further thanks for "benefactions" from various booksellers. There are two pages of more formalized "Benefactors," another six of "Subscribers," and then the poems begin – with an "Elegy to William Shenstone, Esq. of the Leasowes." This important first patron having recently died, the tribute is understandable, but one's patience begins to fray when, nine pages later, "Elegy II. Written to William Shenstone" comes into view. Seven pages more, and we meet: "To William Shenstone, Esq., On his Indisposition in the Spring, 1762" – it seems he had had the 'flu, possibly a warning of worse to come; then "Benevolence, an Ode," with its addressees discreetly noted in a footnote. A fifteen-page poem on "Spring" follows, with just a single mention of "Benevolence" (30). The volume's long central poem, "The Leasowes," then celebrates the patron's estate, which Woodhouse genuinely seems to have taken enormous pleasure in. Then we are back to the death of Shenstone, who may also be the addressee of the next poem, "Palamon and Colinet." A further twenty-five pages of poetry are addressed to Lord Lyttelton, followed by a thank-you verse for a gift of books ("Gratitude. A Poem"), verses "To the Right Honourable The Countess of——On the Death of a Daughter," and finally an "Ode to Apollo" written at the request of a "gentleman."

The "creeping humility" thus fills the whole volume, and William Christmas aptly styles him a "sycophant extraordinaire" (Christmas

2001: 192). But did Woodhouse have anything to say, other than that he loved his patrons, down to the very land they walked on? Well yes he did, in fact, and Steve Van-Hagen has recently recovered an extraordinary late work that shows us what it was (Woodhouse 2005). In *The Life and Lucubrations of Crispinus Scriblerus* (the name another interesting labouring-class adaptation of Pope) Woodhouse lays out his life history in verse. It is a fascinating story, and there is much in it about what Van Hagen calls his "radical levelling theology," and his love of poetry and nature (Woodhouse 2005: xxv). Perhaps the most striking self-image, though, comes from precisely the moment when Woodhouse was penning all those poems in praise of patrons and failing to impress Dr Johnson, and tellingly foreshadows John Clare's image of how his own local patrons would haul him off to Stamford and ply him with drink: "I hate Stamford but am draggd into it like a Bear & fidler to a wake" (Clare 1985: 164–5). Woodhouse writes:

> As tutor'd bears are led from place, to place,
> Displaying biped gait, and burlesque grace;
> Their action clumsey, and their shape uncouth,
> While grunting bagpipe greets the gaping youth;
>
> . . . . . .
>
> So was he sent the twofold City through,
> For Cits, like Swains, are pleas'd with something new,
> That each subscriber's eyes might freely range,
> O'er Clown, so clever! Spectacle, so strange!
>
> (2005: 48)

Among many other things he has to say about his life is a devastating portrait of the patron with whom he was most involved, Elizabeth Montagu, and contrastingly much to suggest that his gratitude to Lyttelton, Shenstone et al. was heartfelt and based in a genuine shared love of landscape.

These contrasting volumes, the early occasional poems and the later autobiographical epic, raise essential issues about how we read labouring-class poetry – about what exactly we are looking for in it, and how far the life and its environment may constrain the letters. It might just be coincidental that the patronly object of Woodhouse's greatest scorn is the very same Elizabeth Montagu who is a key figure in the notorious Hannah More/Ann Yearsley dispute; but then again these extraordinary love/hate relationships with patrons do illustrate a significant development in labouring-class poetry. They are the birth-pangs of the nineteenth-century self-taught man or woman of letters, key figures in Romantic and Victorian culture, very much more independent and self-reliant than their predecessors, the patron-bound eighteenth-century "peasant poets."

The two Woodhouse texts offer a good starting point for discussing these issues, of contextualizing and externalizing his life-story and expressed feelings, and opening up important issues of value. Seminar and essay discussions of labouring-class poetry often stay with the seemingly safe documentary evaluation I outlined above in relation to *The Farmer's Boy*. One reason is the general emphasis in English studies in recent years on the documentary, historical contexts and purposes of texts. It is predictably accentuated in the case of a group of writers defined primarily by social class. It may well be argued (as it was, for instance, about Clare's "peasant poet" label in Paul Farley's BBC radio programme on "The Lament of Swordy Well"), that bracketing these writers by their origins continues to damage them. Two teaching approaches, both intertextual, may help by offering positive reasons and ways to identify these writers as a group.

The first is to make comparative study, noting echoes and allusions as well as unintended similarities of theme, style etc., within the labouring-class tradition. For example one could offer a selection of short labouring-class poems (of which there are plenty) or extracts written "at the grave of" or otherwise in tribute to Burns, which might be put alongside Burns poems. This kind of work, easily achievable for short texts using paper handouts and in more sophisticated ways using electronic resources, can help to understand forms of self-definition and self-recognition within the tradition, seen as self-generated rather than externally imposed.

A second approach is to look at examples of the ways in which labouring-class poets use canonical and classical forms and models. As in the Collier/Pope example noted earlier, examining significant engagements with canonical texts, and how such sources are adapted and changed by labouring-class poets, can give a valuable insight into how these poets worked, and how they placed and defined themselves. A simple example I have discussed elsewhere is Clare's jaunty twist on Gray's *Elegy*:

> Full many a flower is born to blush unseen
> And waste its sweetness on the desert air.
> (Gray 1969: 127)

> Full many a flower, too, wishing to be seen,
> Perks up its head the hiding grass between.
> (Clare 1821: II, 176)

Comparative exercises of this sort offer a range of possible approaches to students. This example could be read formalistically, perhaps in terms of how far the tone of Gray's stately syntax, passive phrasing and pathetic fallacy is changed in Clare, or in contextual terms, perhaps (since Clare mentions the "hiding grass") in the political way John Lucas reads Clare's championing of grass as representing the democratic masses of nature (Lucas 1990: 148). (The *Labouring-Class Poets* series, 2003 and 2006, facilitate these two intertextual approaches by offering subcategories in their thematic indexes: "Intertextual Verse: Canonical Writers," "Intertextual Verse: Labouring-class Writers," and "Verse in Traditional Literary and Classical Genres," Goodridge 2003, 2006.)

As this comparison might suggest, questions of value in labouring-class poetry may be taught through the analysis of form, the mixture of high and low culture in the texts, and the use of varying linguistic registers. Maidment usefully isolates three categories of Victorian labouring-class verse: political poetry, "Parnassian" poetry, and homely (including local and dialect) verse (Maidment 1987). Some of the most interesting texts to teach are those in which two or more of these types meet, and in which the ambition and variety of labouring-class poetry may be seen.

These approaches have worked well in the classroom, but they demand a wide range of texts and critical resources, and I should like to conclude by briefly looking at scholarly resources. We have moved so swiftly in scholarship from a position of primitive capital accumulation to our enormous current wealth of electronic and other resources, that it is now quite a task to explain to students just what these resources are and how best to use them. Online subscription databases such as ECCO, EEBO, LION, ODNB and OED, and free text databases such as Project Gutenberg and Google Book Search, head up an array of very powerful tools, offering university undergraduates practically everything they need up to 1800, and most of what they need thereafter. My own compiled *Database of Labouring Class Poets*, now edited by Tim Burke, offers basic details of some 1,500 such poets we know to have flourished between 1700 and 1900 (a leap forward from the scruffy lists of missing poets with which I used to pester the editor of the *DNB* in my postgraduate days). It is now possible for lecturers and students to explore a wide range of labouring-class poets, obtain most of their texts, get precise information about the words they used, and find out exactly what (if anything) has been published by and/or about them in recent decades.

How can these riches be organized into a coherent canon? One answer would be that there is no real need to do this. One of the consistent pluses of teaching labouring-class poetry is the pleasure students get (and positively comment on, in feedback forms) in finding *new* texts and *new* authors of their own: precisely my own starting point. There is much potential in a field like this for students to carry out self-devised research projects, which in some cases (and unusually for undergraduate work) can even find themselves operating beyond the limits of current published scholarship and contributing to new knowledge.

On the other hand, teaching demands a degree of coherence and organization – including intelligent selection from the mass of writing, and proper scholarly presentation, which is why Lonsdale's anthologies retain their sparkle a quarter of a century on. The two most recent contributions to labouring-class poetry scholarship I have seen, Bridget Keegan's study of *British Labouring-Class Nature Poetry, 1730–1837* and Florence S. Boos's anthology, *Working-Class Women Poets in Victorian Britain* offer useful organizational as well as intellectual resources for teaching, and show a range of possibilities for ordering the field (Keegan 2008; Boos 2008). Keegan begins and ends her narrative with two of the three best-known Romantic period labouring-class poets, Bloomfield and Clare (Burns being the third), the pair book-ending a thematic organization coherently based around eco-criticism. Within this structure is sequenced a series of discrete thematic discussions, each represented principally by one, or two for comparative purposes, poets. Boos offers a fine selection of working-class women's poetry, grouped by author but also nested within three thematic fields, "The Rural Poets," "The Factory Poets," and "Lyricists and Feminists." However, the gifted Janet Hamilton is gloriously exempted from this scheme, and wins her own section, outside of (and preceding) the three thematic sections.

There may indeed be a useful lesson for teachers and students here – one that once led to Robert Graves' interrogation by his Oxford tutors ("It appears, indeed, that you prefer some authors to others . . . " 1960: 305). And that is, that some writers – even neglected labouring-class ones, even in an age of literary levelling and mass textual availability – may be more worth reading (and worth reading more of) than others.

Works cited and further reading

Ashraf, P. M. (1975) *Political Verse and Song from Britain and Ireland* (East Berlin).

—— (1978–9) *An Introduction to Working-Class Literature in Great Britain*, 2 vols. (East Berlin).

Bloomfield, Robert (2007) *The Farmer's Boy*, in *Selected Poems*, ed. John Goodridge and John Lucas, rev. edn. (Nottingham: Trent Editions).
—— (2009) *The Letters of Robert Bloomfield and his Circle*, ed. Tim Fulford and Lynda Pratt, electronic edition, *Romantic Circles*, forthcoming.
Boos, Florence S., ed. (2008) *Working-Class Women Poets in Victorian Britain* (Ontario: Broadview Press).
Boswell, James (1953) *Boswell's Life of Johnson*, ed. R. W. Chapman (London: Oxford University Press).
Burke, Tim, ed. *Database of Labouring Class Poets*, comp. John Goodridge http://human.ntu.ac.uk/research/labouringclasswriters/.
Christmas, William (2001) *The Lab'ring Muses: Work, Writing, and the Social Order in English Plebeian Poetry, 1730–1830* (Newark: University of Delaware).
Clare, John (1821) *The Village Minstrel and Other Poems* (London: John Taylor).
—— (1985), *Letters*, ed. Mark Storey (Oxford: Clarendon).
Collier, Mary (1989) *The Woman's Labour*, in *Two Eighteenth-Century Poems*, ed. E. P. Thompson (London: Merlin Press).
Duck, Stephen (1989) *The Thresher's Labour*, in *Two Eighteenth-Century Poems*, ed. E. P. Thompson (London: Merlin Press).
Farley, Paul (presenter) (7 September 2008) "The Lament of Swordy Well" (radio programme, first broadcast on BBC Radio 4).
Goodridge, John, gen. ed. (2003) *Eighteenth-Century Labouring-Class Poets* (London: Pickering & Chatto).
—— (2004), "New Light on George Catcott's 'Obstinate Arguments'", *Thomas Chatterton Society Newsletter*, 2: 4–7.
—— gen. ed. (2006) *Nineteenth-Century Labouring-Class Poets* (London: Pickering & Chatto).
Graves, Robert (1960) *Goodbye to All That* (London: Penguin).
Gray, Thomas (1969) *Elegy in a Country Churchyard*, in *The Poems of Gray, Collins and Goldsmith*, ed. Roger Lonsdale (London: Longmans).
Keegan, Bridget (2008) *British Labouring-Class Nature Poetry, 1730–1837* (Basingstoke: Palgrave Macmillan).
Kovalev, V. (1956) *Anthology of Chartist Literature* (Moscow).
Landry, Donna (1990) *The Muses of Resistance: Laboring-Class Women's Poetry in Britain, 1739–1796* (Cambridge: Cambridge University Press).
Lonsdale, Roger, ed. (1984) *The New Oxford Book of Eighteenth-Century Verse* (Oxford: Oxford University Press).
—— (1989) *Eighteenth-Century Women Poets* (Oxford: Oxford University Press).
Lucas, John (1990) *England and Englishness* (London: The Hogarth Press).
Maidment, Brian, ed. (1987) *The Poorhouse Fugitives: Self-Taught Poets and Poetry in Victorian Britain* (Manchester: Carcanet Press).
—— (2007) "Review of *Nineteenth-Century English Labouring-Class Poets 1800–1900*", in *Studies in Hogg and His World*, 17: 181–6.
Orwell, George (1968) "The Proletarian Writer," in *The Collected Essays, Journalism and Letters of George Orwell II: My Country Right or Left 1940–1943*, ed. Sonia Orwell and Ian Angus (London: Secker & Warburg): 38–44.
Southey, Robert (1831) "An Introductory Essay on the Lives and Works of Our Uneducated Poets," in *Attempts in Verse by John Jones, an Old Servant* (London: John Murray).

Thompson, E. P. (1968) *The Making of the English Working Class*, rev. edn. (Harmondsworth: Pelican Books).
Trotsky, Leon (1970) "Class and Art" in *Writings on Art and Literature*, ed. Paul N. Siegel (New York: Pathfinder Press): 68–85.
White, Simon et al., eds. (2006), *Robert Bloomfield: Lyric, Class, and the Romantic Canon* (Lewisburg, PA: Bucknell University Press).
Williams, Raymond (1973) *The Country and the City* (London: Chatto & Windus).
Woodhouse, James (1966) *Poems on Several Occasions. By James Woodhouse, Journeyman Shoemaker*, 2nd edn. (London: Messrs. Dodsley et al.).
—— (2005) *The Life and Lucubrations of Crispinus Scriblerus: A Selection*, ed. Steve Van Hagen (Cheltenham: Cyder Press).
Worrall, David (1992) "A Bar to BARS: the Voyage of the S.S. 'Romanticism'," *BARS Bulletin*, 2: 4–5.

2
Romantic Theatre

Thomas C. Crochunis

What if realist, social-problem-oriented dramatic forms had only recently been recognized as a significant strand in the history of dramatic writing? What if although teachers had sometimes included a few plays adopting an *outside-in* approach to showing us the world and its conditions, scholars had only recently reclaimed the late-nineteenth century's heyday of realist/naturalist drama and theatre? A Victorianist would find her or himself reevaluating the importance of realist drama – both as an artistic/cultural form and as a feature of the cultural/economic landscape. What changes would need to be made – to existing courses in drama and theatre history, to period studies courses, even to a degree programme's overall curriculum distribution requirements – to ensure students learn enough about this newly recovered historical moment in theatre and drama history?[1]

The hypothetical recovery of realist drama would be complex, but no more so than the pedagogical and curricular reevaluation of the Romantic era and of British theatre history that faces us in response to recent scholarly work on Romantic theatre and drama. Adding a few plays to the Romantic canon will not be sufficient to engage students fully with recent scholarship's new perspectives on the period. Introducing a special issue of *Nineteenth-Century Contexts* (2006), my overview of recent approaches to Romanticism and theatre emphasized that three broad patterns of scholarship have emerged as significant – a "sociological" approach to analysing how various issues affect the relationship between Romanticism and theatre, a new interest in the cultural significance of dramatic genres, and a reconsideration of the status of dramatic scripts. I further observed that, along with these three trends in scholarship, there has been increased awareness of the methodologies needed to develop new histories of the period's theatre and drama

(Crochunis 2006: 281). Romantic theatre studies can challenge students to rethink Romanticism and British literature studies generally, and its methodological turn provides a valuable opportunity to reexamine with students how we read historically situated texts. Initially, it might be tempting to simply add one or two plays to our Romanticism courses, but such minor tinkering will create neither curricula that make sense across literary history nor pedagogy that develops student interpretive processes that can be applied across periods to a more theatre-relevant version of British literary history.

But if the survey results from the London "Teaching Romanticism" conference in 2006 and other revealing artifacts – such as recently published North American and United Kingdom Romantic studies teaching anthologies – are any indication, Romanticists are still groping for ways to enhance the theatre and drama portions of their period studies curriculum. The 2006 survey of UK academics on teaching of Romantic courses/modules documented that drama remains the least commonly taught of the major literary forms. However, a number of respondents mentioned the absence of drama in major period anthologies, noted their desire to incorporate more plays into the Romanticism module/course, and referred to the time limitations that make adding full-length plays and related theatre history to a relatively short course a bit of a struggle ("Survey Results" 2006). Admittedly, the survey focuses only on UK institutions, but it raises similar issues to those I would expect we would find in North American responses to the changing role of drama and theatre in the period. Both informal professional conversation and recent publication initiatives indicate that new attention is being given to solving the curricular and pedagogical issues raised by adapting Romantic studies courses to the unwieldy historical complexity of theatre and drama. And yet, the challenges we face in rethreading British theatre and dramatic history through our curricula and teaching approaches are more complex than adding a few plays or excerpting a few major drama critics and periodical reviews in our Romantic studies courses.

The 2003 publication of *The Broadview Anthology of Romantic Drama* edited by Jeffrey Cox and Michael Gamer provided a text to help teachers of Romanticism easily access a range of plays in various genres both by authors associated with traditionally taught Romanticism and by those writing for the theatre of the era. The Cox and Gamer anthology also includes supporting critical materials and reviews from periodicals that surface the issues surrounding theatre in the era. Though the collection may seem large at ten plays, it is remarkably economical in how much ground it covers through its careful balancing of texts. In addition, the entire collection provides an admirable introduction to the drama and theatre of the era. In addition to including plays by three of the literary "big six" of Romantic studies (Coleridge's *Remorse*, Shelley's *The Cenci*, and Byron's *Sardanapalus*), Cox and Gamer cannily provide plays by the three most important women playwrights of the long Romantic period (Hannah Cowley's *A Bold Stroke for a Husband*, Elizabeth Inchbald's *Every One Has His Fault*, and Joanna Baillie's *Orra*) and further choose four generically rich plays by major theatrical writers of the period (Matthew Lewis' hippodrama afterpiece *Timour the Tartar*, George Colman the Younger's parody of Lewis' play, *The Quadrupeds of Quedlinburgh* and his orientalist melodrama *Blue-Beard*, and Thomas John Dibdin's pantomime *Harlequin and Humpo*). Not only does the anthology admirably supplement the two poetic dramas – Byron's *Manfred* and Shelley's *Prometheus Unbound* – that are commonly included in anthologies of Romantic literature, its selections and supporting materials (headnotes and contemporary reviews and critical commentary) also speak to each other in a number of ways that enable creative pairings within our courses.

The majority of teachers of Romantic-period courses may not yet want to provide such a thorough overview of the period's theatre. An alternative approach to using an anthology and reading more broadly would be to apply a more intensive focus to a single play, using it to raise many of the kinds of issues about theatre and drama in the era that are touched on in Cox and Gamer's survey. A good example of a prototype resource that aims to facilitate this kind of work with the period's drama is *Romantic Circles'* Praxis Series 2002 volume on *Obi* edited by Charles Rzepka (Rzepka 2002). Based on the series of presentations in 2000 of the *Obi* texts along with critical commentary, the edition includes digital texts of two versions of *Obi* (a pantomime and a melodrama), video clips from the presentations that annotate the digital scripts, and a series of critical commentaries on the issues surrounding these theatre pieces. The *Obi* volume, then, takes an intensive – rather than an extensive – approach to engage us with the theatre of the era, and in this case the chosen plays provide valuable thematic material for those teaching about the issues surrounding abolition in the Romantic era.

Neither the extensive nor the intensive solution is a perfect one, but each has its merits, for we are still in an awkward moment when it comes to targeting the needs of those who want to teach theatre and drama in the context of a Romanticism course. Cox and Gamer's anthology could likely, for some tastes, be half as long and less costly. And *Obi* might not be the text most would choose as a centerpiece of class work on Romantic theatre, though to be fair the Rzepka volume is primarily intended to document scholarly investigation of this text. Still, the Cox and Gamer text demonstrates that a thoughtful overview of the period's theatre and drama is possible within the scope of a commercial anthology, and the *Obi* volume shows how digital media can help us expand the materials we use to teach Romantic theatre.

In the past ten years, source materials – from plays themselves to critical commentary on performances and plays – have gradually become readily available in texts such as Cox and Gamer's and through online resources such as *Romantic Circles'* Electronic Editions and *British Women Playwrights Around 1800* (Crochunis and Eberle-Sinatra 2008). Romanticists are, however, undecided about what plays are most important to teach: the 2006 UK survey, in which 57 per cent said no plays were taught in Romanticism modules at their institutions, revealed that institutions that do teach Romantic drama in their Romanticism course range across no less than twenty-three different plays (interestingly 9 of 10 from the Cox/Gamer anthology); 18 of 88 respondents teach *Manfred*, with 5 to 7 teaching *The Cenci, DeMonfort, The Borderers*, and *The School for Scandal* and others teaching a variety of other plays. This data indicates that despite some hesitation to make the Romantic theatre leap, faculty are still experimenting with which plays fit within the shifting curriculum. With the era's dramatic canon still in flux, often teachers select dramas that help them introduce or develop some of the themes that have become central to Romantic studies in the past twenty years or so – for example, gender relations, colonialism and race, and the politics of revolution. To teach plays within thematic curricular contexts, many teachers no doubt need to compile resources that help connect the plays to other texts in their courses.

Finding appropriate classroom texts is not the only impediment that keeps theatre of the Romantic era from becoming an integrated part of our curricula. Typically, faculty who specialize in Romanticism often do not know well the full history of British drama nor do they possess the pedagogical backgrounds in working with performance texts and histories that are more common among Shakespeare or modern drama specialists. However, a department's drama specialists may be even less likely to know the performance and playwriting of the British Romantic era. Along with this expertise gap, there is the dilemma that Romantic studies, squeezed between the increasingly "long" eighteenth century and the expansive Victorian period, gets too little curricular space to allow for much attention to full-length plays.[2] Even more challenging than fitting full-length plays in a crowded period, the complex theatre history inquiries needed to explore the Romantic era's peculiar hybrid genres and politically and socially complex theatrical culture – documented in recent Romantic era theatre and drama research – present particular challenges to our curriculum and teaching. Romanticists may find it challenging to integrate these unfamiliar materials into courses and units that once played to their strengths as teachers of poetry, prose fiction and political and critical essays; additionally, they may find it difficult to make the case in departmental discussions of curriculum for curricular space outside their period courses for the new theatrical history of the Romantic period.

Faced with some of the logistical and conceptual difficulties that reconceiving our teaching and curriculum can necessitate, Romantic studies faculty might wish that theatre and drama historians would take up the challenge and leave us to our poetry, our Jane Austen, Walter Scott and Mary Shelley, our revolution controversies, discussions of gender roles, and letters and essays on all manner of aesthetic and social questions. But as some of the most provocative scholarship on Romanticism and theatre has amply illustrated, we have much to gain by taking on the complex questions that rethinking the history of British theatre and drama in our period and beyond can open up. Doing so gives us a new perspective on the period and its literary culture, forcing us to reevaluate how we approach some of the themes that have become centrally important to our courses in Romantic studies. Scholarship on Romantic theatre and drama has changed our understanding of the European critical tradition, the problems presented by theatricality in political and social life, women's complex navigations of dramatic criticism and playwriting, the meanings of dramatic genres, the landscape of public theatrical institutions and their significance, and the political valences of theatrical gestures, scenes and images. Transforming our pedagogy and curriculum in light of this scholarship can also stimulate profound reconsideration of the period among our students.

To take a more self-critical view, one might also say that to fail to thoroughly rethink the Romantic period with theatre and drama in mind is to perpetuate the misleading view many students (including perhaps some readers of this essay) have been given of the Romantic era over the course of their educations. Over the years, I have spoken with many scholars of other literary periods who have pleaded utter ignorance of the theatre of the Romantic period. When we do not show our students how British theatre changed from the era of Restoration comedy and heroic tragedy to that of late-Victorian music drama and dramatic realism, we miss an opportunity to make a case for the social and aesthetic importance of the Romantic period to the history of British culture generally. Further, without tracing the performance history of the Romantic era, we can hardly help students make much sense of the performativity of Romantic writing in non-dramatic forms.

Because Romantic drama and theatre is receiving renewed interest outside academia, we have the opportunity to move the history of our period beyond university classrooms and curricula and into the repertories of contemporary theatre companies. Since sometime in 2001, I have had the chance to communicate with directors and dramaturgs who have become interested in the plays of this period. Most of my conversations with theatre artists begin the same way. I receive an email or read about production plans on a website and send an email myself, and soon learn that someone has stumbled upon a play or a playwright that they "had never read in school." Presented with lively dramatic material that they have, in effect, discovered for themselves, these artists typically write with excitement, describing the glimpse the play gave them of an artist, a moment in history, or a dramatic style that is new to them and speaks to them in some way. Our teaching the theatre and drama of the Romantic period – both in our formal courses in universities and through responding to queries by artists interested in developing productions that can speak to audiences now – contributes significantly to the public visibility of our literature studies programmes and to our communities' sense that we have something to contribute. Teaching about the drama and theatre of the Romantic period will make visible to the public at large our contribution. It is in our interest to play this kind of role.

Broad rationales for why Romantic theatre and drama *ought* to be taught are useful up to a point, but thoughtful approaches already being used to integrate drama and theatre into existing curricula make the case most eloquently. In fact, perhaps the strongest rationale for teaching Romantic theatre may be that doing so challenges us to employ teaching methods that can enhance students' learning about all aspects of the period. The complex phenomena surrounding Romantic era theatre and drama invite us to engage students in constructing their own ways of understanding the Romantic era's cultural history rather than simply recording professors' transmissions about the period. When teachers of Romantic theatre work out detailed pedagogical sequences, they illustrate how drama and theatre influence our ways of thinking about the Romantic era and its culture. And so, I want to use positive examples of holistic pedagogical problem solving amidst local institutional conditions to outline what some different approaches have achieved through exploring new pedagogies, classroom activities and curricula. While readers might find that only some of these examples suit their own situations, I hope these sample approaches will inspire development of new teaching strategies that work in a range of situations.

In work on teaching Romantic theatre that I have read in recent years, there are three main strands of pedagogical strategy that stand out – reframing curricula in ways that invite students to participate in rethinking the contexts through which we interpret Romantic theatre and drama, posing of theatre-based problems to engage students with both textual interpretation and historical and aesthetic information, and using concrete interpretive problems related to Romantic theatre and drama to raise fundamental questions for broader literature study. Let me briefly describe examples from recent writing about pedagogical approaches in recent publications.[3]

A number of scholars have reframed courses in theatre history or Romantic studies to encourage students to engage actively in making interpretive connections between Romantic era theatre and other more familiar texts. Catherine Burroughs (1998) offered one of the earliest examples of this when she described an advanced undergraduate course in which she highlighted many of the issues central to Romantic dramaturgy by focusing on women's dramaturgy as both aesthetic theory and practice. Several recent articles illustrate how situating Romantic theatre and drama within courses with different thematic, historical or cultural content helps students to encounter the material from new perspectives. Emily Anderson (2009) describes a graduate seminar on theatre from the Restoration to the Romantic era centered on the interaction of drama and pedagogy. Noting that there are many critical statements by Romantic-period authors about the educative role of theatre in stimulating our reflection about others' passions and our own, Anderson observes that "the key to Romantic pedagogy is not embodiment...but mediated experience," that "we learn about ourselves through others." For Anderson, Romantic drama is a fitting endpoint for an examination of drama's pedagogical potential in the long eighteenth century.

Another compelling thematic reframing of the position of Romantic theatre is Wendy Nielsen's (2009) eight-day unit, "Romantic Revolutions in Europe," exploring the international dimensions of Romantic drama. Nielsen describes how her course explores with students some of the varied elements of Romanticism in a broader European context and then considers these elements in relation to a number of different social upheavals significant to Romantic writing – the French Revolution, the Woman Question (and the roles of women in relation to the French Revolution), and Slavery and Abolitionism (in both England and France). While Nielsen's course only in part focuses on drama – featuring Shelley's *The Cenci* and Inchbald's *The Massacre* – she provides a case example of how drama of the period can be connected thematically while still engaging with some of the complex issues surrounding its negotiations of theatricality in politically charged times. In another example, Amy Muse (2009) reframes dramaturgical history by centering her course on "holy theatre" (a term taken from Peter Brook's *The Empty Space*), or "Theatre of the Invisible-Made-Visible" (Brook 1995). Muse makes Romantic drama central to this "master current" that ranges from Shakespeare's *Hamlet* and *The Tempest* to Strindberg's *The Ghost Sonata*, Beckett's *Waiting for Godot*, and early Sam Shepard. In her rethinking of the dramaturgical lineage in which Romantic drama such as Coleridge's *Remorse* and Baillie's *Orra* participate, Muse draws students into traditions that run counter to realism, that emphasize difficult-to-express affective states, and that use theatricality to engage audiences with character consciousness. Like these colleagues, I have also found that reshaping the curricular context in which we position drama and theatre of the Romantic period can significantly influence student response to the period's drama. In fact, teaching Romantic theatre and drama outside period survey courses may allow us to make compelling thematic connections within or across periods as has some of the most compelling recent scholarship.

Many teachers who have written recently about teaching Romantic-era drama and theatre have noted that studying dramatic scripts benefits from the introduction of performance exploration and dramaturgical or scenic design inquiry grounded in theatre practice; not only do the thinking processes taken from theatre practice help students learn to work through decisions about staging the plays, but they also invite discussions of Romantic-era perspectives on social performance and spectacle, on imagination and interpretation, and on the political valences of public theatre in the period. Drawing on theatre practice as a model for exploration in the classroom helps to provide an experiential framework for developing students' frequently limited knowledge about British theatre history between Shakespeare and Shaw. Through interspersing the reading of plays and Romantic-era commentary on play productions and theatre practices with students' work on performing interpretations of scenes from Romantic era plays, unfamiliar dramatic styles and thematic issues can become matters for inquiry and discussion rather than background to be explained in lectures. Purinton (2004) outlined some of the ways that through projects and activities (many similar to those often used when teaching Shakespeare's plays at the secondary level) she gave students hands-on experience with the dramaturgy and meaning of plays by Joanna Baillie – for example, asking them to "describe how they would film a scene or direct the staging of an act from Baillie's drama in the theatre of her day, or in their own university theatre" (226). Purinton further described working with students on "community" and "readers' theatre" presentations of Baillie's plays for audiences beyond the undergraduate classroom, allowing students to see how audiences unfamiliar with the plays could become engaged by Baillie's exploration of psychological and social issues (234–7). Using theatrical production as an even more fully developed pedagogical strategy, Frederick Burwick, one of the most active practitioners of the staging of plays from the Romantic period within educational settings, writes of a course he designed around the production of James Cobb and Stephen Storace's *The Haunted Tower*, their English adaptation of the Marquis de Sade's *La Tour Enchantée* (Burwick 2009). Burwick cast his play with students from a range of disciplinary backgrounds and explored theatrical history during the process of rehearsal, allowing the students to "learn the material literally from the inside out."

Taking the perspective of the dramaturg as her angle into Hannah Cowley's *The Belle's Strategem*, Melinda Finberg (2009) explores the questions surrounding performance of a single minor character in the play (Kitty Willis). By designing activities for students that lead them to conduct research and interpret the play the way a dramaturg might in working with a director and actors, Finberg demonstrates how the interpretive work that performance demands leads students to contemplate how theatrical meaning making is informed by both diligent work on a script's details and aesthetic choices. In 2008, I worked with Nick Ray, an advanced undergraduate filmmaking student from my university, director Bronwen Carr, and the cast of the Finborough Theatre's 2008 London production of Joanna Baillie's *Witchcraft* to record digital video of rehearsals, interviews and the play's performance. Using the video we recorded, we have begun to develop an early prototype digital resource that can engage students with the interpretive work of a theatre company as it tries to find approaches to making a historically recovered play meaningful to contemporary audiences. Introducing students to theatrical problem-solving processes gives us a powerful set of strategies for using theatre and drama of the Romantic period to promote careful work with texts, practical investigation of historical context, and reflection about how a play's meaning can travel across time.

Several other articles show how topics related to drama and performance in the Romantic era can be used effectively in teaching fundamental interpretive approaches in courses for students early in their course work in the English major. Dawn Vernooy-Epp (2009) describes how she features Baillie's comedy *The Election* early in "Introduction to Literary Studies," a foundational course for English majors, because students come to the play with few preconceptions, and as a result are able to engage directly with Baillie's dramaturgical theory and practice and then to play their own observations about Baillie's play off of critical readings such as Anne Mellor's important early discussion, "Joanna Baillie and the Counter-Public Sphere" (1994). Along the way, Vernooy-Epp guides students in some of the basic elements of literature studies – reading carefully, taking detailed observational notes on challenging readings, and working through in discussion the implications of new perspectives gained from contextual materials. Finally, Noah Comet uses an innovative interpretive exercise involving Hidetoshi Oneda's short film adaptation of John Keats' "La Belle Dame sans Merci" to engage students with the interpretive nuance of Keats' poem (Comet 2009). Comet shows how the essential interpretive issues the exercise raises in discussion in fact connect in important ways to Romantic dramatic criticism, to the problems introduced by performed realization of literary/dramatic meanings, and to Keats' "negative capability" (which is, of course, a critical concept formed in response to Edmund Kean's acting). By developing teaching strategies that both prepare students for further interpretive assignments and reveal how theatre and drama raised significant questions for Romantic-era cultural life, we move beyond treating Romantic theatre as just one more bit of historical period content.

I think it is significant that Romanticists are already energetically exploring many different ways to bring Romantic drama into a range of different levels of courses. Much of what Romantic drama stimulates in terms of pedagogical innovation results in students being asked to learn through hands-on activities. The complexity of the cultural history surrounding Romantic theatre demands that we do more than add new content to our courses; rather we must develop materials and curricular contexts that invite students to engage with theatre history, scholarly criticism and each other, and to reflect on how Romantic-era performances and drama influence their perspectives on the political and psychological issues they see as central to our own time.

Notes

1. My hypothetical question for readers about how they would respond to recovery of a *missing realism* in dramaturgical history is inspired by Amy Muse's adaptation of William Demastes' discussion in his *Staging Consciousness* (2002) of two counter pressures in dramaturgical form – the "outside in" (focused on representing social and experiential reality) and "inside out" (focused on expressing and evoking states of mind and feeling) (Muse 2009). Muse applies Demastes' formulation in describing a drama course that connects Romantic plays to Peter Brook's concept of "holy theatre."
2. Our general period anthologies provide us with concrete illustrations of our curricular dilemma. Longman's portion of their British literature anthology, *The Romantics and Their Contemporaries*, edited by Susan Wolfson and Peter Manning, and Blackwell's *Romanticism: an Anthology*, edited by Duncan Wu, include now only excerpts from Joanna Baillie's "Introductory Discourse" to her 1798 *A Series of Plays* – with none of her plays themselves – and Lord Byron's *Manfred* (1817); the Wu anthology also includes Percy Shelley's *Prometheus Unbound* (1820) (Wolfson and Manning 2006; Wu 2006). (Longman houses the full text of Shelley's play on the anthology's companion website; *The Broadview Anthology of British Literature* provides Baillie's *DeMonfort* online as a companion to her "Introductory Discourse" in the print volume (Black, Connolly, Grundy, et al., 2006). *The Norton Anthology of English Literature*'s 7th edition of volume two includes only Byron's *Manfred* and excerpts from Shelley's *Prometheus Unbound* (Abrams and Greenblatt 2000). Of recent general Romantic period anthologies, Anne Mellor and Richard Matlak's *British Literature 1780–1830* includes the most generous sampling of Romantic era drama – Baillie's full "Introductory Discourse" and *Count Basil* (1798), Byron's *Manfred*, Shelley's *The Cenci* (1819) and *Prometheus Unbound*, Felicia Hemans' *The Siege of Valencia* (1823), and Thomas Bellamy's farcical short play on slavery *The Benevolent Planters* (1789) (Mellor and Matlak 2005). Narrow dramatic selections correspond, I suspect, to the ways users of the anthologies must feel pressured to economize on time and coverage in Romantic studies courses. (There is surprisingly also little drama in the *Longman Anthology of British Literature: the Restoration and the Eighteenth Century*, perhaps because Longman has also published the now dated (1988) *English Drama: Restoration and Eighteenth Century, 1660–1789*; drama's limited representation in core contemporary anthologies is not limited to the Romantic era (Damrosch and Sherman 2006).) Responding to the limited drama selections in major anthologies, in recent years, a wider range of smaller supplementary collections of plays have been edited and published. (See the list of "Related Resources.") When teaching drama in the context of Romantic period courses, many teachers use these supplementary editions, digital play texts, or course pack copies from costly scholarly play editions.
3. Several of these summaries are based on contributions to a 2009 special issue of *Romantic Circles Pedagogy Commons* on "Teaching Romantic Drama" (Crochunis 2009). I encourage readers of this essay to read that issue's contributions in full.

Works cited

Abrams, M. H. and Stephen Greenblatt, eds. (2000) *The Norton Anthology of English Literature*, 7th edn. Vol. 2 (New York: W. W. Norton).

Anderson, Emily Hodgson (2009) "Teaching the Teachings of the Stage: a Graduate Seminar on Restoration to Romantic Drama." Special issue: Teaching Romantic Drama. Thomas C. Crochunis, ed. *Romantic Circles Pedagogy Commons*, http://www.rc.umd.edu/pedagogies/commons/drama/anderson.

Bevis, Richard W. (1988) *English Drama: Restoration and Eighteenth Century, 1660–1789* (London and New York: Longman).

Black, Joseph, Leonard Conolly, Kate Flint, Isobel Grundy, et al., gen. eds. (2006) *The Broadview Anthology of British Literature*, Vol. 4, *The Age of Romanticism* (Peterborough, Ontario: Broadview).

Brook, Peter (1995) *The Empty Space* (New York: Touchstone).

Burroughs, Catherine (1998) "Teaching the Theory and Practice of Women's Dramaturgy," *Romanticism on the Net*, 12, http://www.erudit.org/revue/ron/1998/v/n12/005823ar.html.

Burwick, Frederick (2009) "Teaching Romantic Drama: Production and Performance of *The Haunted Tower*," Special Issue: Teaching Romantic Drama. Thomas C. Crochunis, ed. *Romantic Circles Pedagogy Commons*, http://www.rc.umd.edu/pedagogies/commons/drama/burwick.

Comet, Noah (2009) "'La Belle Dame sans Merci': a Multimedia Experiment in Reading and Seeing," Special Issue: Teaching Romantic Drama. Thomas C. Crochunis, ed. *Romantic Circles Pedagogy Commons*, http://www.rc.umd.edu/pedagogies/commons/drama/comet.

Cox, Jeffrey N. and Michael Gamer, eds. (2003) *The Broadview Anthology of Romantic Drama* (Peterborough, Ontario: Broadview Press).

Crochunis, Thomas C. (2006) "Introduction: When Romanticism Met Theater," *Nineteenth-Century Contexts*, Special Issue: Romanticism and Theater, 28.4: 281–3.

—— and Michael Eberle-Sinatra, gen. eds. (2008) *British Women Playwrights around 1800*, http://www.etang.umontreal.ca/bwp1800/

Damrosch, David and Stuart Sherman, eds. (2006) *The Longman Anthology of British Literature*, Vol. 1C, *The Restoration and the Eighteenth Century*, 3rd edn. (London and New York: Longman).

Demastes, William (2002) *Staging Consciousness: Theater and the Materialization of Mind* (Ann Arbor, MI: University of Michigan Press).

Finberg, Melinda C. (2009) "Staging the 18th-Century Prostitute for the 21st-Century: a Dramaturgical Approach to Teaching Cowley's *The Belle's Stratagem*," Special Issue: Teaching Romantic Drama. Thomas C. Crochunis, ed. *Romantic Circles Pedagogy Commons*, http://www.rc.umd.edu/pedagogies/commons/drama/finberg.

Mellor, A. K. (1994) "Joanna Baillie and the Counter-Public Sphere," *Studies in Romanticism*, 33: 559–67.

—— and Richard Matlak, eds. (2005) *British Literature 1780–1830* (New York: Heinle & Heinle).

Muse, Amy (2009) "Lifting the Painted Veil: Romantic Drama as Holy Theatre," Special Issue: Teaching Romantic Drama, Thomas C. Crochunis,

ed. *Romantic Circles Pedagogy Commons*, http://www.rc.umd.edu/pedagogies/commons/drama/muse.
Nielsen, Wendy (2009) "Romantic Revolutions in Europe: Suggestions for Teaching Drama," Special Issue: Teaching Romantic Drama. Thomas C. Crochunis, ed. *Romantic Circles Pedagogy Commons*, http://www.rc.umd.edu/pedagogies/commons/drama/nielsen.
Purinton, Marjean (2004) "Pedagogy and Passions: Teaching Joanna Baillie's Dramas," in *Joanna Baillie, Romantic Dramatist: Critical Essays*, ed. Thomas Crochunis (New York: Routledge): 315–47.
Rzepka, Charles, ed. (2002) "Obi: a *Romantic Circles* Praxis Volume," *Romantic Circles Praxis*, section ed. Orrin N. C. Wang. 8 Sept 2002, http://www.rc.umd.edu/praxis/obi/
Stillinger, Jack and Deidre Shauna Lynch, eds. (2005) *The Norton Anthology of English Literature: Vol. D: the Romantic Period* (New York: W. W. Norton).
"Survey Results: Teaching Romanticism Questionnaire" (2006) *BARS Website*, http://www.bars.ac.uk/teaching/survey/surveyresults.php.
Vernooy-Epp, Dawn M. (2009) "In Joanna Baillie's *The Election*, Men are Losers: Teaching Romantic Drama in Introduction to Literary Studies," unpublished manuscript.
Wolfson, Susan and Peter J. Manning, eds. David Damrosch and Kevin J. H. Dettmarr, gen. eds. (2006) *The Longman Anthology of British Romantic Literature*. Vol. 2A *The Romantics and their Contemporaries*, 3rd edn. (London and New York: Longman).
Wu, Duncan, ed. (2006) *Romanticism: an Anthology*, 3rd edn. (Oxford: Blackwell).

Related resources

Play texts

Burns, Edward and Paul Baines, eds. (2000) *Five Romantic Plays, 1768–1821* (Oxford: Oxford University Press).
Cox, Jeffrey N., ed. (1992) *Seven Gothic Dramas* (Athens, OH: University of Ohio Press).
Duthie, Peter, ed. (2001) *Plays on the Passions* (Peterborough, Ontario: Broadview).
Finberg, Melinda, ed. (2001) *Eighteenth-Century Women Dramatists* (Oxford: Oxford University Press).
Scullion, Adrienne, ed. (1996) *Female Playwrights of the Nineteenth Century* (London: Everyman).
Wolfson, Susan J. and Elizabeth Fay, eds. (2002) *The Siege of Valencia: a Parallel Text Edition* (Peterborough, Ontario: Broadview).

Collections of criticism

Burroughs, Catherine, ed. (2000) *Women in British Romantic Theatre: Drama, Performance, and Society 1790–1840* (Cambridge: Cambridge University Press).
Crochunis, Thomas C., ed. (2004) *Joanna Baillie, Romantic Dramatist: Critical Essays* (New York: Routledge).
—— guest ed. (1998) *Romanticism on the Net*, 12. Special Issue: British Women Playwrights around 1800: New Paradigms and Recoveries.

Davis, Tracy C. and Ellen Donkin, eds. (1999) *Women and Playwriting in Nineteenth-Century Britain* (Cambridge: Cambridge University Press).
Davis, Tracy C. and Peter Holland, eds. (2007) *The Performing Century: Nineteenth-Century Theatre's History* (Basingstoke: Palgrave Macmillan).
Hoeveler, Diane Long, guest ed. (2003) *European Romantic Review*, 14.1. Special Issue: Romantic Drama: Origins, Permutations, and Legacies.
Moody, Jane and Daniel O'Quinn, eds. (2007) *The Cambridge Companion to British Theatre 1730–1830*. Cambridge: Cambridge University Press.
Nineteenth-Century Contexts, 28.4. (2006) Special Issue: Romanticism and Theater.
Schneider, Matthew, guest ed. (2006) *European Romantic Review*, 17.3. Special Issue: British Women Playwrights, 1780–1830.

3
Scottish, Irish and Welsh Romanticism

Murray Pittock

All literature is a form of travel through time and space. If this is remembered, it is equally the case that criticism must have the same function to pursue it along these same tracks: but the fact that the tracks chosen by criticism across time condition our sense of the space literature occupies can be forgotten. Any refugee from the critical world that preceded the Second World War who came upon a major conference of contemporary Romanticists (say the British Association of Romantic Studies 2007 conference in Bristol) would no doubt be absolutely stunned by the complete absence of Burns and Scott from an assembly of hundreds of papers. In the late 1930s, Burns was clearly one of the major Romantics as measured by the number of articles published on him: lying midway in a group of seven, not six, much-commented on male poets. Meanwhile, Scott's novels were a commonplace of the English grammar school curriculum. Within thirty years, both had more or less been wiped out of the new aestheticized Romanticism, which had abstracted itself from the particularities of Lovejoy's plural Romanticisms, to become an essentialist claim about the nature of the imagination in a particular historic period. This period was never very well-defined: for example, if it began with *Lyrical Ballads* it had no reason to include *Songs of Innocence and Experience*; if it began with the French Revolution, it had no reason to exclude Burns. Blake became a Romantic by virtue of the fact that he survived the publication of *Lyrical Ballads*, not because he was younger than Burns: in fact, he was two years older.

As Sharon Ruston's 2006 survey showed, and as is abundantly clear from other evidence – for example the content of undergraduate readers, those gatekeepers of the academy – this state of affairs has not changed as much as we might expect, twenty-five years after Marilyn Butler and Jerome McGann began to undermine it.[1] A broader, more global

Romanticism has supervened, it is true; postcolonialism has found a number of subjects in the period, not least Jane Austen; women's writing has been reevaluated, as have travel narratives; Southey is back in business, and labouring-class poets have their place in the sun. Yet there are problems: the undergraduate curriculum reflects this imperfectly, while there are relatively few applications in the UK for funded postgraduate research in Romanticism as compared to early modern literature, where the dynamic research agenda of the last twenty-five years seems to have made its way more comprehensively into undergraduate study. Moreover, there are huge gaps in the new Romanticism. Scott studies has taken off again – to an extent – in the USA, but in the absence of wider recognition and dialogue, it often remains a sealed world: in 2007 there was the faintly ridiculous spectacle of the BARS–NASSR conference in Bristol with not a single Scott paper on the programme being succeeded immediately by the Scott conference in Oxford, which had dozens of papers on no-one else. In other words, Romantic studies have still not come close to recognizing Scott's centrality, while Scott studies sail on without taking much notice of Romanticists. This state of affairs, true to an extent of Burns also, is hardly a healthy one. Burns is handicapped by his use of non-standard English, so that the only niche available to him in the new Romanticism is that of peasant or labouring-class poet: but the crucial distinction with Burns is that he manipulates registers of both English and Scots in pursuit of certain effects. This was noticed by Francis Jeffrey as long ago as 1809, so contemporary critics really have no excuse. Scott does the same of course, and so do Edgeworth (with Irish-English) and Hogg: in Scotland in particular, with its long tradition of independent literary language and terms of reference, these approaches have a sophistication which is complex, and which Romantic studies in general show little sign of getting to grips with.

There is no special pleading here. Scott and Burns have been translated thousands of times. Scott was more influential on the Europe of his age than any other Anglophone writer, with the probable exception of Byron. Burns is an iconic figure from Vancouver to Japan, with huge sales in China and Russia, which even issued a stamp in his honour in the 1950s. Yet as I have pointed out elsewhere (Pittock 2003: 195), there are textbooks on the market which purport to cover the period that offer chapters to Stephen Duck and do not mention Burns.[2] On 15 September 2000, the *TLS* ran a big review of Cowper which asked whether he or Smart were the best poet between the death of Pope and *Lyrical Ballads*, effortlessly ignoring the fact that Burns's poems in paperback could be found in competing editions on almost every airport bookstall; in

2009, Burns conferences and events from Beijing to South Carolina will give an appropriate answer to such insularity. People have not given up reading Burns.

For the key problem in many Romantic modules is still arguably the fact that ideas of Romanticism in the British Isles remain trapped on the tracks of an earlier critical paradigm, the end of which elsewhere has led to new dialogues in the fields of class, gender, politics and the public sphere, but which continues to have problems with issues of language and nation. Understanding Romanticism as a dialogue between national traditions and national public spheres (why else were the Edinburgh periodicals so effective at developing, maintaining and exporting their judgements if it was not for the distinctive existence of an Edinburgh public sphere?) is certainly key to deepening and broadening the roads we, as critics, travel down: and more students can be accommodated on a sizeable critical path where many smaller tracks converge.

The question of *more students* was a very important one to me in 2003–04, when I had just taken up post at Manchester as the first professor of Scottish literature south of the border. It was not an uncommon view that few students outwith Scotland would be interested in learning about Scottish literature. This was a view which I think was successfully challenged, both in the Higher Education Association day on "Teaching Irish and Scottish Literature" organized at the University of Manchester in 2005, and in the module, "Scottish and Irish Gothic," which is described below.

One of the important reasons for reconstituting British Isles Romanticisms as a series of dialogues comes from the fact that not all dialogues are between a centrally *English* and marginal *Scottish/Irish/Welsh* literature. There are dialogues over Ossian between Wales and Scotland and Scotland and Ireland, and the National Tale exists as a form in both Ireland and Scotland – and perhaps earlier than both in Wales, as recent work by Sarah Prescott seems to suggest (Prescott 2008). In devising a new final year BA Honours option module, I chose the major dialogue between Scottish and Irish literature, and the dialogue of both with the Gothic, chosen not only for its potential in boosting recruitment, but also because one of the ways that I argue that a national literature can best be defined is in the manner of its inflection of genre. Irish Gothic has been termed almost a "national genre" by writers such as Jarlath Killeen (2005), while its particular inflections have been explored by critics such as Vera Kreilkamp (1998) and Luke Gibbons (2004). Scottish Gothic has been less well explored and evaluated, but work by Ian Duncan (1994), Fiona Robertson (1994) and the present author have all helped to model some of its distinctive features in the Romantic period, particularly in the work of Hogg and Scott. In choosing both a generic and a national point of dialogue for Scottish literature, the intention was to broaden the critical path and promote student recruitment, while retaining intact the concept of Scotland's literature as a national and relational entity, not simply a subdivision or margin.

Recruitment in fact exceeded my expectations. With the cap of fifty students being reached in both 2004 and 2005, "Scottish and Irish Gothic" was one of the largest of all Honours modules at Manchester, especially considering that it was principally concerned with Romantic and nineteenth-century literature.

Despite its success in attracting students, the delivery of the course presented a number of problems. Students arrived on it with no background to speak of in the national literatures concerned, which they were expected to study at a relatively advanced level; they had a clear need of supportive background information, which must not turn into history, in a course that was both critical and theoretical; and, given the exigencies of student numbers, they were taught in two large groups of twenty-five or so in two-hour sessions.

The introductory session consisted of the distribution of an extensive handout on major Gothic themes and tropes with instructions for further reading, and an interpretative *cover* handout which suggested which of these themes might be identified in the texts set. There was a general if short lecture of about 30–40 minutes on these themes and tropes, linking them with a range of contemporary cinema, before moving into the question of national inflection of the Gothic and its implications: do certain Gothic themes stand for aspects of a national political and cultural experience?

In the individual meetings of the class which followed on from this first meeting, a pattern was established whereby the meeting began with two (or very occasionally three) presentations, each of which tackled an aspect of the text. There was then a question and answer session on these presentations, which in turn was followed by a thirty-minute lecture which covered both the critical issues raised and others which were important in the context of a *national* Gothic: for example, the references to dates in *Carmilla* and the role of a repressed native aristocracy; the symbolic importance of Laura's half-Styrian ancestry, and so on. At about five minutes to the end of the first hour, the class was divided into three groups. Three questions were offered to the groups: one might be on Gothic themes, one might be on national symbolism and one at least was always a close reading. Each group chose one of these topics, and the tutor then left the room for twenty minutes. On returning, each group took it in turns to make the points which had been raised in their discussion. This did not usually take place through a spokesperson: most members of the group made individual points. The tutor placed these points on the board, within a matrix headed by considerations of themes in the plot, Gothic themes and national inversions of the Gothic. The questions were so framed as to provide many opportunities for connexions to be made in the ensuing discussion, and this indeed turned out to be the case – not infrequently the groups would enter into debate with one another as to the relevance of these connexions. At the end of each session (which usually ran for the whole two hours, and normally threatened to overrun) students were able to understand and relate the literary dilemmas of the text to its genre, and its genre to the conditions of its own national inflection.

For many students of non-Scottish background taking Scottish literature modules, the Scots language often proves to be a major obstacle. To take the example of one text, in dealing with James Hogg's *Confessions of a Justified Sinner*, a number of the students voiced a concern common among non-Scottish students taking Scottish literature about the author's use of Scots: that it was redundant, indulgent or unnecessary in some way. Those familiar with more generic Anglophone usage are often prepared to accept non-standard language if it appears that the writer in question has only a grasp of dialect: such a view is taken, for example – erroneously – of Burns. But if it is absolutely clear that the author can write high quality metropolitan literary English, there is often a concomitant feeling among non-Scots students that since they can write the standard, it is an indulgence not to: a reaction not unlike that shown to Welsh speakers who converse in the language while being able to speak English. One of the paradoxes of this point of view is that Hogg, who was far more of a "peasant poet" in literal terms than Burns, is not usually classified as such because his poetry is more or less in standard English. The use of Scots in *Confessions* therefore, is an obstacle to understanding to those not familiar with the language within their own environments.

It was particularly important for the students to cross this hurdle successfully if they were to understand that variable register was one of the key ways in which Scottish literature marks social and national allegiances within a text. The peasant voice (for example in the story of the Deil at Auchtermuchty) acts as a kind of choric commentator in Hogg's text; orality is preferred to print. Wringhim's work as a printer's devil is a grimly humorous parody of the reality of his demoniacal fall:

his reliance on a misreading of sacred scripture shows the limitations of a text-based (and therefore standardized) understanding of language. The Enlightenment writers promulgated the spread of a standardized English language in order to facilitate communication, trade and social homogeneity: Hogg shows that a homogenous language fails to prevent fanaticism, dysfunction and all kinds of social evil, at the same time challenging empiricism by his multiple narratives and undercut witness statements. Arabella Logan and Bell Calvert go to Bogle Heuch (incidentally a real place in Scotland), not understanding that what they will meet there is the supernatural, bogles in fact. They have lost touch with the language of the country, though not as seriously as Wringhim has.

The students were exposed to passages in the text where they could clearly see the functionality of Scots as a code or commentary for common sense and autochthonous authenticity, which is set against existential, empirical or theological definitions of self. At the end of the book, the Enlightenment narrator of the first part of it goes with a friend to visit James Hogg, a character in his own novel who speaks Scots to them and in general acts truculently towards their Edinburgh airs and graces. At the beginning of the book, John Barnett tells young Wringhim that he is a "gowk": a word meaning fool, but also cuckoo. The implication that he is a changeling (cf. John Wyndham's *Midwich Cuckoos*) as well as a fool is only possible through the Scots word, which in addition carries the secondary implication that Wringhim cannot (being a changeling in the nest who appears like a true chick) be as much of a fool as he seems. The adopted son who destroys his family and ultimately himself was to be an important theme for Emily Brontë, but as well as understanding that Hogg's *Confessions* has a central role in Anglophone literature which goes well beyond Scotland, it was also important for the students to realize that Hogg, typically for a writer utilizing Scots, varied register for purposes of thematic depth and artistic ambiguity. This eighth type of ambiguity broke through the surface of standard English to provide the key to another world in which the altermentality, the other-mindedness, of Scottish literature was part of its self-conscious establishment of its own rights as a national literature.

In encountering this, students deepen their understanding of the nature of literary language and its functions. It is not easy to realize fully that Wordsworth's "real language of men in a state of vivid sensation" is nothing of the kind until one encounters the multiple registers and evasive code-switching of his Scots and indeed Irish contemporaries.[3] There were Cumbrian dialect poets of course: but Wordsworth's aspirations to be a national poet could lead – in England – in one direction only, to standard English. The fact that there was an alternative national model available outwith England is one which helps students come to terms with the idea of dialogue between national literary traditions.

Language issues were also key to the approach taken in another successful module, "Writing and Identity in Scotland and Ireland, 1700 to the Present," a fourth year Honours course which I convened at the University of Strathclyde from 1996 to 2003. "WISI" was the first undergraduate course in the UK to place Scottish and Irish literature in a dialogic relationship, and two examples of this were its use of song traditions from Scotland and Ireland (recordings of songs were also played in the Manchester module) and the relationship between Scotland, Ireland and the Union as manifested in Susan Ferrier's *Marriage* and Maria Edgeworth's *Castle Rackrent.*

The student body at Strathclyde were more homogenous in a number of ways than that of Manchester, where students tended to be (very roughly) around 60 per cent from the north and 40 per cent from the south of England in the class. A few of the northerners in particular took the class because they regarded themselves as members of the Irish diaspora, but the number of such students was usually small. In Strathclyde by contrast, most of the students came from west or west central Scotland, with a few from the North of Ireland. The diversity of the group chiefly resided in the fact that there were a significant number of mature students, often from working-class backgrounds, and also that a largeish proportion of the student body from Scotland was of Irish cultural background. Quite often this group would know some of the songs which were discussed in class, and here by contrast with Manchester the issue was defamiliarizing the familiar rather than familiarizing students with the unfamiliar. Encountering these songs as literary texts was not an approach that these students had hitherto been familiar with: in doing so, they not only reencountered the signifiers of their own background, identity and self, but also interrogated them as badges of collectivity and pride. This was very interesting to see: but surely even more important was the confidence that a number of students gained that street literature was real literature: that there was no disconnection between their cultural background and their encounter with the curriculum, but that on the contrary *literature* was a ground of encounter for cultural representation and self-representation. The mirror to nature was not a trope but a description. They had walked first down the critical track in the time and space of their own lives.

This effect depended on the homogeneity of the student body. Just as at Manchester transferable codes (for example, the deployment of non-standard language in texts) and multiple connexions between different ways of reading engaged the majority of a diverse group, so at Strathclyde a significant number of the students could be bonded to the interest in the material by specificity of reference. They engaged with and intensified the cultural specificity of their own backgrounds, rather than disengaging from them to examine the unexpected and unfamiliar. In both cases, however, there was a violation of expectations as to what *literature* consisted of. For those students at Strathclyde who had previously studied little or no Scottish or Irish literature (a sadly not unfamiliar occurrence) the sense of self-discovery and self-authentication was sometimes intense, almost as if they had found a voice they feared prohibited in *literature* as a prestige product: the voice of their own lives, the performance of a national culture.

This was particularly striking in the case of *Castle Rackrent*. The unreliable voice of Thady – after Gulliver perhaps the first classic unreliable narrator in fiction – speaks a subaltern language which the footnotes and glossary seek to corral and control in the name of what Joep Leerssen has termed "auto-exoticism," the strategy by which the Ascendancy voice finds a post-Union role for itself as the uniquely qualified interpreter of the strange world of native Irishness (Leerssen 1996). The internal exotic, Thady, is thus presented to the British reader. But of course, the tale Thady tells, of his own family's victory over the Ascendancy Rackrents, who long ago abandoned the Catholic faith for the estates they have now lost, is suspect on every level from timescale to outcomes. In keeping with Edgeworth's mocking sally at English prejudice in *An Essay on Irish Bulls, Castle Rackrent* presents the internal triumph of the subaltern voice over the penal restrictions of footnote and glossary just as it presents the external story of the triumph of Jason over the Rackrents. On another level, like Burns's "Tam o'Shanter," Thady's narrative's triumph over its footnotes is a version of the collected evading the Romantic collector's grasp through opacity of linguistic reference and cultural practice.

Some mature students were deeply struck by this element in the text. Brought up in an education system which had censored the use of Scots in the classroom every bit as forcefully as any Irish *bull* was ever sneered at, they understood at once Thady's language's role as a domestic, patronized and to an extent private language, the censored speech they kept for home and friends. Those of Irish origin may well have understood this on a double level. The embedded quality of Gaelic speech in both Scots and Hiberno-English – for example, the use of the definite article with day, as in "it's a fine day the day" – also no doubt helped the students understand Thady's speech in relation to their own. In this way, outstanding work was done by some students whose general level of work was not so high: the theme of language and nation in Edgeworth was one to which their own experience responded deeply, as would not necessarily have been the case in another student body.

The language issue is of course even more stark with writing in Gaelic or Welsh. At Strathclyde, writers such as Aoghan Ó Rathaille and Eoghan Rua Ó Súilleabhain were taught in translation (usually with the Gaelic in facing text), and comparison was offered between the Gaelic and English versions of Roisin Dubh, Mangan's "Dark Rosaleen." The purpose of including such authors was not simply to provide variety, but to indicate the strength of different languages within the national literature, and to stress the importance of crossovers in theme and genre between Gaelic and Anglophone writing. For example, James Thomson and Allan Ramsay influenced Alasdair MacMhaighstir Alasdair, who included quite a number of English loan-words in his verse as well as being influenced by Thomson's *Seasons*. In turn, MacMhaighstir Alasdair's *Birlinn Clann Raghnaill* ("Clanranald's Galley") seems to have influenced Macpherson, besides the Gaelic originals on which Macpherson himself drew (Black 2005).

If the presence of multiple languages complicates the picture in Scotland and Ireland, it is even more marked in Wales. Iolo Morganwg is a figure at the crossroads of dialogues on Romanticism within the British Isles, with particular relevance to (for example) Chatterton and Macpherson. Now that more secondary work is available on Iolo, the unfinished "History of the Bards" is more accessible as a concept, as is Iolo's role as founder of bardic traditions and his use of them to forge Welsh nationality, or at least a rather partisan version of it, which privileged south Wales (Glamorgan in particular) over the north of the country. At the same time, for most students the language question would be an issue. One way to examine Iolo's contribution, then, would be through the concept of the bard: adopted to describe Shakespeare in the wake of Ossian, conferred on Turlough Ó Carolan in Ireland as a defence mechanism against Ossianism, and utilized by Iolo (as by Burns and Blake) to suggest both indefinite antiquity, renewal and potential futurity. The *bard* would thus become (particularly in the context of Percy's attempt to use the term "minstrel" to suggest that Anglo-Saxon culture transcended its Celtic antecedents) a concept at the core of a course concerned with identities in creation, tension and dialogue across the British Isles. The new research projects led by Claire Connolly at Cardiff (on Welsh and Irish Romanticism) and Mary-Anne Constantine at the Centre for Advanced Welsh and Celtic Studies/Y

Ganolfan Geltaidd (on Wales and the French Revolution) have the potential to develop a number of new ways of approaching these questions: indeed Cathryn Charnell-White's *Bardic Circles* (2007) can itself form a basis for examining Iolo and Burns as involved with projecting themselves as *national bards* in parallel ways.

It is this central concept of dialogue that is so often absent from the conventional critical track of Romanticism because it remains at undergraduate and even sometimes taught postgraduate level too heavily dependent on an outworn (or, more often, inadequately reinterpreted) version of the Romantic critical paradigm. In recent years, large international reception studies of Macpherson and Scott have been published, and the author is currently engaged on another reception project on Burns in the shape of the AHRC-supported Global Burns Network. Yet this activity seems so often to happen in a vacuum. It would be preposterous in any other period of Anglophone literature to find three writers of demonstrably global significance (Scott, Burns and Macpherson) excluded from the curriculum, and indeed from much critical inquiry. That they are so is a sign of the continuing confusion between aesthetic and period characteristics in a Romanticism which claims to have outgrown the former and expanded the latter. In November 2007, Amazon listed twenty-three separate editions of Burns's work, more than 75 per cent of them in paperback, and most of them can be bought for under ten pounds. Recent companions and bibliographies from the major presses allot him about one-seventh of the space offered Clare or Southey, and as little as 4 per cent of that given to Blake.[4] The buying and critical publics operate in different worlds: but the business of teaching and evaluating literature is to promote dialogue, not to repress it; to guide others through the time and space in which literature exists, not to deny its existence. Romanticism must be more open to nation, language and dialogue to appeal to the student body of today and the researchers of the future. In the reclamation of the relationship of national Romanticisms lies one of the most important means to free the study of literature from 1746–1848 from the limited purview from which it still too often suffers.

Notes

1. Sharon Ruston's survey of UK Romanticism teaching was unveiled at the Higher Education Association "Teaching Romanticism" day in London on 17 March 2006, and subsequently published in the *BARS Bulletin* (Ruston 2006:

10–2). Full details of the survey results are available on the BARS website ("Survey Results" 2006).
2. For example, David Womersley (2000).
3. The phrase is from the Preface to *Lyrical Ballads* (1802) (Gill 1990: 595–603).
4. For example, the *Cambridge Companion to British Romanticism* (Curran 1993) and the Clarendon Press *Literature of the Romantic Period: a Bibliographical Guide* (O'Neill 1998).

Works cited

Black, V. Ronnie (May 2005) "Sharing the Honour," unpublished paper, Association for Scottish Literary Studies Crossing the Line conference, Sabhal Mor Ostaig.
Butler, Marilyn (1981) *Romantics, Rebels and Reactionaries* (Oxford: Oxford University Press).
Charnell-White, Cathryn (2007) *Bardic Circles* (Cardiff: University of Wales Press).
Curran, Stuart (1993) *The Cambridge Companion to British Romanticism* (Cambridge: Cambridge University Press).
Duncan, Ian (1994) "The Upright Corpse: Hogg, National Literature and the Uncanny," *Studies in Hogg and His World*, 5: 29–54.
Gibbons, Luke (2004) *Gaelic Gothic* (Galway: Arlen House).
Gill, Stephen (ed.) (1990) *William Wordsworth* (Oxford: Oxford University Press).
Killeen, Jarlath (2005) *Gothic Ireland* (Dublin: Four Courts).
Kreilkamp, Vera (1998) *The Anglo-Irish Novel and the Big House* (New York: Syracuse University Press).
Leerssen, Joep (1996) *Remembrance and Imagination* (Cork: Cork University Press).
McGann, Jerome (1983) *The Romantic Ideology* (Chicago: University of Chicago Press).
O'Neill, Michael, ed. (1998) *Literature of the Romantic Period: a Bibliographical Guide* (Oxford: Oxford University Press).
Pittock, Murray (2003) "Robert Burns and British Poetry," *Proceedings of the British Academy*, 121: 191–211.
—— (2008) *Scottish and Irish Romanticism* (Oxford: Oxford University Press).
Prescott, Sarah (2008) *Eighteenth-Century Writing from Wales: Bards and Britons* (Cardiff: University of Wales Press).
"Survey Results: Teaching Romanticism Questionnaire" (2006) *BARS Website*, http://www.bars.ac.uk/teaching/survey/surveyresults.php.
Robertson, Fiona (1994) *Legitimate Histories* (Oxford: Oxford University Press).
Ruston, Sharon (Autumn 2006) "Teaching Romanticism," *BARS Bulletin and Review*, 30: 10–2.
Womersley, David, ed. (2000) *The Blackwell Companion to Literature from Milton to Blake* (Oxford: Blackwell).

4
European Romanticism

David Higgins

Given that many British Romantic writers were strongly influenced by Continental literature and philosophy, and that some of them (most obviously Byron and Scott) had a strong impact on European culture in the first half of the nineteenth century, it is unfortunate that undergraduates are rarely encouraged to consider Romanticism in a transnational context.[1] The aim of this essay is to offer a detailed examination of the problems and opportunities arising from teaching an undergraduate course on European Romanticism, based on my experience of teaching such a course at two British universities. I hope that it will encourage others to develop courses in this area, or, at least, to do more to encourage students to consider British Romanticism in relation to European culture. With increasing academic interest in the forces of transnationalism and globalization, this is a particularly apposite time for the study of Romanticism as a European phenomenon. As Peter Mortensen puts it, "studying literature in a migratory age . . . cannot but heighten our consciousness of the ways in which literary innovation was always, to a certain extent, the product of complex cultural intersections whose faultlines rarely, if ever, coincided with the borders of modern nation states" (2004: 6). Similarly, Michael Ferber notes that in American (and I would add British) universities, "there is now a strong trend towards diversity and 'world literature' as well as a growing awareness that English Romanticism is not fully comprehensible outside its greater European context" (2005b: xxix).[2] Furthermore, some significant recent publications, most notably *A Companion to European Romanticism* (Ferber 2005a) and the anthology *European Romantic Poetry* (Ferber 2005b), have made important primary texts and background material much more accessible to the anglophone reader than was previously the case.[3]

For some time before developing *European Romanticism*, I felt frustrated with the parochialism of much teaching and research in the area of Romanticism, including my own. One of the pleasures of teaching this course has been that I have been forced to read and reread some important European literature, deepening my understanding of European *and* British Romanticism. Given that I work in an English department, and I have tended to teach the course to students who had taken (or were in the process of taking) courses on British Romanticism, my approach is inevitably Anglocentric. However, this essay will examine broad issues that are applicable to a range of learning and teaching contexts: putting together a syllabus that is both coherent and wide-ranging; encouraging students to consider the relationships between literature from different countries; and helping students to address the crucial question as to whether Romanticism can be understood as a coherent phenomenon across Europe.

This question was not fully addressed by the first European Romanticism course I designed, to be taught to second-year undergraduates over one semester. I realize in retrospect that it was put together using four main criteria: *feasibility, range, coherence* and *contextual engagement.* (Such criteria might apply to many literature courses.) To start with *feasibility*, the temptation with such a broad topic is to try to include too much. But having been guilty in the early stages of my teaching career of overloading students, I tried to be as selective as possible in setting reading. I also needed to take account of library resources, which, in British universities at least, are often poor when it comes to European Romantic literature. Reliable English versions of the primary texts are also not always easily available, although a good range of translated European works are published in Penguin Classics and Oxford World's Classics.[4] Despite these limitations, I tried to not to make the course too "thin," given that its *raison d'être* was to explore, under the rubric of "European Romanticism," a wide *range* of different themes, texts, authors, genres and countries. Inevitably, though, one will end up with substantial omissions and certain countries will be underrepresented, or absent.

Somehow this *range* had to lead to a certain *coherence*. The course needed to help students to make connections between different texts, countries and themes. I tried to pick texts that I thought would work well together, and to identify some broad themes: revolution; the self and nature; genius and imagination; and sensibility. So far, so predictable, but I also wanted to include the more grotesque and ironic strands of Romanticism, so that students gain a sense of its complexity and inner tensions. Students sometimes see the Romantics as a po-faced bunch obsessed with mountains and sincerity, and it seems important to do as much as possible to complicate that oversimplification. *Contextual engagement* can also help with this. There is obviously a limit to how much one can expect of busy students but, for the course to be viable, they needed to be encouraged to consider Europe-wide events and processes (most obviously the French Revolution and the career of Napoleon), while also being aware to some extent of the specific national contexts in which texts were written. For example, it helps with Goethe's *Sorrows of Young Werther* if students understand that in the late eighteenth century "Germany" was not a fully-fledged nation state but a loose confederation that made up part of the Holy Roman Empire, and that middle-class German literature, particularly *Sturm und Drang*, articulated burgeoning nationalistic sentiment against the French-speaking nobility (Boyle 1991– vol. 1, chapter 1; Elias 1994: 3–28). Similarly, it is difficult successfully to engage with Gogol's fantasies of life in Saint Petersburg without an awareness of the importance of bureaucratic hierarchy in nineteenth-century Russia, and the status of that city as the most "modern" and outward-looking part of the nation (Berman 1988 is particularly useful here).

When I moved institutions, and had the opportunity to reconfigure *European Romanticism*, I added a fifth criterion: the course needed to be *critically reflective*. It began to seem important that neither tutor nor students should simply assume that there was such a thing as "European Romanticism," but consider it as the result of an ongoing process of cultural construction that began with the writings of the Jena Circle (most notably Friedrich Schlegel) at the end of the eighteenth century and continues to the present day. Sadly lacking in the course's first incarnation, I decided to add a seminar examining literary and artistic theory from the Romantic period, and also a concluding seminar in which we were to examine several critical texts that wrestled with the question of the coherence/existence of "European Romanticism" (for example, Bone 1995; the introduction to Ferber 2005a; and Lovejoy 1924). This new focus is made explicit in the description I now provide to students who might wish to choose this course.[5]

The next stage was to devise a detailed course outline. The syllabus below assumes ten weeks of teaching. It also assumes a number of favourable conditions: motivated students who are able to get through a fair amount of reading; a reasonable amount of contact time; no problems with copyright or the availability (or the expense) of texts; and no serious clashes in terms of material with other courses taught in the same department. In practice, of course, all syllabi are the result of compromise, but this one is fairly close to the *European Romanticism* course that I taught most recently. There are inevitably many significant omissions, but I think it strikes a good balance between diversity and coherence, and would be interesting and enjoyable to teach and study.[6]

Week One (Introduction): Jean-Jacques Rousseau, *Reveries of the Solitary Walker*.
Week Two: Johann Wolfgang von Goethe, *The Sorrows of Young Werther*; Friedrich Gottlieb Klopstock, "The Spring Festival"; Ossian (James Macpherson), "The Songs of Selma."
Week Three: Friedrich Schiller, *The Robbers*.
Week Four: George Gordon, Lord Byron, *Childe Harold's Pilgrimage*, Canto III; Allesandro Manzoni, "The Fifth of May"; Alphonse De Lamartine, "Man" (excerpt).
Week Five: Germaine De Stael, *Corinne, Or Italy*; Letitia Landon, "The Improvisatrice."
Week Six (Nature and the Self): Frederike Brun, "Chamouny at Sunrise"; Samuel Taylor Coleridge, "Hymn Before Sunrise, in the Vale of Chamouny"; Joseph von Eichendorff, "Departure"; William Hazlitt, "On Going a Journey"; Nikolaus Lenau, "Loneliness"; Eduard Mörike, "The Beautiful Beech"; Alexander Pushkin, "Autumn."
Week Seven (Romantic Theory): extracts from Victor Hugo, Novalis, Friedrich Schlegel, Percy Bysshe Shelley and Wilhelm Wackenroder.
Week Eight: Nikolai Gogol, "Nevsky Prospect," "Diary of a Madman," and "The Nose"; E. T. A. Hoffman, "The Sandman" and "The Golden Pot."
Week Nine: Mikhail Lermontov, *A Hero of Our Time* and "The Poet's Death."
Week Ten: Conclusion: a European Romanticism?
(All the poetry, except for that of Byron and Coleridge, can be found in Ferber 2005b.)

I knew that I wanted to start the course with two giants of late eighteenth-century European culture: Rousseau and Goethe. But which texts? I eventually settled on Rousseau's *Reveries of the Solitary Walker* (having rejected *Julie* and *The Confessions* as too long), and Goethe's *The Sorrows of Young Werther*. Both explore themes that resonate throughout European Romantic literature: sensibility; solitude; tensions between nature and culture; and the importance of the imagination. They also raise important issues to do with autobiography, persona and irony.

Rousseau, I hoped, would link particularly well later in the module to Byron's *Childe Harold's Pilgrimage* and to the texts that we were to examine in the seminar on "Nature and the Self."[7] Similarly, I thought that students might be able to make interesting connections between *Werther* and Schiller's *The Robbers*; the utterances on art and the imagination that we were to examine in the seminar on "Romantic Theory"; Lermontov's *A Hero of Our Time*; and Gogol's "Nevsky Prospect." In the *Werther* seminar(s), we also consider poems by Klopstock and "Ossian," which are important to the relationship between Werther and Lotte. (We might also look at the five sonnets written from Werther's perspective in Charlotte Smith's *Elegiac Sonnets* (1784).) Issues related to intertextuality and adaptation run through the whole module.

The Robbers is an important play that influenced many European writers and which helps students to (among other things) engage with political issues that lurk more implicitly in *Werther* and the *Reveries*. We continue to look at the relationship between literature and politics in the following seminar, on the third canto of Byron's *Childe Harold's Pilgrimage*, which meditates on the Battle of Waterloo and the rise and fall of Napoleon. Reading this alongside Manzoni's "The Fifth of May" helps students to get a sense of the hold that Napoleon had over the European imagination. I have also found that showing students a range of images of the French Emperor, from David's great propaganda paintings to patriotic British caricatures, helps them to engage with how he is represented in literature. (Time permitting, it is also helpful for students to read for this seminar an extract from Lamartine's "Man," which offers an interestingly ambivalent response to Byron.) In Week Five, we take a very different approach to Napoleonic Europe, examining the relationship between national and individual genius and the construction of gender roles in De Stael's *Corinne*. Issues of adaptation are raised by comparing the novel to Letitia Landon's poem "The Improvisatrice," which draws heavily on its plot and themes.[8]

Weeks six and seven are thematic. The seminar on "Nature and the Self" revisits ideas about solitude and the natural world from Rousseau, Goethe and Byron by examining several poems and Hazlitt's essay "On Going a Journey," a remarkable meditation on travel and the imagination that alludes to a number of Romantic writers, including Rousseau. The relationship between Brun's "Chamouny at Sunrise" and Coleridge's "Hymn Before Sunrise, in the Vale of Chamouny" (which partly plagiarizes Brun) often provokes interesting discussions about poetic "influence." The following seminar, on "Romantic Theory," looks at a range of extracts on art, poetry, and the imagination from writers of the period and is vital preparation for our consideration of the concept of European Romanticism in the concluding seminar.[9]

Rather idiosyncratically, the final two weeks of the course focus mainly on Russian literature, exploring authors who are not always described as "Romantic." (Pushkin would be a more obvious candidate.) However, Gogol's St Petersburg tales, although they might seem to look forward to Dostoevsky and Kafka, also mine a rich vein of fantasy and fairy tale that was an important aspect of European Romantic literature. They would work well, I think, in conjunction with one or two of E. T. A. Hoffman's fantastical short stories, and "Nevsky Prospect," indeed, contains characters called Hoffman and Schiller. The way in which this story portrays Piskarev's idealization of the woman he pursues offers a fascinating comparison with *Werther*. Lermontov's *A Hero of Our Time* is an appropriate final text for the module. I like to teach it alongside his poetic response to Pushkin's death in a duel, "The Poet's Death," in part because it offers an interesting gloss on the duel between Pechorin and Grushnitsky. In some respects Lermontov's novel seems archetypically "Romantic": it is set in exotic space at the edge of "civilization"; its protagonist is a self-consciously Byronic hero; and it is written as a confession. And yet, its complex structure and Pechorin's scepticism might be seen to work against the valorization of sincerity and idealism often associated with Romanticism. If nothing else, the novel should remind students of the difficulties of generalizing about such a diverse set of texts and writers.

I want now to give some specific examples of how I have taught certain texts and themes. At both institutions, I have delivered *European Romanticism* principally through seminar discussion (ten to twenty students). I try to avoid lecturing in seminars as much as possible and generally proceed through a combination of open discussion and group work (the balance of this depends on the size and ability of the seminar group). It strikes me, though, that this course that would particularly benefit from some contextual lectures, and also from a degree of flexibility in delivery. For example, at my current institution, option courses tend to be taught through a one-hour seminar every week. However, there are also five "extra" hours over the semester, which can be used to supplement the course's delivery. Because I had a small number of students, I was able to add an extra seminar to some weeks of the semester; this helped when trying to examine and compare closely related texts such as De Stael's *Corinne* and Landon's "The Improvisatrice."[10]

The first week of my current *European Romanticism* course contains two one-hour seminars. (If student numbers were higher, this might need to be changed to a seminar and a lecture.) I email students at least a week before teaching starts, so that they know that they have to had read Rousseau's *Reveries*. The first seminar begins with the usual introductions and administration (answering questions about the assessment and so on). I also like to give a start-of-course "pep talk," in which I emphasize the importance of the seminar as a forum for relaxed, friendly, but intellectually challenging debate. The *Reveries* is quite a tricky text for students, who might be reasonably confident about how to approach a novel or a sonnet but less sure about how to deal with a collection of meditative, digressive autobiographical essays. In such cases, it is often best to start with something easy and familiar, so I ask students to think about the "I" of the *Reveries* as a *constructed persona*, like a character in a novel. Using the whiteboard, we discuss what we make of this persona, unpacking the terms that students shout out ("sensitive," "paranoid," "lonely," etc.). In the subsequent seminar, we do some more detailed analysis of the *Reveries*. I tend to let the students decide which "Walks" we are going to focus on; the most popular tend to be the "Fifth Walk," in which Rousseau reminiscences about his happy existence on the "Île de la Motte," and (interestingly) the botanizing "Seventh Walk." The exploration of solitude and the self in the "Fifth Walk" gives an excellent foundation for discussions later in the course:

> I liked then to go and sit on the shingle in some secluded spot by the edge of the lake; there the noise of the waves and the movement of the water, taking hold of my senses and driving all other agitation from my soul, would plunge it into a delicious reverie in which night often stole upon me unawares. The ebb and flow of water, in continuous yet undulating noise, kept lapping against my ears and my eyes, taking the place of all the inward movements which my reverie had calmed within me, and it was enough to make me pleasurably aware of my existence, without troubling myself with thought. (Rousseau 2004: 86–7)

The move from active ("I liked") to passive ("taking hold," "stole upon me") in the first sentence exemplifies the way in which this passage celebrates the self-forgetfulness encouraged by solitary reverie in nature.[11] The physical "lapping" of the water is also a mental phenomenon which gently replaces the troubled "inward movements" of Rousseau's mind. Thus the apparently egoistic fantasy of the "Fifth Walk," in which the self is entirely detached from society and becomes "self-sufficient like God" (Rousseau 2004: 89), leads to a dreamlike state in which intense and painful self-consciousness is dissipated. This paradox is important to several texts later in the course (most obviously *Childe Harold's Pilgrimage*).

In the following week, we examine *The Sorrows of Young Werther*, which has a number of interesting similarities to the *Reveries*, not least the sense of alienation felt by both protagonists. We begin by discussing Werther's character, perhaps again using the whiteboard; some students find him attractively sensitive, others annoyingly self-obsessed. This leads nicely into an examination of the novel's form: how does it affect our relationship to the characters and events? Should we assume that the novel is straightforwardly endorsing Werther as a sentimental hero? We then move to talking about the novel's treatment of desire: why does Werther fall in love with Lotte? Does falling in love necessarily have much to do with the other person? The novel's fragmentary structure makes it easy to pick out short extracts for close reading, such as the passages for 13, 16 and 18 July, in which Werther enthuses about his "sacred" love for Charlotte, using all kinds of interesting metaphors. Students also often respond well to extracts from Roland Barthes's *A Lover's Discourse*, which uses Werther as one of a range of examples he draws on in anatomizing the various "figures" that constitute being in love:

> Werther wants *to be pigeonholed*... [He] wants a place which is already taken – Albert's. He wants to enter into a system... For the system is a whole in which everyone has his place (even if it is not a good place); husbands and wives, lovers, trios, marginal figures as well... everyone except me. (Barthes 1990: 45)

This "system," in *Werther*, is not only a system of desire, but a political and social system from which the bourgeois intelligentsia feel excluded: an exclusion that is manifest in Werther's humiliation at court. We have here, then, an intertwining of the personal and political, which is crucial to understanding the literature of the period. The pains and pleasures of these dual exclusions echo throughout the module, and help students to place the course texts in dialogue. For example, comparing the account of Werther's suicide and funeral, with its devastating final sentence ("No priest attended him" (Goethe 1989: 134)), to the more obviously ironic account of Piskarev's suicide in "Nevsky Prospect" sheds light on both texts. Similarly, *Werther* is an invaluable referent when considering the romantic posturing of Grushnitsky from "Princess Mary" in *A Hero of Our Time*.

I hope that it is not too bathetic to admit as we come towards the end of this essay that I may not teach *European Romanticism* again in its current form. Having moved from a small department where students have quite limited course options to an exceptionally large one in which the free market reigns, I have found that the course does not attract as many students as I would like. The other Romantic-period option that I teach, *Byron and the Shelleys*, fares much better. One reason for this is that last year *European Romanticism* ran "in competition" with several other attractive Romantic-period options, but perhaps an explicitly European course will never attract that many students whose primary focus is studying English (or, more properly, anglophone) literature. Still, it may be that the course needs to build up momentum at my "new" institution: several students have told me that they are disappointed that *European Romanticism* will not be running next year. I may also need to rethink the module and "sex up" its rather unexciting description. Whatever happens, I will be teaching European Romantic texts in future. I am currently considering putting together a module on Romantic autobiography, which would examine British texts alongside Rousseau and Goethe. I am also thinking of a module on Byron and Byronism which would, in part, address his impact on European writers like Lermontov and Stendhal. I do not exaggerate when I say that teaching European Romanticism has fundamentally changed the way in which I conceive teaching British Romantic authors.

But what do the students make of all this? Anonymous module feedback suggests that they have generally found the course enjoyable and stimulating, but also that they have understandably found some of the material difficult and struggled at times with moving between texts from different countries. Library resources have also been raised as an issue, although this is a hardy perennial of student feedback forms. Whatever the challenges of the course, I have found that as it progresses most students are able to make increasingly cogent connections across texts and cultures. In the final seminar, I write a list of the authors studied on the left-hand side of the whiteboard. I ask students to shout out what they think are the significant themes or issues that we have examined on the course and I write these on the right-hand side. Then we start to connect up themes to authors (and themes to themes, and authors to authors), and quickly end up with a messy whiteboard, but a strong sense of shared interests among European authors of the period.

In this final seminar, we also discuss the concept of "European Romanticism" with reference to critical work on the subject. Students find particularly helpful Michael Ferber's introduction to *A Companion to*

European Romanticism, which uses Wittgenstein's idea of "family resemblances" as a way of making sense of the similarities and differences between Romantic authors (Ferber 2005a: 1–9).[12] The last time I taught the course I designed my own student questionnaire to supplement my university's. One of the questions was "Does it make sense to talk about 'Romanticism' as a Europe-wide phenomenon?" Most students seemed to agree that it did. One wrote, "Certainly and I wouldn't have thought so prior to this module. Thematically and theoretically the artists are all linked under the umbrella of 'Romanticism' and we have proved that." It is of course hard to imagine that a highly selective literature course taught by an individual academic could prove very much at all, and perhaps this student had not fully taken on board some of my caveats about the constructedness of Romanticism. Still, there is something cheering about such confidence and about the student's awareness that their own views had changed. I hope that all of us had learnt from the module the extent to which European authors and texts of the Romantic period were in dialogue with one another, and the limitations of examining literature solely through the lens of national culture and tradition.

Notes

1. I am grateful to Ashley Chantler for his helpful comments on an earlier draft of this essay.
2. This trend is also apparent in recent critical interest in "Transatlantic Romanticism": see Manning 2005, Newman et al. 2006, Pace et al. 2005. It is a sign of the times that the two biggest Romanticism conferences of 2008 were entitled "Romantic Diversity" and "(Trans)National Identities / Reimagining Communities."
3. Other significant recent publications include Gogol 2003, Mortensen 2004, and Vincent 2004. See also the Continuum series "The Reception of British and Irish Authors in Europe", which includes useful edited volumes on Austen, Byron, Coleridge, Ossian, Scott and P. B. Shelley.
4. I have tended to supplement the course's main primary texts with a photocopied "course pack" to be purchased by the students at cost price, although one has to be careful here with copyright.
5. The Romantic period (circa 1770–1840) was one of great cultural, social and political change. Its defining event was the French Revolution of 1789–93, which led to the growth of various revolutionary and reformist movements across Europe. This period of socio-political turmoil was accompanied by an extraordinary flowering of innovative art and literature. Although the notion of "Romanticism" as a coherent and definable cultural form is problematic, there is no doubt that in Europe during this period, writers, artists and thinkers were engaging with a range of similar themes: the self and nature,

revolution, the importance of the imagination, sentiment and feeling, the irrational (dream, the supernatural, etc.), and the exotic. This module will consider these themes in a transnational context, examining and connecting a wide range of Romantic texts (in translation) by authors from various European countries. We will also interrogate the very idea of "Romanticism," discussing how it was constructed and imagined by writers at the time, as well as by modern critics.

6. I do not claim that this is the best of all possible *European Romanticism* courses; it is easy to imagine an excellent course with the same title that looks at none of the texts I teach. It could consider, for example, Rousseau's *Julie* or the *Confessions*, Goethe's *Faust*, Chateaubriand's *René* and *Atala*, Kleist's short stories, Tieck's "Eckbert the Fair" and Fouqué's "Undine," Stendhal's *The Charterhouse of Parma*, Scott's *Ivanhoe*, Manzoni's *The Betrothed*, Pushkin's *Eugene Onegin*, and poetry by (say) Burns, Espronceda, Heine, Lamartine, Leopardi and Mickiewicz. This course would not be thematically identical to mine but there might be a surprising number of similarities.
7. For a fine account of Rousseau's impact on the British Romantics, particularly as an autobiographer, see Dart 1999.
8. See Riess 1996: 814–17 for some interesting comments on what Landon "does" to *Corinne*.
9. Useful inspirations for the seminar on Romantic theory include Donnachie and Lavin (2003) and Furst (1980).
10. I do not have space in this essay to discuss assessment patterns, but the course is currently assessed by a four-thousand word essay, based in part on a two-thousand word unassessed essay. I have found that having the chance to comment on this essay and discuss with students how they might revise and expand it has been very helpful and resulted in some strong assessed work.
11. In this move from active to passive, Peter France's translation is true to the original text.
12. In an essay published in the same year as Ferber's, Christopher Bode also talks interestingly about European Romanticism in terms of Wittgenstein's "family likenesses" (2005: 135).

Works cited

Barthes, Roland (1990) *A Lover's Discourse* (Harmondsworth: Penguin).

Berman, Marshall (1988) *All That is Solid Melts into Air: the Experience of Modernity* (Harmondsworth: Penguin).

Bode, Christopher (2005) "Europe," in *Romanticism: an Oxford Guide*, ed. Nicholas Roe (Oxford: Oxford University Press): 126–36.

Bone, Drummond (1995) "The Question of a European Romanticism," in *Questioning Romanticism*, ed. John Beer (Baltimore: Johns Hopkins University Press): 123–32.

Boyle, Nicholas (1991–) *Goethe: the Poet and His Age*, 2 vols. (Oxford: Oxford University Press).

Dart, Gregory (1999) *Rousseau, Robespierre and English Romanticism* (Cambridge: Cambridge University Press).
Donnachie, Ian and Carmen Lavin, eds. (2003) *From Enlightenment to Romanticism: Anthology*, 2 vols. (Manchester: Manchester University Press).
Elias, Norbert (1994) *The Civilising Process*, trans. Edward Jephcott (Oxford: Blackwell).
Ferber, Michael, ed. (2005a) *A Companion to European Romanticism* (Oxford: Blackwell).
—— ed. (2005b) *European Romantic Poetry* (New York: Pearson Longman).
Furst, Lilian R., ed. (1980) *European Romanticism: Self Definition: an Anthology* (London: Methuen).
Goethe, Johann Wolfgang von (1989) *The Sorrows of Young Werther*, trans. Michael Hulse (Harmondsworth: Penguin).
Gogol, Nikolai (2003) *The Collected Tales of Nikolai Gogol*, trans. Richard Peaver and Larissa Volokhonsky (London: Granta).
Lovejoy, Arthur (1924) "On the Discrimination of Romanticisms," *PMLA*, 39: 229–53.
Manning, Susan (2005) "Americas," in *Romanticism: an Oxford Guide*, ed. Nicholas Roe (Oxford: Oxford University Press): 149–62.
Mortensen, Peter (2004) *British Romanticism and Continental Influences* (Basingstoke: Palgrave Macmillan).
Newman, Lance, Chris Koenig Woodyard and Joel Pace, eds. (2006) *Sullen Fires Across the Atlantic: Essays in Transatlantic Romanticism, Romantic Circles Praxis Series*, http://www.rc.umd.edu/praxis/sullenfires/.
Pace, Joel, Lance Newman and Chris Koenig Woodyard, eds. (2005) *Transatlantic Romanticism: a Special Issue of Romanticism on the Net*, 38–9, http://www.erudit.org/revue/ron/2005/v/n38-39/index.html?lang=en.
Riess, Daniel (1996) "Laetitia [*sic*] Landon and the Dawn of English Post-Romanticism," *Studies in English Literature, 1500–1900*, 36: 807–27.
Rousseau, Jean-Jacques (2004) *Reveries of the Solitary Walker*, trans. Peter France (Harmondsworth: Penguin).
Vincent, Patrick (2004) *The Romantic Poetess: European Culture, Politics and Gender, 1820–1840* (Lebanon, NH: University Press of New England).

Further reading

Bainbridge, Simon (1995) *Napoleon and English Romanticism* (Cambridge: Cambridge University Press).
Bassnet, Susan (1993) *Comparative Literature: a Critical Introduction* (Oxford: Blackwell).
Cranston, Maurice (1994) *The Romantic Movement* (Oxford: Basil Blackwell).
De Stael, Germaine (1998) *Corinne, or Italy*, trans. Sylvia Raphael (Oxford: Oxford University Press).
Furst, Lilian R. (1979) *Romanticism in Perspective* (London: Macmillan).
Goethe et al. (2000) *German Romantic Fairy Tales*, ed. Carol Tully (Harmondsworth: Penguin).
Hobsbawm, E. J. (1988) *The Age of Revolution: Europe, 1789–1848* (London: Abacus).

Lermontov, Mikhail (2001) *A Hero of Our Time*, trans. Paul Foote (Harmondsworth: Penguin).

O'Neal, John C. and Ourida Mostefai (2004) *Approaches to Teaching Rousseau's* Confessions *and* Reveries of the Solitary Walker (New York: MLA).

Porter, Roy and Mikulas Teich, eds. (1988) *Romanticism in National Context* (Cambridge: Cambridge University Press).

Schiller, Friedrich (1979) *The Robbers and Wallenstein*, trans. F. J. Lamport (Harmondsworth: Penguin).

Wellek, René (1949) "The Concept of 'Romanticism' in Literary History," *Comparative Literature*, 1: 1–23, 147–72.

5
Gender and Sexuality

Sharon Ruston

I do not ask students anymore whether they call themselves feminists, because the results are depressing. The last time I asked, only one of a hundred plus first years put her hand up; it may be that students were embarrassed to admit their feminism in front of their fellow students. As my deliberate gendering here suggests (*fellow*), I wonder whether, as with mixed school classes, women are embarrassed to speak up, which is depressing in itself, but I am not sure that this is necessarily the case. There are many female students now who would object to being known as a feminist. For them feminism is both militant and irrelevant. I will not rehearse the full trajectory here, but just briefly glimpse at the range of pop culture constructions of feminism that students have been confronted by in recent years in order to see why this might be the case. We have moved from the liberating effects of *The Female Eunuch*, to drunken and loutish 1990s "ladettes" in the tabloids and the dubious freedoms asserted by The Spice Girls' and Lara Croft's "girl power." In our present students' adulthood the pop band Girls Aloud's explanation of sexual difference in their 2006 song *Biology* ("You can't mistake my Biology / The way that we walk / The way that we talk / So easily caught") offers them a simple account of femininity as biologically determined.[1] Suffice to say the students I teach often think feminism is a thing of the past, that its battles have been won, and that they would not want to associate themselves with its heroines and their ideals.

Much of this, of course, is misunderstanding; when I tell them that at root being a feminist means believing that women are equal to men, students no longer have a problem with it. Often my objective, which I am explicit about in my classes and lectures, is to persuade them that being a feminist still has relevance to their lives: I point out to them that perhaps the battle has been won by the wrong side. Persuading people that the sexes are treated equally in society now might just be the master stroke of patriarchy. We have seen a palpable shift in the fact that there are now very few Women's Studies departments in Higher Education Institutions in the UK; there is however an equally clear upsurge of interest in gender studies, including masculinity studies (which may, of course, be the study of dead, white men by another name), and of queer studies. Modules on these topics routinely attract large numbers of students and often involve, to some degree, teaching of feminist theory.

In this essay I argue for the full inclusion of women writers on Romanticism modules, that these writers should be integrated within such modules rather than taught as a separate entity, and that both gender and sexuality are to be regarded as only one aspect of a writer's identity. I give examples from my current teaching that examine the cultural construction of gender, and then move to consider how modules on the gothic perhaps offer more scope for the teaching of sexuality. I explore the trajectory of critical opinion, from the earliest calls for the need to read women writers to very recent new assessments of the potential that queer readings have for gothic texts of this period. Finally, I end with a case study from a lecture and seminar in which I show how women's bodies were a site of contention and suggest ways that this material might be used in evaluating the behaviour of female characters studied on the module.

At my institution we have a second-year, survey module called "Romanticisms." As the title suggests, this module has always (since before my time) emphasized the plural nature of the concept of Romanticism; as A. O. Lovejoy would have it: "When a man is asked . . . to discuss romanticism, it is impossible to know what tendencies he is to talk about, when they are supposed to have flourished, or in whom they are supposed to be chiefly exemplified" (1924: 66–7). In the module I consider this plurality in a rather more positive light than Lovejoy did: we interrogate the concept of "Romanticism" and try to establish coherence in its characteristics and themes. I try to give a sense of the people who created "Romanticism"; those Victorian and twentieth-century critics who, with hindsight and agendas of their own, gave the literature of around 1780 to 1830 this label. The students hear very different voices with entirely opposite ideas, such as looking at extracts from both Burke and Paine in one lecture, reading versions of the Christian's and the atheist's sublime in another, and comparing examples of society and solitude in Romantic literature in yet another. When I had the opportunity to revise the module substantially, I started with a few rules: there would be as nearly as possible equal numbers of female and male authors covered, and this sense of balance would be evident in paired lectures; for example, a lecture on "Romantic Femininities" is matched with one on "Masculinities"; there is also a separate lecture on "Romantic Sexualities."

In my previous institution, there was a week set aside for lectures on "Women in Romanticism" and "Women Romantic Poets." Given an opportunity to create a module I really approved of in my next post I determined instead to fully incorporate female authors on topics such as "Revolution," "Imagination," "Nature." We have another level-two survey module called "Gothic Fictions," which starts in the eighteenth century with Horace Walpole's *The Castle of Otranto*, but moves into the twentieth century; this is far more popular than "Romanticisms." For this reason "The Gothic" only has one lecture on Romanticisms; clearly this is an area in which issues of gender and sexuality feature prominently, and we do discuss gothic tales in seminars, such as William Beckford's *Vathek*, William Godwin's *Caleb Williams* and S. T. Coleridge's "The Rime of the Ancient Mariner." Since I teach on both modules, I can ensure that issues of gender and sexuality are fully represented in my lectures on Romantic-period texts on the "Gothic Fictions" module too.

I teach the Romantic period as a time in which the idea that women should have rights was first seriously mooted and this same idea ridiculed. I also emphasize this period as a time when the construction of gender was first understood, or in Mary Wollstonecraft's words, the way that females "are made women of when they are mere children" (1997: 245–46). I show examples to prove the very real sense of gender difference in writings of these times, from the authors themselves and their reviewers. In other words, when female poets are assessed it is *as* a female poet. We look at the outraged response of John Wilson Croker to Anna Barbauld's political poem *Eighteen Hundred and Eleven*, for example:

> We had hoped, indeed that the empire might have been saved without the intervention of a lady-author . . . a confident sense of commanding talents – have induced her to dash down her shagreen spectacles and her knitting needles, and to sally forth . . . in the magnanimous resolution of saving a sinking state. (Anon.: 309)

Maria Edgeworth, though privately, called Croker's review "ungentlemanly," while Henry Crabb Robinson similarly described an attack on Barbauld by Coleridge as "unhandsome and unmanly" (cited in Newlyn 2000: 38–9). Even in these defences of Barbauld, then, the students can see that the critic's gallantry, clearly a gendered notion, is the main issue. We examine other reviews that show that even when female authors are approved of, it is within the same parameters. George Gilfillan's approbation of Felicia Hemans is a good example of this:

> We have selected Mrs Hemans as our first specimen of Female Authors, not because we consider the best, but because we consider her by far the most feminine writer of the age. All the woman in her shines.... you see a graceful and gifted woman, passing from the cares of her family, and the enjoyments of society, to inscribe on her tablets some fine thought or feeling, which had throughout the day existed as a still sunshine upon her countenance or, perhaps as a quiet unshed tear in her eye. (1847: 360–61)

This quotation usually raises a laugh. I ask the students whether the gender of an author matters to them now, whether they think they can tell which gender the author is if they do not already know, and whether they think that these are reasonable grounds on which to judge a poet's work. I tell them that it has been argued that the former quotation was responsible for ending Barbauld's poetic career, and there is no laughing at that (Newlyn 2000: 164–9).

When we discuss William Beckford I offer them salacious gossip, which they enjoy, telling them about the infamous three-day long party held to celebrate Beckford's twenty-first birthday at Fonthill Abbey. We still do not know much of what went on during that time, or can only surmise what went on by its repercussions: Beckford's removal to Europe in disgrace. Asking students whether biography should matter to the interpretation of texts is one way of trying to make connections with a literary theory module taught in the first year; similarly I reintroduce them to Judith Butler's *Gender Trouble* in our discussions of the construction of gender, and return to Eve Kosofsky Sedgwick in my lecture on James Hogg's *Confessions of a Justified Sinner* on the gothic module (Butler 1990; Sedgwick 1985). I try not to subsume queer studies into my lectures on gender, but to recognize the complicated (and not always conciliatory) relationship they have with each other. Class is also entangled in this complex web of identity, but again the idea of class, at least to my current students, seems to be from a time long ago, and, they believe, has had little to do with their experiences so far in the world. William Godwin's *Caleb Williams*, one of three novels taught on the "Romanticisms" module, offers just such a tangle of ideas: we look at issues of class, gender and sexuality in the novel and in readings of the novel, alongside its political message and its attempt at historical intervention as a reflection of "Things as They Are." Still, the idea persists that this is more like "Things as They Were" for the students I teach.

It has been over twenty years since Stuart Curran's ground-breaking work argued that with the omission of women writers from the Romantic canon, "[m]anifest distortions of the record have accrued." In reality, we now know that female novelists and playwrights outnumbered male, and, "[i]n the arena of poetry... the place of women was likewise, at least for a time, predominant, and it is here that the distortions of our received history are most glaring. Its chronology has been written wholly, and arbitrarily, along a masculine gender line" (Curran 1988: 187). Despite the substantial research that, since Curran's essay, has resulted in the often full inclusion of women writers in Romantic critical thinking, female authors often remain underrepresented in university teaching. I begin my lecture on "Romantic Femininities" with facts of this nature, drawing largely from Paula Feldman and Theresa M. Kelley's work: revealing that, despite what students may think they know, Felicia Hemans was one of the best-selling writers of the Romantic period, her work "admired by Byron, Shelley, Wordsworth, Matthew Arnold, William Michael Rossetti, George Eliot, Elizabeth Barrett"; that Walter Scott (often another unknown name to students coming to the module) "called Joanna Baillie 'the best dramatic writer' in Britain 'since the days of Shakespeare and Massinger"'; that Wordsworth's famous "Preface" to the *Lyrical Ballads* "appropriated without acknowledgement" Joanna Baillie's plea for a more natural language to be used in literature (Feldman and Kelley 1995: 2, 4, 5). As the need to explain who Scott is indicates, usually I have to explain what the "canon" is in order to be able to demonstrate its constricting effects. I seem each time to end up telling them that when I went to university the Romantic-period module I was taught (called "From Gray to Lord Byron") included none of these women writers, and was largely concerned with what were then called the "pre-Romantics" and the "big six" poets: Blake, Wordsworth, Coleridge, Byron, Shelley and Keats. It did not just omit women, of course; there were no novels, no plays, and no black writers.

So, I have to teach students what the canon was in order to show them how far we have come from its clutches. Yet it does appear from the survey conducted in 2006 that some institutions have not thus escaped, and perhaps have not attempted to challenge the canon in the same way ("Survey Results" 2006). Those students who already have a degree of knowledge about the literature of the period are often disappointed that we will not be studying in much detail the literary *greats* of whom they have heard. More students still come to university because they wanted to study William Wordsworth, for example, than Felicia Hemans, despite the updating of A-level texts. When redesigning the "Romanticisms" module I could not fit all of the so-called "big six" into our twelve week semester, so made room by not teaching (in seminars at least) Byron and Keats. What one hopes, of course, is that students will find more than ample recompense in the authors one introduces them to for the first time: in this case, Jane Austen, Joanna Baillie, Anna Barbauld, Felicia Hemans, Charlotte Smith and Mary Wollstonecraft.

Anne Mellor's important 1993 book *Romanticism and Gender* was one of the first to consider how seriously the map of Romanticism was changed by the inclusion of female writers. Mellor was also the editor of the ground-breaking collection of essays *Romanticism and Feminism*, published in 1988, a volume which, as she put it, "marks the coming of age of a feminist criticism of the major texts of the English Romantic period" (Mellor 1988: 3). In her later book, Mellor wrote of two kinds of Romanticism, a "masculine" and a "feminine" Romanticism:

> When we look at this female-authored literature, we find a focus on very different issues from those which concerned the canonical male Romantic poets... even a cursory, introductory survey reveals the significant differences between the thematic concerns, formal practices, and ideological positionings of male and female Romantic writers. (Mellor 1993: 2–3)

Mellor does of course recognize the "deeply problematic" model she adopts in using such polarized positions (1993: 3). In "Romanticisms" we test this theory out: do the female writers that we look at examine different concerns to the male ones? Are the concerns of "masculine" Romanticism necessarily connected to the sex of the author? What do we do with Keats's "effeminacy," as explored by Susan J. Wolfson and other critics (Wolfson 1990)? Do women and men of the period tend to write in different genres? Is genre gendered? Are authors writing specifically for a male or female reader? It is the case, as Mellor pointed out, that when women of the period are given "equal weight" in our consideration of Romanticism, a "paradigm shift" occurs: for one thing, poetry has to share curriculum space with novels and plays (1993: 1).

It is perhaps testament to our changed notions on gender in Romanticism that where there were once separate anthologies, Duncan Wu's *Romanticism: an Anthology* (first edition, 1994) and *Romantic Women*

Poets: an Anthology (1997) there is now one, *Romanticism: an Anthology* (1998, 2005). This is the anthology, which we use for "Romanticisms" and which the 2006 Teaching Romanticism Questionnaire found to be the one most used in UK institutions ("Survey Results" 2006). Nearly everything that we need is in this anthology, though admittedly I designed the module partly with use of the anthology in mind; with regard to women writers on the course, we have to provide photocopies of Hemans's "Casabianca," Barbauld's "A Mouse's Petition," and students are asked to buy the Broadview edition of Joanna Baillie's *Plays on the Passions* and a scholarly edition of Jane Austen's *Mansfield Park*. I discuss Mellor's ideas of two separate strands of Romanticism in week nine, in the "Romantic Femininities" lecture. Up to that point, women and men have been integrated into themed lectures: for example, in the lecture dealing called "Nation and Nationalism," we look at texts from Wordsworth ("The Discharged Soldier"), Byron (an extract from *Childe Harold's Pilgrimage: Canto the Third*) and Hemans, ("Casabianca"). Issues of gender are raised alongside those of nationalism in discussions of these texts.

Of course, my teaching is hugely indebted to the researchers who have recovered women's writing of the period, and have helped me (since my first university degree) to think about these writers on their own terms, as well as in relation to the male writers I knew far more about. Here I am specifically thinking of Jennifer Breen's anthology *Women Romantic Poets, 1785–1832* (1994); Paula R. Feldman and Theresa M. Kelley's edited collection of essays *Romantic Women Writers: Voices and Countervoices* (1995); Vivien Jones's edition of source texts, *Women in the Eighteenth Century: Constructions of Femininity* (1990); Stuart Curran's work (1998, 1993); Fiona Robertson's edition *Women's Writing, 1778–1838: an Anthology* (2001). Much of the initial work was done on Romantic women writers in the early 1990s, and Anne Janowitz's editing of the *Essays and Studies* volume "Romanticism and Gender" in 1998 is a sign of the times. Since then there have been important works of criticism of individual women writers, which are too numerous to list here. It is the case, though, that there has been some movement away from the ideas presented in early work on specifically women Romantic writers. For example, as Carolyn Franklin writes in *Mary Wollstonecraft: a Literary Life*:

> Feminist critics such as Anne Mellor and Mitzi Myers, in order to trace a specifically female literary tradition, have also sought to homogenize all women writers at the cost of eroding the ideological

> differences between them. It is important to situate an intellectual like Wollstonecraft amongst the whole range of writers and thinkers, male and female, with whom her texts engaged, for she played a part in the public sphere and not in a separate women's arena. (Franklin 2004: x)

For this reason, other aspects of identity besides the fact of their femaleness are not forgotten when discussing women writers on our module, such as Barbauld's identity as a Unitarian, Hannah More's political conservatism and religious orthodoxy, or Ann Yearsley's class.

The division of literature into *male* and *female* has survived more convincingly perhaps in gothic studies, since Ellen Moers's *Literary Women* first coined the phrase "female gothic" (Moers: 1976). While Radcliffe has been seen as the archetypal author of this "female" gothic and Matthew "Monk" Lewis of the "male" gothic, it is generally acknowledged that these binaries are not necessary linked simply to the gender of the author. Of course, the very categories upon which the gothic is based, Burke's division into the sublime and the beautiful, themselves "ultimately reproduce dominant cultural representations of sexual difference" even while not seeming explicitly to speak of such matters (Jones 1990: 4).

Gothic has also been far more accepting, I would argue, of queer studies than has traditional Romanticism. The idea of the *gothic* can itself be considered a queer concept: othered from a *normal* self, gothic fiction has always been interested in issues of authenticity, sincerity, transgression and ambivalence. If we look at the representations of gender in gothic characters, Ann Radcliffe's heroines are often strong-willed and determined; Caleb Williams can be seen as effeminate and weak; Hippolita and Mathilda in Horace Walpole's *Castle of Otranto* are regarded as examples of exaggerated gender stereotyping by the students, though their passivity and submission are balanced by the vivacity and forwardness of Isabella and Bianca.

Where Moers attributed Mary Shelley's gothic vision to the simple fact that she was a woman, Robert Miles has argued that "female" gothic arises from "social repression": "[t]he greater the social repression, the more authors' minds were forced into roundabout ways of addressing their experience, the more articulate their texts, and the more significant and representative their evasions" (Miles 1994: 131, cited in Fincher 2007: 3). This leaves the way clear for extending our idea of social repression beyond the forms that this took for women, to take in "the prohibition of sexual desires" for both men and women (Fincher 2007:

3). Max Fincher discusses *The Castle of Otranto, Vathek, The Monk, Caleb Williams, Lara* and *The Giaour*, and *The Vampyre* in his book *Queering Gothic in the Romantic Age*, considering in many of these cases "writers whom we suspect of same-sex desires and whose writing is ambiguous or complicated" with the expectation that "their writing will in covert ways signify for a queer reader" (2007: 3). Ignoring the biography of the authors, Fincher's is a fruitful and suggestive study of recurring motifs of secrecy, the gaze, shame, and their links to same-sex desire and homophobia in these texts.

Christopher Nagle asserts that the study of Romanticism is still characterized by "traditional narratives of rupture and revolutionary innovation", its "critical and methodological orthodoxies... more resistant to change perhaps than [the study of any other period] at present" (Nagle 2007: 3). In *Sexuality and the Culture of Sensibility in the British Romantic Era*, he imagines that:

> A new story could be told that takes into account both [Percy Bysshe] Shelley and [Anne Batten] Cristall, for example, without resorting to tired commonplaces about older and younger "generations" (often with their own respective "circles"), or to newly familiar and equally unimaginative models positing distinctive "masculine" and "feminine" varieties of Romanticism. (2007: 3)

Instead he believes that "[s]ensibility provides... the discursive infrastructure of Romanticism itself" (2007: 4). Its importance to Romanticism has long been clear, and its importance to gender issues equally so. Indeed, Claudia Johnson thought that the point when male writers, such as Edmund Burke, appropriated the female language and gestures of sensibility was the first sign of "a wedge between sex and gender" (Johnson 1995: 17, cited in Nagle 2007: 9). Sensibility was connected in the period with the body; for people living in the Romantic period, it denotes a peculiar "receptivity of the senses" (Barker-Benfield 1992: xvii). It is this link between women's bodies and their behaviour that I wish to explore for the remainder of this essay; this is an area that I find interests students particularly and which helps convince them both of the importance of this moment in history and literature, and of its relevance to their lives.

In my lecture "Femininities," I try then to explore some of the ways in which women writers negotiate and elude the strict cultural definitions of women that they were subject to. I make the point that the women writers we will look at (Barbauld, More, Smith, Wollstonecraft) are writing from a number of perspectives, and that while some seek to undermine and subvert contemporary notions of women's inferiority to men, others intend to confirm that idea. I look at the ways in which these women engage with and work within so-called masculine genres, and the strategies they employ to discuss those issues which are forbidden to them as woman writers. I begin in rather a conventional way with that infamous passage from Richard Polwhele's poem, *The Unsex'd Females*, which laments the current state of affairs: "Survey with me, what ne'er our fathers saw, / A female band despising NATURE'S law" (cited in Jones 1990: 186). This immediately leads into to a discussion of what was felt to be "natural" to women in this period, and the links made between the bodies of women and judgement of their mental capacities.

We look at passages in Wollstonecraft's *Vindication* where she attempts to prove that the mind has no sex, that characteristics such as reason and virtue should not be considered "manly" but as human. She wishes "to prove that the prevailing notion respecting a sexual character," or that women and men have different natures, is "subversive of morality" (1997: 103). Thomas Laqueur first claimed in 1987 that "[s]ometime in the late eighteenth century human sexuality changed" (1987: 1). Londa Schiebinger has examined the many and varied efforts to describe a new "distinctively female body," and attempts to "discover 'the essential sexual difference"' between men and women (citing anatomist Jakob Ackermann) (1991: 189). This is a topic that never fails to elicit a response from any class: are women and men innately different? Is there a link between biology and behaviour? I ask them Schiebinger's rather mischievous question: do they think there might be "a connection between eighteenth-century movements for female equality and attempts on the part of anatomists to discover a physiological basis for women's 'inequality'?" (1986: 42). To which there is usually a resounding "yes."

I show the students how women's bodies as much as their minds were the site of contention in the period. We look at passages from conduct books such as John Gregory's, which advised women not to "dance with spirit," and which so angered Wollstonecraft (cited in 1997: 137). In the seminar following the lecture we can discuss Wollstonecraft's belief that not allowing women the fresh air and exercise granted to boys actually changed their body shapes, while the lack of mental exercise reduced them to the capacities of children: their "limbs and faculties are cramped with worse than Chinese bands" (1997: 153). There are obvious parallels with the fashion-conscious world in which students live. We then examine those characters in Romantic novels who evince the behaviour Wollstonecraft most disparages, those who "use art and feign a sickly delicacy in order to secure her husband's affection," particularly looking at the healthy, the sickly and the hypochondriac women in Austen's *Mansfield Park* (1997: 138).

Just as now, in the Romantic period there was assumed to be a natural and innate link between sex and gender, a belief that gendered behaviour, in modern terms, was biologically determined. Physiology and anatomy then and now were bent on proving this: for instance, after Samuel Thomas von Soemmering noted that women's skulls were heavier than men's in proportion to their total body weight the Edinburgh anatomist John Barclay argued that this was evidence of their infantilism, since children's skulls are similarly proportioned (Scheibinger 1991: 207). The childishness of women, which Wollstonecraft railed at in *Vindication*, and which we can explore in the characters of, for example, Maria and Julia Bertram in *Mansfield Park*, was in part understood as the result of their bodies. From such examples it is an easy step to think again about the ways that our bodies are still held responsible for our actions, the way that, as quoted in earlier, Girls Aloud have told students that it is impossible to mistake their biology.[2] I hope by these means to reinvest their study of Romanticism with a feminist agenda, asking the female and male students, by considering this critical moment in history, to reassess the way that their own and others' identities are constructed and to beware current attempts to circumvent politics in favour of the pop-science answers offered by the media and contemporary culture.

Notes

1. Of course, I like to think that today's students are astute in their readings of gender representations presented by popular culture. The challenges and opportunities for feminism posed by contemporary popular culture are discussed in essays included in Gillis, Howie and Munford 2004.
2. I should point out that Girl's Aloud are not sole authors of the lyrics for their single "Biology": the credits list "Brian Higgins, Girls Aloud, Tim Powell, Nick Coler, Shawn Lee."

Works cited

Anon. [Wilson Croker, John] (1812) Review of Anna Barbauld, *Eighteen Hundred and Eleven, A Poem*, *Quarterly Review*, 7: 14 (June): 309–12.

Baillie, Joanna (2000) *De Monfort*, in *Plays on the Passions*, ed. Peter Duthie (Ontario, Canada: Broadview Press).
Barker-Benfield, G. J. (1992) *The Culture of Sensibility* (Chicago and London: University of Chicago Press).
Breen, Jennifer, ed. (1994) *Women Romantic Poets, 1785–1832* (London: Everyman).
Butler, Judith (1990) *Gender Trouble* (New York: Routledge).
Curran, Stuart (1988) "The I Altered," in *Romanticism and Feminism*, ed. Anne K. Mellor (Bloomington: Indiana University Press): 185–207.
—— (1993) "Women Readers, Women Writers," in *The Cambridge Companion to British Romanticism*, ed. Stuart Curran (Cambridge: Cambridge University Press).
Fincher, Max (2007) *Queering the Gothic in the Romantic Age: the Penetrating Eye* (Basingstoke: Palgrave Macmillan).
Franklin, Carolyn (2004) *Mary Wollstonstonecraft: a Literary Life* (Basingstoke: Palgrave Macmillan).
Feldman, Paula R. and Theresa M. Kelley, eds. (1995) *Romantic Women Writers: Voices and Countervoices* (Hanover, NH: University Press of New England).
Gilfillan, George (1847) "Female Authors, no. I. – Mrs. Hemans," *Tait's Edinburgh Magazine*, 14: 359–63.
Gillis, Stacey, Gillian Howie and Rebecca Munford (2004) *Third Wave Feminism: a Critical Exploration* (Basingstoke: Palgrave Macmillan).
Greer, Germaine (1970) *The Female Eunuch* (London: McGibbon and Kee).
Janowitz, Anne, ed. (1998) "Romanticism and Gender," *Essays and Studies*, 51.
Johnson, Claudia (1995) *Equivocal Beings: Politics, Gender, and Sentimentality in the 1790s* (Chicago: Chicago University Press).
Jones, Vivien (1990) *Women in the Eighteenth Century: Constructions of Femininity* (London and New York: Routledge).
Laqueur, Thomas (1992) *Making Sex: Body and Gender from the Greeks to Freud* (Cambridge, MA: Harvard University Press).
—— (1987) "Orgasm, Generation, and the Politics of Reproductive Biology," in *The Making of the Modern Body*, ed. Catherine Gallagher and Thomas Laqueur (Berkeley: University of California Press): 1–41.
Lovejoy, A. O. (1924; repr. 1970), "On the Discrimination of Romanticisms," in *Romanticism: Points of View*, ed. Robert E. Gleckner and Gerard E. Enscoe (New Jersey: Prentice Hall): 66–81.
Mellor, Anne K. (1993) *Romanticism and Gender* (New York and London: Routledge).
——, ed. (1988) *Romanticism and Feminism* (Bloomington and Indiana University Press).
Miles, Robert (1994) "Introduction," *Women's Writing*, 1: 131–41.
Moers, Ellen (1976) *Literary Women* (New York: Doubleday).
Nagle, Christopher (2007) *Sexuality and the Culture of Sensibility in the British Romantic Era* (Basingstoke: Palgrave Macmillan).
Newlyn, Lucy (2000) *Reading, Writing, and Romanticism: Anxieties of Reception* (Oxford: Oxford University Press).
Robertson, Fiona (2001) *Women's Writing, 1778–1838: an Anthology* (Oxford: Oxford University Press).

Schiebinger, Londa (1986) "Skeletons in the Closet: the First Illustrations of the Female Skeleton in Eighteenth-Century Anatomy," *Representations*, 14: 42–82.
—— (1991) *The Mind had no Sex? Women in the Origins of Modern Science* (Cambridge, MA and London: Harvard University Press).
Sedgwick, Eve Kosofsky (1985) *Between Men: English Literature and Male Homosocial Desire* (New York: Columbia University Press).
"Survey Results: Teaching Romanticism Questionnaire" (2006) *BARS Website*, http://www.bars.ac.uk/teaching/survey/surveyresults.php.
Wolfson, Susan J. (1990) "Feminizing John Keats," in *Critical Essays on John Keats*, ed. by Hermione de Almeida (Boston: G. K Hall): 317–56.
Wollstonecraft, Mary (1997) *Vindication of the Rights of Woman*, in *The Vindications*, ed. D. L. Macdonald and Kathleen Scherf (Ontario: Broadview).
Wu, Duncan, ed. (1994; later edns 1998, 2005), *Romanticism: an Anthology* (Oxford: Blackwell).
—— ed. (1997) *Romantic Women Poets: an Anthology* (Oxford: Blackwell).

Further reading

Fay, Elizabeth (1998) *A Feminist Introduction to Romanticism* (Oxford: Blackwell).
Janowitz, Anne (2004) *Romantic Women Poets*, Writers and their Works (Plymouth: Northcote House).
Jones, Vivien, ed. (2000) *Women and Literature in Britain, 1700–1800* (Cambridge: Cambridge University Press).
Mason, Emma (2004) *Women Poets of the Nineteenth Century*, Writers and their Works (Plymouth: Northcote House).
Shiner Wilson, Carol and J. Haeffner, eds. (1993) *Re-Visioning Romanticism: British Women Writers 1776–1837* (Philadelphia: University of Pennsylvania Press).

6
Slavery, Empire, Race

Brycchan Carey

In *Romantic Colonization and British Anti-Slavery*, Deirdre Coleman points out that "by 1820 Britain ruled 200 million people, over a quarter of the world's population," and that it was difficult to find anyone not involved in some way or another with the "imperial system" (2005: 237). As with people, so with literary texts: it is correspondingly difficult to find novels or extended poems written between 1750 and 1850 that make no reference, however fleeting, to Britain's burgeoning empire, be it in the Americas, Asia or the Pacific. By the start of the eighteenth century, the trickle of literature concerned with empire had become a flood, and by the end of the eighteenth century the flood had become a deluge. Non-fictional texts poured forth from the press and included voyage narratives, autobiographies, histories, natural histories, geographies and ingenious schemes to enrich the nation. These, in turn, inspired novels, poems and plays about colonies, hoped-for colonies, colonists and the colonized. Together, fiction and non-fiction lauded the benefits to both Britons and native peoples of rational government based on sound commercial principles. Just as often, however, they lamented the depredations that colonization made on the colonized and, in a related set of rhetorical manoeuvres, they increasingly questioned slavery and the slave trade.

By the end of the eighteenth century, colonial literature was as vast and as various as the expanding empire, and the ubiquity of the theme and the quantity of the available material can make the task of choosing appropriate texts to teach seem overwhelming. Modules can be organized by area, chronology, genre, culture or religion, or by any combination of the above, but the matter is complicated since none of these are stable criteria. Take the category of *area*, for example. It might seem on the face of it to be a simple matter to define what parts of the world were colonized in the Romantic period, and what parts were colonizers, but this matter becomes contested before one even leaves the British Isles. Many people would accept that eighteenth-century Ireland, Scotland and Wales were to some extent subject to English colonization, but the question is less routinely discussed in relation to the Channel Islands, or to Cornwall, which, in the words of Alan Kent, "*is* and *is not* an English county. It *is* and *is not* mentioned in the same breath as Wales, Scotland and Éire" (Kent 2000: 11). A module on English colonization in the Romantic period might thus look very different to a module on British colonization, and would raise rather different questions. A Highland family evicted from their land in the 1790s, as many were, might be discussed only as victims of English colonization in the former module. Students on the latter module might be equally interested in their role as settlers in Nova Scotia. Likewise, the shifting relationship between Britain and its American colonies, from Canada to the Caribbean, is particularly difficult to assess. The United States, for example, was postcolonial in regard to the United Kingdom after 1776, but a colonizing power in regard to the Native American nations it conquered throughout the eighteenth and nineteenth centuries, and taking this into account makes teaching some of the most important English-language texts of the Romantic period more complex than is often realized; authors as central to the American tradition as Benjamin Franklin and Washington Irving were both postcolonial and international. Finally, Britain's Atlantic empire was, by the late eighteenth century, only part of its operations overseas. British activities in India, Africa and the Pacific Ocean were all attracting the attention of authors and the reading public. A module on the literature of the Pacific would be as viable for this period as a module on the literature of the Atlantic. Likewise, a term reading Scottish literature of the Romantic period would be as productive and as diverse as a term reading American Romantic literature.

Faced with a bewildering choice of material, there are, it seems to me, two main strategies for presenting colonial literature of the Romantic period to students. The first is to incorporate the literature within an existing Romantic survey module. Many tutors will find that they are already teaching Blake's "The Little Black Boy," Coleridge's "The Rime of the Ancient Mariner", Burns's, "The Slave's Lament –," or Wordsworth's *The Prelude*. It is not difficult to address the colonial elements of these poems in lectures, or to raise the topic in seminars. Tutors might also choose to augment this reading with further texts: Southey's many anti-slavery poems, Hannah More's, *Slavery, A Poem*, or much of Byron's later poetry all offer opportunities to discuss colonial themes within a traditional framework. Even if the topic is not explored in depth in class, students can be given the opportunity to explore the material in more depth in essays or other assessment.

The other approach is to specialize on a much narrower area of literature such as Anglo-American writing, the literature of Scotland, Ireland and/or Wales, exploration and encounter (for example in the Pacific or in Africa), representations of Asia (or more narrowly either India or China) or writing and religion – which might include European missionary literature or European engagements with non-European religions. In an essay of this length there is room only to consider one such module in any depth. Since it reflects both my own research interests and my teaching experience, I here offer a detailed commentary on a hypothetical module that explores the relationship between literature and slavery in the years 1766 to 1831. There is a rich vein of material available. Arguments either for or against Britain's continuing involvement in the slave trade and, later, slavery itself prompted more poems, novels, pamphlets, sermons and periodical articles than any other colonial topic in the period. The following is a suggested syllabus for a twelve-week module that examines a small selection of this literature.

Week 1: Sarah Scott, extracts from *The History of Sir George Ellison* (1766).

Week 2: John Bicknell and Thomas Day, *The Dying Negro* (1773).

Week 3: Thomas Clarkson, *An Essay on the Slavery and Commerce of the Human Species* (1786).

Week 4: Hannah More, *Slavery, A Poem* (1788) and Ann Yearsley, *A Poem on the Inhumanity of the Slave Trade* (1788).

Week 5: Newspaper reports from the Burney Collection of William Wilberforce's abolition speech in Parliament, 12 May 1789.

Week 6: *The Interesting Narrative of the Life of Olaudah Equiano, or, Gustavus Vassa, the African* (1789).

Week 7: Shorter abolitionist verse: William Cowper, "The Negro's Complaint," "The Morning Dream," and "Sweet Meat has Sour Sauce: or, the Slave Trader in the Dumps" (1788); William Blake, "The Little Black Boy" (1789); Robert Burns, "The Slave's Lament –" (1792).

Week 8: Samuel Taylor Coleridge, "Lecture on the Slave Trade" (1795).

Week 9: William Wordsworth, "To Thomas Clarkson. On the Final Passing of the Bill for the Abolition of the Slave Trade" (1807); "To Toussaint L'Overture" (1807); extracts from *The Prelude* (1805 Text) Book X, lines 203–28 (1805, 1st published 1926) and *The Prelude* (1850 Text) Book X, lines 237–65 (1850).

Week 10: Jane Austen, *Mansfield Park* (1814).
Week 11: *The History of Mary Prince* (1831).
Week 12: Film: *Amazing Grace*. Dir. Michael Apted (2007).

This syllabus is composed of texts that are available either in print or online. Many, such as those by Wordsworth and Austen, are easily found, but for the less well-known writing some digging will be required. Tutors and students with access to online databases such as *Eighteenth-Century Collections Online* and *Seventeenth and Eighteenth Century Burney Collection Newspapers* will be at an advantage, although most of the suggested texts can also be found in recent printed sources – examples of which are given in the "Further Reading," below. To date, the most comprehensive student reader on literature and slavery is Karina Williamson's *Contrary Voices* (2008), but many tutors might find her selection chronologically too broad for a module centred on the Romantic period. It is probable, therefore, that the tutor will need to compile some sort of module pack. Creating this can become an activity in itself, both for tutors and for students. Hunting down and making available reliable versions of elusive texts has satisfactions for tutors, but can also be a useful way to introduce students to practical questions of research, textual provenance and successful editorship as well as to more theoretical debates such as canon formation. In the main, this approach works well with smaller and more advanced classes; larger groups and those at an earlier stage of their degree programme are often better served by a more traditional handout. Whatever texts are ultimately selected, it is worth remembering that the texts I have suggested are by no means exclusive, but instead represent a small sample of generically diverse writings that, between them, help the student to build up a picture of the history and culture of the abolition movement. Few of the texts are irreplaceable and tutors may have strong reasons for wanting to substitute them with those that reflect their own particular interests. Some might well want to include dramatic texts, for example (although my experience is that there are few abolitionist plays that really engage undergraduate students). Likewise, some might want to include a sample of proslavery literature, or a philosophical discussion of the idea of race. Examples of all of these can be found in the readers listed in the Further Reading.

As well as focusing geographically on the Atlantic world, the module follows a chronological rather than a thematic or generic arrangement. In this case, the choice is not arbitrary. The central aim of the module is to chart literary engagement with an historical problem and to assess the extent to which writers influenced the outcome of that problem. For that reason this is unavoidably an historicist module. Nevertheless, the relationship between writing and historical events should never be taken for granted, and students should be encouraged to ask questions about that relationship from the start. On the most basic level, students might investigate the extent to which abolitionist writing reflects the realities of the slave trade or a life in enslavement. It will become apparent to most students, after even relatively cursory historical research, that most abolitionist literature, consciously or otherwise, misrepresents both Africa and Africans, and this in itself is a valuable learning process for literary students unused to questioning the accuracy of historical documents. Having understood this, most students will readily grasp abolitionist literature's status as rhetoric (or, to the more cynical, propaganda) which allows for a variety of analyses and questions. Among these, students might ask why literary forms such as poetry and the novel are being used to do political work, who was being addressed in this literature, how these texts have been constructed to operate on the reader, and whether the texts in any way changed the debate. This final point leads students into a more complex engagement with the texts in which they can be read as discursive and intertextual. A module of this length, on a relatively narrow theme, provides an ideal opportunity to see how the texts largely reflect each other rather than historical realities, and even to see how some historical realities eventually came to reflect the texts themselves.

Not all students will want to focus on the texts' status as historical discourse: one of the most frequent comments I receive in student evaluation of a module such as this is that there is too much concentration on history (which students invariably refer to as *background*) and not enough on literature, by which they mean poems, plays and novels. Care must be taken to explain in advance why there is an emphasis on abolitionist history, but nevertheless this module is a fruitful place to challenge students' preconceptions of what constitutes *history* and what *literature*, and to replace a simplistic notion of *background* and *foreground* with a more sophisticated discursive model. Even so, traditionally literary concerns cannot be abandoned without some risk of alienating students. To that end it is useful to remember that the science of political persuasion – rhetoric – shares its origins and its terminology with the art of critical analysis. Comparing an extract from a poem with an extract on a related theme from an abolitionist tract, or a newspaper report of a parliamentary speech, allows students to discover that similar rhetorical techniques are employed in superficially dissimilar literary forms. Similarly, students learn that political writers of the period were just as likely to make appeals to sentiment, or to invoke the sublime, as literary writers were to tackle political subjects in verse or in the pages of a novel. By the end of this module students should thus be able to demonstrate a sophisticated understanding of the interrelationship of literary and political texts in the period.

Of course, many of these issues will also arise on modules that focus on other historical or political moments, whether in the Romantic period or elsewhere, and clearly a module on the literary implications of the French Revolution, or the literature of the Anti-Corn Law League, would require just as much attention to ideas and practices of rhetoric and representation. While few students have a view one way or another on the Corn Laws, however, almost all have very strong views on race and colonization. The issues that the literature of slavery and abolition raise are more strongly inflected by matters of current concern, are often emotive, and have the potential both to unite and to divide students in ways that can surprise or which challenge the expectations of both tutor and students. This has distinct advantages in class in that it makes engaging students with the subject easier than is often the case with other topics. Although many students find the language of abolitionist literature difficult, while the images the literature presents of downcast slaves and heroic saints can be read anywhere on a spectrum from laughable to sinister, the subject matter nevertheless speaks to current concerns about racism, inequality and the conduct of nations on the international stage. Lively debate is almost guaranteed in class.

The subject matter also presents challenges. One of the main difficulties, both in classroom discussion and in writing essays, is that some students seize an opportunity to discuss current political problems instead of addressing the Romantic era. It is not always easy to achieve a balance with this since, as I have already suggested, the relevance of the module to current concerns is one of the principal reasons many students are drawn to it in the first place, as well as being one of the aspects of the module that generates lively discussion. But it is necessary at times to remind students that their focus is the past, not the present. In addition, students may need direction with the difficult task of assessing the Romantic era with some measure of objectivity. Students often judge eighteenth-century figures by twenty-first-century criteria and would, for example, brand Wilberforce an unmitigated racist and hold Pitt responsible for genocide. Other students take the opposite tack and exonerate all Romantic-era figures, no matter how heinous their crimes, on the grounds that they were *of their time*. Neither position is very useful, except in that they might initiate classroom discussion. If they do, the tutor will need to guide discussion away from such simple assertion and towards a more complex analysis of the texts in which the students ask why, if slavery and the slave trade were the normal practice of the day, some people questioned their legitimacy while others did not.

The same holds true for the situation that many tutors fear: the moment when sensitivities over ethnic and racial identities come to the surface – which can sometimes happen very suddenly. Tutors do need to anticipate that the material being discussed often represents views that most people today find repugnant and that it will therefore prompt strong feelings in many students. It is not unusual for students to articulate a sense of frustration or even anger at the racial ideologies being expressed in eighteenth and nineteenth-century writing on race and slavery, particularly when discussing material that attempted to defend the slave trade. Some eighteenth-century language can cause embarrassment or offence. The word *negar* in particular, which is pronounced exactly as *nigger*, is now taboo. In discussion, it is worth pointing out that while many white authors used it, as they thought, neutrally, black people were not comfortable with the word even in the eighteenth century. As the African-born letter-writer Ignatius Sancho explained to the writer Lawrence Sterne in 1766, "I am one of those people whom the vulgar and illiberal call '*Negurs*' " (Sancho 1998: 73). Sancho's intervention can be seen as one of the first by many Africans and people of African descent to declare the word offensive. Rather than avoiding difficult language and concepts, tutors can in this way draw attention to the means by which language has been an ideological battleground from the outset.

At the other end of the spectrum, some students, usually unconsciously, articulate views that may seem archaic or out-of-place at best; offensive at worst. On rare occasions, class discussion can become tense and tutors do need to be prepared for the possibility that one or more students might say things that other members of the class find offensive. Although such occurrences are rare, I have witnessed a student accuse another of "being obsessed with race" and, on another occasion, one accuse another of "having a chip on his shoulder." In one memorably awkward seminar, a student explained to an astonished class that "black men can't help wanting to have sex with white women; it's been scientifically proved – it's in their genes." When challenged, the student stood by her guns, and even cited an article from a well-known British tabloid newspaper that had published a pseudoscientific article making that claim. In the main, moments such as these are self-correcting in that the students themselves establish a dialogue and return the language and discourse to a balanced socially-acceptable norm. Occasionally, however, the tutor will need to act as a referee. It has not been my experience that students use seminars on a module such as this to advance a consciously racist agenda. It has often been my experience, however, that students inadvertently articulate racist views that they have unconsciously absorbed from a variety of sources, including peers, parents and, as we have seen, tabloid newspapers. A well-prepared tutor should read the dailies often enough to be able to counter the racist arguments that some newspapers routinely perpetuate. Indeed, it may be a useful exercise to ask students to analyse recent passages dealing with race from a tabloid newspaper, both to hone their critical skills and to alert them to the nature of the rhetorics to which they are being exposed.

Thus prepared, the tutor will ask the students to read the texts and bring their thoughts to class. The texts in this reading list have been selected both for their importance to the debate about slavery and for their likely ability to engage students. I begin with extracts from the first few chapters of Sarah Scott's, *The History of Sir George Ellison*. This novel was one of the first to question whether slavery, as it was then practiced, was a humane system. Students may be disappointed or even outraged to find that it is not a text of radical antislavery – indeed, it suggests only a scheme to ameliorate slavery, not to abolish it – but it is useful to ask students at this stage to examine their own expectations and assumptions, and to try to imagine how the book might have been received in its own time. The novel also introduces students to some key themes of the module: like many of the later writers, Scott phrases her arguments in the language of sensibility; she imagines a plantation she has never seen; she represents Africans very differently to Europeans; and she attempts to draw parallels between arguments based in humanitarianism and economic utility. It might be useful at this point to ask students to identify the key themes, arguments and tropes of the novel, and to return to and build on that list as the module progresses. They will find very quickly that abolitionist writers use very similar strategies, and this emerges in week two with John Bicknell and Thomas Day's poem *The Dying Negro*, which was inspired by an actual newspaper report and which itself went on to inspire numerous other representations of the enslaved as sentimental heroes, suffering quietly but sometimes making the only kind of violent protest that was acceptable to Europeans – suicide. Like Scott, Bicknell and Day use a sentimental register, imagine plantations that they have never seen, and make use of both economic and humanitarian arguments. They also construct an image of an African that was quite distinct from their representations of Europeans but which went on to influence much abolitionist writing. Students might thus find it useful to chart the ways in which Bicknell and Day construct their portrait of a "dying Negro."

Scott, Bicknell and Day were all writing before an organized abolition movement took shape in Great Britain; indeed, they were in part responsible for bringing slavery to public attention. The next five weeks of the module concern texts written at the height of the movement by authors who in most cases knew each other well and who often collaborated. The first of these, Thomas Clarkson's *Essay on the Slavery and Commerce of the Human Species*, brought together most of the main arguments against the slave trade and became a handbook for abolition activists. The book started life as an undergraduate essay, which might help students realize that the work they do at university can be life-changing, but since Clarkson's original essay was 50,000 words in length, and the book version is even longer, choosing a relevant passage for class discussion can be difficult. Most literature tutors will want to avoid Clarkson's economic or religious analyses, for example, although these were important aspects of the abolition debate. The section that I have found most useful is chapters 1–2 of Book Two, in which Clarkson dramatizes the effects of the slave trade on an African village. His representation of Africa is purely imaginary and his method of arguing is entirely sentimental. Indeed, he seems to abandon all appeal to reason when he argues that "where the conduct of men is so manifestly impious, there can be no need, either of a single argument or a reflection; as every reader of sensibility will anticipate them in his own feelings" (Clarkson 1786: II, ch. 2). Asking students why Clarkson adopts such a sentimental tone in what is otherwise a solidly empirical essay is a fruitful starting point for classroom discussion – that I have discussed at length elsewhere (Carey 2005: 130–7)

Week four marks a return to more traditionally literary forms with Hannah More and Ann Yearsley's rival poems on the slave trade, both written in 1788 at the height of the abolition agitation. Contemporaries immediately contrasted these poems and students will want to as well, not least because of the social differences and personal animosities of the authors. Unlike the labouring-class Yearsley, More was a close friend of William Wilberforce. Wilberforce did not produce a major antislavery text at any point of his career, nor do we have reliable versions of any of his parliamentary speeches. What we do have are many contrasting accounts in newspapers and parliamentary journals which are now more widely available in electronic forms than they were until very recently. Students may wish to contrast different versions or to look in depth at only one, while those who do have access to the full range of databases may find that charting the course of the debates in parliament and the papers is a very rewarding research activity. In either case, they will discover that although Wilberforce was an expert rhetorician, by failing to vote against the slave trade in 1789–92, the British government legitimized it more fully than they ever had done before. This is an irony that would not have been lost on Olaudah Equiano, whose *Interesting Narrative* is the reading for week six. Published to coincide with Wilberforce's 1789 parliamentary speech, this autobiography (students may debate whether the term "slave narrative" is useful or appropriate) is now justly famous. Some classroom discussion must be dedicated to the debate over Equiano's identity and nativity prompted by Vincent Carretta's discovery of manuscripts that seem to contradict Equiano's own account of his childhood in Africa (Carretta 2005: 319–20). To discuss only this, however, would be a disservice to what is a complex work, by turns a voyage narrative, a conversion narrative, an economic treatise and an abolitionist tract. As with the shorter abolitionist verse that is discussed in week seven, Equiano's *Narrative* is unlikely to present problems for most English tutors since in both cases, we see political points being presented in a predominantly literary form. Students should by now be used to analysing the interplay of sentiment and economics, humanitarianism and pathos, that these texts deploy. The week on shorter verse is, accordingly, a good moment to assess progress so far and to ask whether, by 1792, we can talk of a fully fledged literature of antislavery.

Samuel Taylor Coleridge's "Lecture on the Slave Trade" marks the first of two weeks dedicated to the response to the abolition movement by those traditionally central figures of Romanticism, Wordsworth and Coleridge. Coleridge's lecture, delivered at Bristol Library in 1795, was neither particularly original nor particularly influential but it was in many ways typical of the thousands of antislavery lectures that were delivered up and down the country in the 1780s and 1790s. Students will note one important digression in the lecture from the mainstream of abolitionist thought that they have so far encountered, however, since Coleridge attacks abolitionists for "bustling about and shewing off with all the vanity of pretended Sensibility" (Coleridge 1971: 246). Does Coleridge's lecture mark a turning point in the literature of antislavery, students may ask, or does it merely rearticulate the same arguments in the language of a new generation? It may be useful to compare the lecture with Coleridge's recently translated Greek "Ode on Slavery" to see how radical his thinking actually is (Basker 2002: 446–9). Wordsworth too wrote about slavery, including a confessional passage in *The Prelude* in which he admits to having felt lukewarm about the abolition campaign, but his feelings appear more than merely lukewarm in his poems "To Thomas Clarkson" and "To Toussaint L'Overture," both written in 1807, the year in which the British slave trade was abolished. Most students will spot that these poems are sonnets, but the significance of that (if any) is less obvious. Why would Wordsworth present political biography in the form of Elizabethan love poetry? Here, a discussion of a form that is relatively familiar to students can lead into a discussion of a subject matter that is far from familiar.

After 1807, there was a brief lull in popular agitation against slavery; indeed, the condition of the enslaved appears to have been all but forgotten by the general public. Jane Austen's novel *Mansfield Park* (1814) is a useful reminder of the ways in which colonial realities are taken for granted in this period. Students will need to read the novel carefully to note, as Edward Said has argued, that the novel depends on the understanding that plantation money finances British aristocratic life (Said 1993: 95–116). Whether students ultimately agree with Said is perhaps not important: to the scholar, Austen emerges as an author with an attitude to slavery complicated by her connections to the largely anti-abolitionist Tories and the predominantly abolitionist Royal Navy. Students might want to draw a starker picture, seeing Austen as either fully committed to the slave economy or, by contrast, opposed to it in subtle and ironic ways. Both readings, and neither, are possible, and discussion should draw out those ambiguities. This will contrast strongly with the reading for week eleven. *The History of Mary Prince* appeared in 1831, at a time when antislavery campaigners were pushing hard for the complete eradication of slavery throughout the British Empire. This account of the life of Mary Prince, born a slave in Bermuda, was, like Equiano's *Interesting Narrative* four decades earlier, an important part of the debate. What is less clear is in whose voice Prince's story is being told. Unable to write herself, Prince's narrative was recorded by an amanuensis who ordered and altered the story in subtle and less than subtle ways. As students will have seen many times on this module, British abolitionists had appropriated the voice of an enslaved person.

This module ends with a film, Michael Apted's *Amazing Grace*, which was released in 2007 at the time of the two-hundredth anniversary of the abolition of the British slave trade. Having spent twelve weeks reading abolitionist literature, students will recognize many of the historical figures portrayed in the film. Centring on Wilberforce, there are also roles for Clarkson, Equiano, Pitt, More and others. Unless they have not been paying attention over the past weeks, students will be astonished to note that the film is historically inaccurate in many respects, from trivial details to grand narratives. Spotting the mistakes is not difficult and can be quite amusing, but students may be interested in discussing a wider point. Apted misrepresents abolitionist history, but is his ahistorical approach essentially any different from the ways in which abolitionist writers represented themselves or the ways in which they represented the enslaved? Students might ask themselves what this film tells us about the legacy of the abolition movement in the twenty-first century, and what it tells us about the relative importance of factual accuracy and narrative presentation or, to use the cliché, between rhetoric and reality. Ultimately, they might conclude, the literature of antislavery – then and now – is about changing hearts and minds rather than about establishing and presenting facts.

Works cited

Basker, James, ed. (2002) *Amazing Grace: an Anthology of Poems About Slavery, 1660–1810* (New Haven and London: Yale University Press).

Carey, Brycchan (2005) *British Abolitionism and the Rhetoric of Sensibility: Writing, Sentiment, and Slavery, 1760–1807* (Basingstoke: Palgrave Macmillan).

Carretta, Vincent (2005) *Equiano, the African: Biography of a Self-Made Man* (Athens, GA: University of Georgia Press).

Clarkson, Thomas (1786) *An Essay on the Slavery and Commerce of the Human Species, particularly the African, translated from a Latin Dissertation, which was Honoured with the First Prize, in the University of Cambridge, for the Year 1785, with Additions* (London: J. Phillips). Accessed from: http://oll.libertyfund.org/title/1070.

Coleman, Deirdre (2005) *Romantic Colonization and British Anti-Slavery* (Cambridge: Cambridge University Press).

Coleridge, Samuel Taylor (1971) "Lecture on the Slave Trade," in *Lectures 1795: On Politics and Religion*, ed. L. Patton and P. Mann (Princeton: Routledge and Princeton University Press): 235–51.

Kent, Alan M. (2000) *The Literature of Cornwall: Continuity, Identity, Difference, 1000–2000* (Bristol: Redcliffe Press).

Said, Edward (1993) *Culture and Imperialism* (London: Chatto and Windus).

Sancho, Ignatius (1998) *Letters of the Late Ignatius Sancho, An African*, ed. Vincent Carretta (London: Penguin).

Further reading

Carey, Brycchan, ed. "Slavery Poems", http://www.brycchancarey.com/slavery/poetry.htm.

Carretta, Vincent, ed. (1996) *Unchained Voices: an Anthology of Black Authors in the English-Speaking World of the Eighteenth Century* (Lexington: University Press of Kentucky).

"Documenting the American South," University of North Carolina at Chapel Hill, http://docsouth.unc.edu/. Slave Narratives online.

Engerman, Stanley, Seymour Drescher and Robert Paquette, eds. (2001) *Slavery: a Reader* (Oxford: Oxford University Press).

Gregg, Stephen, ed. (2005) *Empire and Identity: an Eighteenth-Century Sourcebook* (Basingstoke: Palgrave Macmillan).

Kitson, Peter, Debbie Lee, et al., eds. (1999) *Slavery, Abolition and Emancipation: Writings in the British Romantic Period*, 8 vols. (London: Chatto and Windus). This text provides facsimiles of many primary sources.

Morgan, Kenneth, et al., eds. (2003) *The British Transatlantic Slave Trade*, 4 vols. (London: Pickering and Chatto).

Richardson, Alan, ed. "Editing Anti-Slavery Poems Project," http://www2.bc.edu/~richarad/asp.html.

Williamson, Karina, ed. (2008) *Contrary Voices: Representations of West Indian Slavery, 1657–1834* (Kingston, JA: University of West Indies Press).

Wood, Marcus, ed. (2003) *The Poetry of Slavery: an Anglo-American Anthology 1764–1866* (Oxford: Oxford University Press).

Part II

Approaches to Teaching Romanticism

7
Teaching Romanticism and Visual Culture

Sophie Thomas

To teach Romantic period literature and visual culture together is to approach the subject in a way that responds to the broader cultural preoccupations proper to that literature. It is of course only one possible interdisciplinary approach, and a strong case could made for readings of Romantic texts that are attentive to history, politics, the natural sciences, sexuality and so on. I will argue below that the relationship of Romantic literature to questions of visuality is a close and productive one, but I would like to begin by addressing the more general problem of disciplines and their boundaries – or, to put it differently, how one thinks of interdisciplinarity and its potential gains. Interdisciplinarity has been as often contested for offering conceptual support to intellectual alliances that are more convenient than necessary, as praised for enabling more subtle and complete understanding. However, interdisciplinarity responds to the inherent limitations of disciplines not simply by making connections and fostering dialogue between them, or by allowing more (or more probing) questions to be asked than a given discipline may allow on its own, but by opening up a potentially "undisciplined" space in the areas in between.[1] To some extent, this space is what Roland Barthes refers to when he argues that interdisciplinary study is not about confronting "already constituted disciplines"; rather, "Interdisciplinary study consists in creating a new object, which belongs to no one" (Barthes 1986: 72).

What does it involve to teach Romantic literature in a way that asks "undisciplined" questions? At a minimum, it means not teaching literature per se, but its broader cultural and historical context, which would involve some unsettling of the discipline. In the case of visual culture, I would claim that questions of visuality (of perception and representation, of vision and the imagination) are central preoccupations of Romantic writing, and of the aesthetic (and ideological) concerns that accompany it. Arguably, then, the questions raised by visual material are being raised and debated in literary materials too – and not least when those materials take an *anti*visual stance. Wordsworth's claim in *The Prelude* that the eye is the "most despotic of our senses" (1805, 11: 173) offers an obvious point of reference for students who are very familiar with the contemporary version of the debate about the power of the imagination, set against the field of the image; what they rarely appreciate is how far reaching the historical, cultural and technological determinants of that debate really are.

While courses that approach English Romanticism with broader questions of vision and visuality in mind are few and far between, it has been a long-standing practice to teach aspects of Romantic literature and painting alongside one another. Such courses aim, often very effectively, to explore elements of a common cultural context, and identify shared preoccupations. The MLA "Approaches to Teaching World Literature" Series, in its volumes on aspects of Romanticism and on specific Romantic poets, dedicates chapters to approaching their work through the visual arts. As a point of departure, it is instructive to identify the principles that govern these chapters.

Stephen C. Behrendt's essay on "Teaching the Gothic Through the Visual Arts" uses visual media, primarily paintings and prints, to sharpen students' responses to key aspects of Gothic literature (Behrendt 2003). Images, with which he argues students engage more readily and often "more probingly" (2003: 66), help convey such central concerns as: the creation of environments that are threatening or which evoke terror (Piranesi's *Imaginary Prisons*); an appreciation of the sublime and its aesthetic and psychological effects (Poussin's *Winter; or, The Deluge*); themes of decline and decay as present in scenes of ruin such as those of Hubert Robert; historical and political determinants such as those connected with the Industrial Revolution (Philippe De Loutherbourg, Joseph Wright of Derby); the question of nature (Caspar David Friedrich), or the unnatural; fantasy, nightmare, misogyny (Fuseli). The point for Behrendt however is not that the images the students encounter are themselves necessarily Gothic, nor that they illustrate the Gothic in some essential way; rather, these paintings "reveal important intellectual and aesthetic analogies to the themes, subjects, and phenomena we typically associate with the literary Gothic" (2003: 71). These works were produced during a period characterized by major upheaval across Europe in political, social and economic structures, and the juxtaposition of these two forms affirms that while one might well study Gothic literature on its own, it is at the same time part of a wider cultural debate about humanity itself during a period of crisis and historical transition.

Three further MLA "Approaches to Teaching" volumes, those devoted to Wordsworth, Byron and Keats, all contain chapters that specifically cover teaching their poetry with the visual arts – and all of them, written by Nicholas Warner, share a set of presuppositions about the capacity of visual material to enrich students' understanding of texts. In the case of Wordsworth, the approach is comparatist and focuses first on painters whose work bears thematic affinities with the poet's, such as Constable, whose landscapes Warner suggests are analogous to Wordsworth's spots of time – and Gainsborough, whose attention to rural (and often humble) subjects raises questions that can be useful for teaching some of the poems in *Lyrical Ballads* (Warner 1986). Secondly, Warner covers poems, such as "Elegaic Stanzas," that address or describe a work of art. For a poet such as Keats, whose relationship to the visual arts is closer and more directly informative of his poetic imagery and aesthetic theory, this second category particularly is considerably larger (Warner 1991a). With Keats, there are affinities in mood and subject matter with a broad range of paintings, sculpture and classical architecture, and a clear set of influences (for example, Poussin's *The Empire of Flora* on "Sleep and Poetry"). From the extensive area of "interart affinities," Warner moves toward a consideration of Keats's "iconic" poems – poems that convey or respond to an actual (or imaginary) work of art, from the Elgin Marbles, to Titian's painting, to that famous urn. He observes that students exposed to such material, who are led to reflect on the relations between verbal and visual media, appear to be better able to grapple with the larger issues of aesthetic representation that revolve around reality, temporality and the imagination.

In Byron's case, Warner focuses on three different areas of "interart" study, of which the first two will be familiar (Warner 1991b). The first involves affinities apparent in the poet's work, in "attitude, subject matter, or mood," with certain Romantic artists: preoccupations with individual freedom, political rebellion, war, Napoleon, nature and so on, all animate the work of painters such as David, Ingres, Gros, Goya, Géricault, Delacroix and Friedrich, as does a shared concern with the sublime (perhaps most apparent in Turner's shipwrecks and snowstorms), and with particular places, such as Venice (1991b: 45). Whether it is the dramatic alpine settings of *Manfred* or the shipwreck scene in *Don Juan*, or the question of orientalism encountered in such works as *The Giaour*, Warner contends that by selecting and presenting visual material that focuses on the theme or issue of a certain passage, students are motivated "to closer, more considered readings, and rereadings of Byron's text" (1991b: 48). The second area of interest is in Bryon's "iconic" poems. *Childe Harold's Pilgrimage* is the obvious focus here, with its passages on famous statues such as the *Horses of St. Mark*, the *Venus de Medici*, the *Apollo Belvedere*, and the *Dying Gladiator*: much can be learned not just about Byron's attitude to sculpture, but also about his views on antiquity and history.

The third area of special interest is illustration, which Warner had also found instructive in relation to Keats (though principally in connection with Victorian and Pre-Raphaelite responses to his poems). Byron however was one of the most often illustrated writers of his own period, perhaps most famously by Turner, Delacroix and Cruikshank, and a number of pertinent questions can be raised with regard to the selection of scenes for illustration, their tendency to emphasize, suppress or distort aspects of the text, and whether or not they enhance our understanding of style, structure and meaning. Larger, more theoretical, questions can also be posed about "the clash or complementarity between text and illustration," about what can be learned from relations between visual and verbal media (Warner 1991b: 49). As with Behrendt's use of visual material to support his teaching of the Gothic, Warner's overall point in all of these areas is to link Byron with "a pervasive cultural phenomenon in European art and vividly demonstrate some of the ways that literary-artistic study can be integrated into the broader framework of cultural interpretation" (1991b: 49).

In these "Approaches" texts on the canonical poets, the co-relation of poetry and painting as "sister arts" is more-or-less taken for granted. A great deal of productive discussion will no doubt arise when the visual arts are juxtaposed with Romantic texts. As I suggested above, however, there are other aspects of visuality, and of visual culture that are central to Romanticism. We can learn much from, and indeed take further, Raymond Williams's claim that broader cultural analyses can "reveal unexpected identities in hitherto separately considered activities" (Williams 1965: 63).[2] Any analysis of high culture, on these grounds, ought to take into account elements of popular culture and everyday experience; it is not enough, thus, to approach visuality in literature through other "high" forms such as painting. One may also do so through popular visual entertainments and public spectacle, travel literature, print culture, visual media and technology. For lack of a better term, I prefer to use "visual culture" in order to include these diverse aspects of visuality (figurative, as well as literal), in addition to painting, exhibitions and poetry about paintings. The benefit of teaching Romanticism in this way lies not simply in registering a shared set of preoccupations, nor in approaching it from a comparative or contrastive angle.[3] Pictures, and indeed all visual media, pose their own interpretive challenges and do not simply restate the contents of a text. Nor do they permit themselves to be subordinated to texts in a straightforward way. Rather, that "text" may find itself replaced with – or preoccupied by – a new or further set of questions. Moreover, acts of perception and interpretation, in relation to visual materials, can (quite literally) foreground the way they are themselves situated, in cultural and historical terms.

My reflections on teaching Romantic literature alongside Romantic visual culture come principally from my experience with an MA course I first designed on "Romanticism and Visual Culture" in 1999. The course has been offered since on two different interdisciplinary MA programmes at the University of Sussex: one in Nineteenth Century Literature and Culture, and the other in Literature, Film and Visual Culture. The Nineteenth Century MA focuses on literary texts but situates them in terms of their interactions with other contemporary cultural forms and intellectual debates, surrounding for example developments in science and evolutionary theory, psychology and sexology, religion and anthropology. The second MA programme is designed for postgraduates with intellectual interests that cut across the disciplines of English, Media, Film and Image Studies. It is not period specific, and explores the convergence between literature and visual culture from the late eighteenth century to the present. Broadly put, it addresses the theoretical as well as the historical interconnections between literary and visual representation, and aims to offer students a fresh understanding of the theoretical exchanges between visual and textual analysis.

In the context of this second MA programme, my course on Romanticism and visual culture deals with material that is the most historically distant, and with a period that tends to fall outside, or rather before, the primary field of visual culture studies, since it obviously predates the development of photography and the cinema. One impetus for the course is simply to show students how the period in fact gave rise to an extraordinary array of popular spectacles dependent on evolving visual technology, some of which clearly anticipate photography and cinema. The course investigates these developments and their impact on paradigms for viewing predominant in the late eighteenth century. It also examines the relationship between the visual media of the period and the treatment of the visual in canonical Romantic texts, and to this end we address figurative as well as more literal interconnections between the visual and the imaginary. These broader connections and concepts are familiar to students even though they lack the historical background.

With the course's position on two different MA programmes comes a difference in the interests of the students: those mainly interested in Romantic and nineteenth-century culture, and those more interested in contemporary visual culture. Having these two constituencies seems not to present a problem; in both camps moreover, it is common to have students with a limited (or even no) background in Romanticism. On balance, however, there is no reason why this course, or elements of it, would not work well pitched at undergraduates. Because there is a wide variety of material to work with, it is also the case that particular elements do lend themselves to extracting for Romantic literature courses that have a different, or more general, focus. For example, I usually include a component on visual culture in undergraduate teaching of Romanticism, usually in the form of a lecture on prints, painting or on popular visual technologies.

Ease of access to visual material and improved IT provision in the seminar room have made this course more straightforward to teach. On a practical note, I rely less now on slides and overheads, and more on PowerPoint or Keynote for presenting images and related material, some of which is readily available on the internet. There are a number of sites where students can locate supplementary materials. *The Midley History of Early Photography* website, for example, contains a great deal of historical information on the development of the diorama (R. D. Wood). *The William Blake Archive* is probably the easiest way for students to see different editions of his illuminated books and an extensive range of his drawings, paintings and engravings (Eaves, Essick, Viscomi). *Romanticism on the Net* and *Romantic Circles* both contain a number of helpful resources for students that are relevant to visual culture (see particularly Halliwell and Haywood 2007; Miles 2005).

Broadly, my course on Romanticism and visual culture, which is run as a seminar course, falls into three sections. The first introduces students to key aspects of eighteenth century aesthetic theory, picturesque tourism, the Grand Tour, and to prominent paradigms for viewing, including a consideration of the cultural impact of major museums and public galleries established at this time. We begin, quite literally, with opportunities for viewing – by exploring all opportunities for visual engagement, and more specifically, by thinking about shows, exhibitions and visual display of various kinds proper to the eighteenth century. I ask students to look at Richard Altick's *The Shows of London* to get a preliminary sense of the array of spectacles available to the viewing public and I also ask them to read C. Suzanne Matheson's entry on "Viewing" in *An Oxford Companion to the Romantic Age* and the chapter in Gillen D'Arcy Wood's *The Shock of the Real: Romanticism and Visual Culture, 1760–1860*, on prints and exhibitions. Over the next few weeks, we focus on the aesthetic categories of the sublime and the picturesque, and then on a consideration of land and landscape, including an examination of prospect poems, and the gender and class politics surrounding prominent paradigms for viewing. We consider the phenomenon of the picturesque tour, with its accompanying guidebooks, view points, and visual paraphernalia such as Claude glasses and mirrors. This topic is taught through a fairly typical split between literature and theory (cultural, aesthetic, political, etc.), with visual examples, as well as wide array of prospect and landscape poems, from Gray, Wordsworth, Coleridge and Charlotte Smith.

Following this, we take forward questions of viewing and landscape into a number of related concerns surrounding the Grand Tour, focusing on Rome and its ruins, and on newly discovered archaeological sites such as Pompeii and Herculaneum. Tourism, and with it class and gender, remains a key topic, but the focus is on the kinds of visual questions raised by ruins in relation to history, and raised pointedly by the experience of visiting sites that have an established image repertoire (as well as a long textual history). In addition to reading a wide range of material on the Grand Tour and on the significance of Rome, for example, in the Romantic period, students read selected texts by Byron, Keats and Shelley.

The second section of the course looks more closely at the emergence of popular visual media, such as the panorama, the diorama and the phantasmagoria, and at this point there is a significant shift in focus. What I am most interested in getting to students to think about here is the desire that drives the development of these technologies either to possess fully the visual by creating a full or immersive illusion (in, for example, the case of the panorama), or to create and manipulate the field of the visual (in the case of the diorama). The content of both of these shows exploited public interest in exotic and/or distant locations, picturesque landscapes, and gothic scenes, as well as in recent historical events. The phantasmagoria, with its origin in Revolutionary Paris during the 1790s, and in the technology of the magic lantern, makes for an interesting discussion of the politics as well as the aesthetics of projective technologies, and Terry Castle's chapter on "Phantasmagoria and the Metaphorics of Modern Reverie" in *The Female Thermometer* offers a good point of departure (1995). Wordsworth's response to the shows and spectacles of London in Book Seven of *The Prelude* is the standard point of reference for the resistance to the visual that arises in response to the public's insatiable appetite for spectacle. Though he is himself fascinated and diverted by the shows of London, his account relates clearly to a preference for the exercise of the imagination that will become a more important topic in later weeks.

At this point we turn to the theatre, not so much to convey an overview of theatre in the Georgian period, as to examine its engagement with the visual. Coleridge's *Remorse* is used to explore relevant debates about dramatic illusion, set against the public appetite for sensational stage spectacle. Students also read Byron's verse dramas to explore the idea of "mental" theatre. Closet dramas, works intended to be read privately rather than staged publicly, and which often engaged abstract, psychological themes that were arguably unrepresentable, raise important questions about anti-theatricality, antivisuality and the imagination. I also ask students to read the chapter on theatre and painting from Wood's *The Shock of the Real* to get a sense of other visual contexts in which to consider theatre – to see, for example, how images of the individualized celebrity actor, and famous theatrical moments, were widely reproduced in paintings and prints.

Elements of this discussion cross over effectively to a session spent examining the phenomenon of the literary galleries, such as Boydell's Shakespeare Gallery – a commercial gallery that displayed specially-commissioned illustrations for a deluxe edition of Shakespeare's plays. Luisa Calè's approach to Fuseli's Milton Gallery in her recent study is helpful here (2006). She examines how the burgeoning exhibition culture of late eighteenth-century London refined the interaction between the visual and verbal, and turned, in Fuseli's phrase, "readers into spectators." The material for this week gives us the chance to think more about illustration, but also to reconsider the importance of the gallery in reconfiguring the relationship between painting, literature and culture. Christopher Rovee's *Imagining the Gallery: the Social Body of British Romanticism,* is also a useful resource for considering how the space of the exhibition gallery, and more specifically portraiture, became an "index" to the re-imagining of the national community in Romantic Britain (2006).

While literary examples and responses are important throughout, Romantic writers are more explicitly the focus of the last third of the course, where engagement with visual matters may be direct, or metaphorical, or conceptual. One important topic addressed is ekphrasis, as many texts of the period take visual artifacts, and artworks, as their subjects. Primary examples are drawn from Keats, Wordsworth, Hemans and Shelley, where the relationship of visual to textual forms raises engaging questions about temporality, cultural domination, and aesthetic representation. Reading Blake in the context of a course such as this makes it possible to consider more fully the relationship of the visual to the visionary in his "illuminated books," and in his practice as an illustrator. On the theoretical issues raised by the relationship of text to image in Blake's poems, W. J. T. Mitchell's *Picture Theory* and *Blake's Composite Art* are particularly effective for helping students to see how his work complicates the assumptions of the "sister arts" tradition, and how text and image can work with each other by working *against* each other in productively contrary ways (Mitchell 1994, 1978).

In other canonical Romantic writers, the visual is more entirely a conceptual or metaphorical issue, and in this final part of the course we address literary material that explicitly investigates the relationship between poetry and the eye, or between images of the natural world and the eye (and I) of the poet. Many Romantic poems, such as Wordsworth's, involve perception, memory and the processes of composition. P. B. Shelley's work offers rich opportunities for considering the relationship between visions and the visual, particularly where the ideal knowledge which the poet seeks is on the one hand unseeable, but on the other, is mediated by the language of visual perception. Returning again to the problem of the resistance to the visible in Romanticism, students come to appreciate the extent the which the exercise of the imagination is not so much opposed to, as fundamentally intertwined with, visible manifestations and visual language.

Perhaps inevitably, there are many more elements that one could include – for example, I would like to do more with the topic of illustration, possibly also with scientific displays, with maps, and questions of empire and race. Other courses, such as Noah Heringman's on "Romanticism and Visual Culture" at the University of Missouri-Columbia (also taught at graduate level), offer different emphases. Heringman spends more time on Blake and uses his writings on art alongside Lessing's *Laokoon*, and Reynolds' *Discourses* as key sources for aesthetic theory. He also teaches a unit on political cartoons, a unit on Ann Radcliffe and the picturesque that addresses scenic design in stage adaptations of her novels, and a section on the controversy over the Parthenon sculptures after their arrival in England. Luisa Calè's teaching of Romantic visual culture, at Oxford and now at Birkbeck College, University of London, includes closer attention to the sublime and its anti-pictorial thrust, to practices of literary visualization inherent in texts, to nature commodified by technological and cultural practices, and to galleries, museums and visual displays as sites of sociability and intertextual dialogue.

What is shared among these courses, and my own, is a conviction that elements of visual culture do not merely supplement or handily illustrate a study of literary Romanticism, but provide students with a fuller picture of its central conceptual preoccupations. This conviction animates much recent research on the subject as well, as Laurie Garrison's excellent overview – "The Visual Subject, *c.*1810–1840: Trends in Romanticism and Victorianism" (2007) – demonstrates. Studies that are generally helpful include William Galperin's examination of the "return" of the visible in British Romanticism (1993) and Gillen D'Arcy Wood's exploration of the significance of prominent visual modes for larger cultural debates (Wood 2001). Wood's *The Shock of the Real* points to a widening gulf between Romantic theories of artistic production that emphasized original genius and an idealized view of the imagination, and a burgeoning visual culture industry that traded on mass reproduction, spectacle and simulation. When viewed in this context, Wood argues that much Romantic aesthetic ideology should be regarded as a response not only to the Enlightenment rationalism of the eighteenth century, which is the model that tends to predominate in Romantic studies, but also to the paradigm shifts produced by the emergence of modern visual culture (Wood 2001).

My own research in this area was closely tied at its inception to the designing of this course, and has been shaped by it ever since. In my study *Romanticism and Visuality: Fragments, History, Spectacle*, I argue that the prominence of figurative and metaphoric uses of sight in literary texts of the period argues for an interest in acts of seeing that intersected, often producing conflicting effects, with a correspondent interest in acts of the imagination (Thomas 2008). In the Romantic period there is a more palpable antagonism between visual display and imaginative endeavour – an antagonism, however, that is not simply negative or combative, but generative. When Romantic texts are situated alongside prominent visual media, it becomes possible to "see" the impact made by the paradigms and procedures of visual modes on the writing of the period. Students can readily appreciate how those visual modes were conceived in terms that emphasized, in a thematic as well as material way, the very nature and limits of visuality.

One should note, in closing, that the course I have sketched out here is structured around the very problematic it addresses. The tension between the visual and the imaginary, or visual and textual culture, has an analogy in how the format of the course involves moving between textual and visual material, and asks students to negotiate those very shifts and interrelationships for themselves. What results is a view of Romanticism that is in keeping with Barthes's suggestion that interdisciplinary study gives rise to a new and undisciplined space, a new object, belonging to no one (Barthes 1986). That the space of Romanticism might itself be always contested, always in the making, always – as in Wood's configuration – figured by a tension between the historical and the modern, becomes apparent in a direct and powerful way (Wood 2001).

Notes

1. See Moran 2002: 15. The indeterminacy of interdisciplinarity relates to the ambiguity of the prefix "inter," for as Geoff Bennington has noted, it can refer to bringing things together (as in "intercourse," or "international") as well as to keeping them apart (for example, "interval," or "intercalate"). See "Inter," in McQuillan 1999: 104.
2. See Moran 2002: 58, for a discussion of the terms "literature" and "culture" in connection with this claim. I take it for granted here that these are contested terms.
3. W. J. T. Mitchell's 1990 essay "Against Comparison: Teaching Literature and the Visual Arts" is particularly instructive on this point (Mitchell 1990). See also Morris Eaves's chapter "The Sister Arts in British Romanticism" in the *Cambridge Companion to British Romanticism* for some penetrating remarks on the consequences, as profound in the Romantic period as now, of the separability and *inseparability* of words and images (Eaves 1993).

Works cited

Altick, Richard (1978) *The Shows of London* (Cambridge, MA and London: Harvard University Press).

Barthes, Roland (1986) *The Rustle of Language*, trans. Richard Howard (Oxford: Basil Blackwell).

Behrendt, Stephen C. (2003) "Teaching the Gothic Through the Visual Arts," *Approaches to Teaching Gothic Fiction: the British and American Traditions*, ed. Diane Long Hoeveler and Tamar Heller (New York: Modern Language Association of America): 66–72.

Calè, Luisa (2006) *Fuseli's Milton Gallery: "Turning Readers into Spectators"* (Oxford: Oxford University Press).

Castle, Terry (1995) *The Female Thermometer: Eighteenth-Century Culture and the Invention of the Uncanny* (New York and Oxford: Oxford University Press).

Eaves, Morris (1993) "The Sister Arts in British Romanticism," *Cambridge Companion to British Romanticism*, ed. Stuart Curran (Cambridge: Cambridge University Press): 236–69.

—— Robert N. Essick, and Joseph Viscomi, eds. *The William Blake Archive*, http://www.blakearchive.org/.

Galperin, William H. (1993) *The Return of the Visible in British Romanticism* (Baltimore: Johns Hopkins University Press).

Garrison, Laurie (2007) "The Visual Subject, c. 1810–1840: Trends in Romanticism and Victorianism" *Literature Compass*, 4/4: 1078–91, http://www3.interscience.wiley.com/journal/117994462/abstract.

Halliwell, John and Ian Haywood, eds. (May 2007) "Romantic Spectacle," *Romanticism and Victorianism on the Net*, 46, http://www.erudit.org/revue/ron/2007/v/n46/index.html.

Labbe, Jacqueline (1998) *Romantic Visualities: Landscape, Gender, and Romanticism* (Basingstoke: Macmillan – now Palgrave Macmillan).

McQuillan, Martin et al., eds. (1999) *Post-Theory: New Directions in Criticism* (Edinburgh: Edinburgh University Press).

Matheson, C. Suzanne (2001) "Viewing," *An Oxford Companion to the Romantic Age: British Culture 1776–1832*, ed. Iain McCalman (Oxford: Oxford University Press).

Miles, Robert, ed. (December 2005) "Romantic Technologies: Visuality in the Romantic Era," *Romantic Circles Praxis Series*, http://www.rc.umd.edu/praxis/.

Mitchell, W. J. T. (1978) *Blake's Composite Art: a Study of the Illuminated Poetry* (Princeton, NJ: Princeton University Press, 1978).

—— (1990) "Against Comparison: Teaching Literature and the Visual Arts," *Teaching Literature and Other Arts*, ed. Jean-Pierre Barricelli et al. (New York: Modern Language Association): 30–7.

—— (1994) *Picture Theory: Essays on Verbal and Visual Representation* (Chicago and London: The University of Chicago Press).

Moran, Joe (2002) *Interdisciplinarity* (London and New York: Routledge).

"Romanticism and Visual Culture," Graduate Centre in the School of Humanities, University of Sussex, http://www.sussex.ac.uk/gchums/1-3-22.html.

Rovee, Christopher (2006) *Imagining the Gallery: the Social Body of British Romanticism* (Stanford, CA: Stanford University Press).

Thomas, Sophie (2008) *Romanticism and Visuality: Fragments, History, Spectacle* (New York and London: Routledge).

Warner, Nicholas O. (1986) "Wordsworth and the Sister Arts," *Approaches to Teaching Wordsworth's Poetry*, ed. Spencer Hall and Jonathan Ramsey (New York: Modern Language Association): 60–2.

—— (1991a) "Keats and the Visual Arts," *Approaches to Teaching Keats's Poetry*, ed. Walter H. Evert and Jack W. Rhodes (New York: Modern Language Association): 86–91.

—— (1991b) "Teaching Byron in Relation to the Visual Arts," *Approaches to Teaching Byron's Poetry*, ed. Frederick W. Shilstone (New York: Modern Language Association): 45–9.

Williams, Raymond ([1961] 1965) *The Long Revolution* (Harmondsworth: Penguin).

Wood, Gillen D'Arcy (2001) *The Shock of the Real: Romanticism and Visual Culture, 1760–1860* (New York and Basingstoke: Palgrave – now Palgrave Macmillan).

Wood, R. D. *The Midley History of Photography*, http://www.midley.co.uk/.
Wordsworth, William (1979) *The Prelude 1799, 1805, 1850*, ed. Jonathan Wordsworth, M. H. Abrams and Stephen Gill (New York and London: W.W. Norton & Company).

Further reading

Crary, Jonathan (1990) *Techniques of the Observer: On Vision and Modernity in the Nineteenth Century* (Cambridge, MA and London: MIT Press).
De Bolla, Peter (2003) *The Education of the Eye: Painting, Landscape and Architecture in Eighteenth-Century Britain* (Stanford, CA: Stanford University Press).
Kroeber, Karl and William Walling, eds. (1978) *Images of Romanticism: Verbal and Visual Affinities* (New Haven: Yale University Press).
Sha, Richard (1998) *The Visual and Verbal Sketch in British Romanticism* (Philadelphia: University of Pennsylvania Press).

8

Teaching Wordsworth in the Lakes: the Literary Field Trip

Sally Bushell

> And to that place a Story appertains,
> Which, though it be ungarnish'd with events,
> Is not unfit, I deem, for the fire-side
> Or for the summer shade.
>
> (Wordsworth 1992: 253)

This chapter will consider the importance of place (the Lake District) for teaching Wordsworth's poetry. It is concerned with trying to articulate exactly how we can go about teaching literature about place, in place, and how our discipline might learn from, or respond to, the model of fieldwork provided by Geography. Whilst the first two parts of the chapter are concerned with the forms of interpretation and understanding involved in responding to literary works through place, the final section is more practical, presenting two different ways of teaching Romanticism in the Lakes.[1]

Wordsworth stands as an example of a poet for whom place is an essential element in his work and who also writes specifically about the place in which he lives (Grasmere), where the majority of his manuscript materials are still held today by the Wordsworth Trust. The opening to "Michael," with its place-specific description and use of the second person address, further reminds us of the poet's heightened alertness to his own future readers:

> If from the public way you turn your steps
> Up the tumultuous brook of Green-head Gill,
> You will suppose that with an upright path
> Your feet must struggle [...]
>
> . . . . .

> [...] although it be a history
> Homely and rude, I will relate the same
> For the delight of a few natural hearts,
> And with yet fonder feeling, for the sake
> Of youthful Poets, who among these Hills
> Will be my second Self when I am gone.
>
> (Wordsworth 1992: 53)

Wordsworth himself initiates the model of reading his poetry within the landscape of its writing, as recorded by Coleridge: "On this blessed calming Day – sitting on the very sheepfold dear William read to me his divine Poem, Michael. – The last day of the year" (Coleridge 1957: I, 1782). Whilst, of course, we do not *have to* seek out the originating object for Michael's sheepfold in order to respond to Wordsworth's poem "Michael," this paper will consider what happens if we *do* visit it. How does a heightened awareness of actual place enrich a student's understanding of Romantic texts?

A sense of place

There have been various attempts to articulate a specifically literary response to place and the problem of representation. In his well-known essay "The Sense of Place" Seamus Heaney distinguishes between:

> two ways in which place is known and cherished, two ways which may be complementary but which are just as likely to be antipathetic. One is lived, illiterate and unconscious, the other learned, literate and conscious. In the literary sensibility, both are likely to co-exist in a conscious and unconscious tension: this tension and the poetry it produces are what I want to discuss. (1980: 131)

Heaney sets up a dialectic between place as event, directly experienced, and the writing of that place and sees such a dialectic as an essential dynamic within the production of a certain kind of poetry. The poet speaks for, and out of, a particular situation but that act of speaking places him apart.

In *Romantic Ecology*, Jonathan Bate takes Heaney's two categories one stage further in response to Wordsworth's "Poems on the Naming of Places." In his final chapter he draws upon Edward Thomas to make a useful distinction between three ways of responding to place in terms of "knowing"; "naming" and "recording" and three corresponding literary forms – the "dwelling poem"; "naming poem"; "prospect poem" (1991: 87, 103). He states that:

> there is the poet's rootedness, his *knowing* of place; his localness, his *naming* of places . . . and his specificity, his *recording* of "times and places of composition." Knowing, naming and recording are closely related, but there is a progression through these categories towards the personal and towards consciousness, even self-consciousness. The people who know places best, who are most rooted in them, tend not to be those who give them names. (87–8)

Bate argues that his first and third categories (*knowing, recording*) correspond to Heaney's two, and that the middle category (*naming*) functions for Wordsworth "as a mediation between the first and third, resolving the tension" (88). Where *knowing* constitutes a directly rooted sense of place, an everydayness without self-consciousness, *recording* stands against it as a highly self-conscious literary act. "Naming" for Bate allows Wordsworth to unite and connect the two extremes: it is through naming poems that Wordsworth "establishes and seeks to protect and preserve a sacred secluded place" (94). Drawing upon Hartman's essay on inscription, Bate articulates a "sacramental attitude to place" from which both the distinctive Wordsworthian voice, and the Romantic lyric emerge (Bate 1991: 92; Hartman 1970). However, although Bate makes a fluent and well-argued case for the centrality of naming to Wordsworth, in his concern to assert Wordsworthian ecocritical credentials he tends to gloss over the problematic nature of the relationship between literary representation and the lived experience of place.[2] So, for example, if the tension between lived and learned responses to place is capable of being "resolved" where does that leave the poetry which, according to Heaney, is created through such tension?[3]

Heaney's and Bates's definitions are concerned primarily with the problematics of a relationship between actually experienced and represented place for the *poet*. Their focus is on poetic self-identity in relation to the people that inhabit place more unthinkingly than the poet does and the texts which are produced either embody or explore some of the contradictions involved. However, neither account is concerned with the role of the *reader* in relation to the place-specific text, or in how we interpret the actual through the imagined by revisiting the geographical sites that initially stimulated representation.

The literary field trip

What, then, is the purpose of the literary field trip? How does it divide itself between a shared experience of an event (either that of the poet, living and composing in that place, or of the reader reexperiencing it in the present) and the written meaning held in the text relating to it? A topographical or geographical understanding is not generally considered essential to literary interpretation. Literature does not demand to be "read in the field" and the reasons for doing so may even be considered suspect – inclining towards authorial reification or a model of "literary pilgrimage." One way to begin to address such questions is by looking at a comparable model in the discipline of Geography, a discipline that has undergone considerable change and re-definition in the last thirty years.

Geography traditionally defined itself as "either a physical (environmental) science, a social science or some combination of the two" with a scientific research practice based on logical empiricism, involving the collection of data in "objective" measurable ways (Clifford and Valentine 2003: 2). Whilst such a method worked more or less unproblematically for physical geography, human geography underwent first a quantitative turn in the 1950s (attempting to be more rigorous in its practices) and then a cultural turn in the 1970s and 80s. Disciplinary self-definition was challenged by a phenomenological approach, asserting the necessarily subjective nature of all human endeavour, with a resulting shift away from quantitative methods towards the qualitative. Cultural geography, in particular, "changed from a relatively self-contained subdiscipline into one that embraces concerns that span the sciences, social sciences and the arts and humanities" (Doel 2003: 502).

When we look across from Literary Studies to Geography to learn about fieldwork, two alternative possible models emerge. The more traditional disciplinary approach offers a clear scientific methodology for extracting data in the field. Within such an account the literary work falls into a category of *stored data* in which there is a danger of the objectivity of the researcher being influenced by the materials:

> a major characteristic of data-collection based on stored materials is the intervention of another filter. In these circumstances, rather than observing phenomena directly, the researcher relies on the presumably accurate sensing and recording by another person. (Stoddard 1982: 183)

At the cultural studies end of the discipline, however, the world is understood in the poststructuralist terms of its signifying codes so that "everything is a text" and "a text is anything that *responds* to the call of an interpretative gesture" (Doel 2003: 506). Such an account demands that:

> a geographical analysis of cultural texts and competing discourses needs to follow as rigorously as possible the spatial, temporal and social traces of both real and imagined signifying structures: representations and practices. (Doel 2003: 508)

This position collapses disciplinary boundaries, so that what we might be doing on a literary field trip potentially becomes identical with a cultural geography field trip, since both may be interested in a represented sense of place rather than the actual or *real* and neither necessarily has to be located on site. Perhaps tellingly, however, this approach seems less inclined to articulate any kind of field work methodology. We need, then, to look more attentively at the traditional model in order to try and articulate a literary alternative.

In *Field Techniques and Research Methods in Geography*, Robert Stoddard defines his focus as "geographic facts" which "pertain to phenomena occurring within their earthbound setting" (1982: 9). Field work is defined against and alongside laboratory work as a contextualized practice. His account is centred on the need to accurately measure and classify data numerically in order to generate accurate information for an area and to articulate clear stages of fieldwork. Lounsbury and Aldrich similarly give a straightforward list of the required stages of field research:

1) a clear statement of the problem,
2) determination of the research area,
3) formulation of hypotheses,
4) identification of the necessary data,
5) categorization or classification and scale of data to be obtained,
6) acquisition of the data,
7) processing and analysing the data, and
8) formulation of the answers to the question or problem as first stated. (1979: 12)

In this account, the authors propose the setting of a variety of exercises and problems in the field, as well as the value of thinking in terms of three phases of response (in the classroom; actual fieldwork; analysis of data). They strongly emphasize the importance of work in the field being "problem oriented" with the initial research problem being of crucial importance in determining the quality and success of the fieldwork (1979: 20).

Where this kind of Geography field work is primarily visual and observational, concerned with measuring and recording, a literary field trip is more concerned with the layering of imagined, represented, textual and actual experiences of a site for both writer and reader. If the aim of the literary field trip is the bringing together of written meanings within the shared space of production and representation, then the primary purpose of such field work must be, not the collection of measurable data, but a concern with more abstract enrichment and enlargement of understanding in response to both literature and place. We might say that where the primary focus of the geographic field trip is that of place (even in the broadest sense of the cultural, social and ethnographic meanings that emanate from a place) the primary focus of the literary field trip must be interpretation of the literary work (even if literary studies is also interested in the cultural, social and historical conditions for it). It would seem appropriate, therefore, to try to clarify the interpretational underpinnings of the literary field trip, and the assumptions that follow from a particular interpretational model. We need to turn briefly to hermeneutics.

A hermeneutics of place

In *Truth and Method,* Hans-Georg Gadamer builds upon Heidegger's account of being as a state of anticipated openness in order to explore interpretation itself as endlessly open to revision. For Gadamer, the work of art "becomes an experience that changes the person who experiences it" (2003: 102). Interpretation occurs as a constant circle (the hermeneutic circle) of anticipated meanings which, when they do not match our expectation, demand that we adjust our own initial assumptions: "interpretation begins with fore-conceptions that are replaced by more suitable ones" (267). The hermeneutic circle involves a constant movement between part and whole, so that:

> The anticipation of meaning in which the whole is envisaged becomes actual understanding when the parts that are determined by the whole themselves also determine the whole. (291)

Experience thus occurs by negation and the sum of experience is not knowledge so much as openness and the ability to recognize and confront prior prejudices within ourselves. For this reason Gadamer places considerable emphasis on the value of asking the right question: "In order to be able to ask, one must want to know, and that means knowing that one does not know" (363). Gadamer also transposes his model into a spatial, environmental metaphor of expanding horizons. The horizon is "the range of vision that includes everything that can be seen from a particular vantage point" (302). Since we are always situated within our own historical present we can never escape from this context, but we can attempt to "transpose ourselves into alien horizons" (304). Gadamer connects this image to the larger hermeneutic model when he states:

> We started by saying that a hermeneutical situation is determined by the prejudices that we bring with us. They constitute, then, the horizon of a particular present, for they represent that beyond which it is impossible to see. (306)

Enlarged understanding means that our horizon constantly has the potential to expand further even though we remain within it: "The horizon is, rather, something into which we move and that moves with us" (304).

It is worth looking also at the prior interpretative model against which Gadamer explicitly defines himself: the Romantic hermeneutics of Friedrich Schleiermacher. He defined two key aspects to interpretation through the hermeneutic circle: understanding of the part (grammatical: text) and of the whole (technical: author, context, life). His account was strongly linked to the individuality of the author and the need to try and understand the work of art through attempted re-construction of all the original contexts of authorial knowledge and production in order for understanding to be achieved: "The task is to be formulated as follows: To understand the text at first as well as and then even better than its author" (Schleiermacher, 1977: 112). At the heart of Schleiermacher's account lies what Gadamer calls "con-geniality" – a kind of affective or psychologically-experienced act of connection with the past. For Gadamer this is not an achievable goal: "It is quite mistaken to base the possibility of understanding a text on the postulate of a 'congeniality' that supposedly unites the creator and the interpreter of a work" (2003: 187).

Although Schleiermacher's account is easily discredited in these post-authorial times, the concept of a reconstructed (authorial and super- or post-authorial) experience presents us with a possible model of interpretation for understanding a creative as well as represented literary response to environment. The idea that by reconstructing certain *conditions* a shared experience can be created, between someone in the present and someone in the past, may be of use when we think about the relationship between actual and textual place, or between past and present inhabitation of it through the medium of text. Schleiermacher's account is at fault in that its focus is too firmly upon the mind of the author as the prime focus of interpretation but the value of an affective engagement with the past, particularly through the medium of place, remains.

Central to the literary field trip must be the multi-layered temporality of the literary work. In the case of Wordsworth, we can also factor in the manuscript object, since both it and the final published text are vitally connected to a specific location which is also bound up with poetic self-identity and production. If we return to Wordsworth's "Michael" then (and assuming that students have previously read the poem) one could begin by interpreting the original context of literary production using Dorothy Wordsworth's Journal (as "stored data"). Dorothy records Wordsworth's difficulty in writing the poem and his situating of that writing very specifically within the landscape, close to the place where "Michael" lived and beside the sheepfold which functions as a symbolic object within the final poem. She richly describes their search for an actual sheepfold as Wordsworth begins writing the poem:

> A fine October morning – sat in the house working all the morning. Wm composing – Sally Ashburner learning to mark. After Dinner we walked up Greenhead Gill in search of a Sheepfold.... The Colours of the mountains soft & rich, with orange fern – The Cattle pasturing upon the hill-tops Kites sailing as in the sky above our heads – Sheep bleating & in lines & chains & patterns scattered over the mountains. They come down & feed on the little green islands in the beds of the torrents & so may be swept away. The Sheepfold is falling away it is built nearly in the form of a heart unequally divided. (Wordsworth, D. 2002: 26)

Next, using archive materials held at The Wordsworth Trust, students can revisit Wordsworth's writing of the poem by working with the first draft manuscript notebook (DC MS 30), as a site of writing which is itself situated within the landscape of its creation and which bears its own history. Although there is not space here to discuss it, this manuscript involves the writing of "Michael" over and across a printed copy of Coleridge's *Poems* (1796), which raises all kinds of issues about the 1800 edition of *Lyrical Ballads* and the replacement of "Christabel" by "Michael," as well as about the physical and psychological contexts for creativity. It is also worth noting that the description of the sheepfold, and the narrative connected with it does not appear at all in the surviving first draft text.[4]

Next, in more literal, physical terms, we can revisit the place to which we know Wordsworth walked, on an almost daily basis, as he struggled to write the poem (the valley of Greenhead Ghyll) and if we wish we can try to search for the ruins of a sheepfold which remain there. Figure 8.2

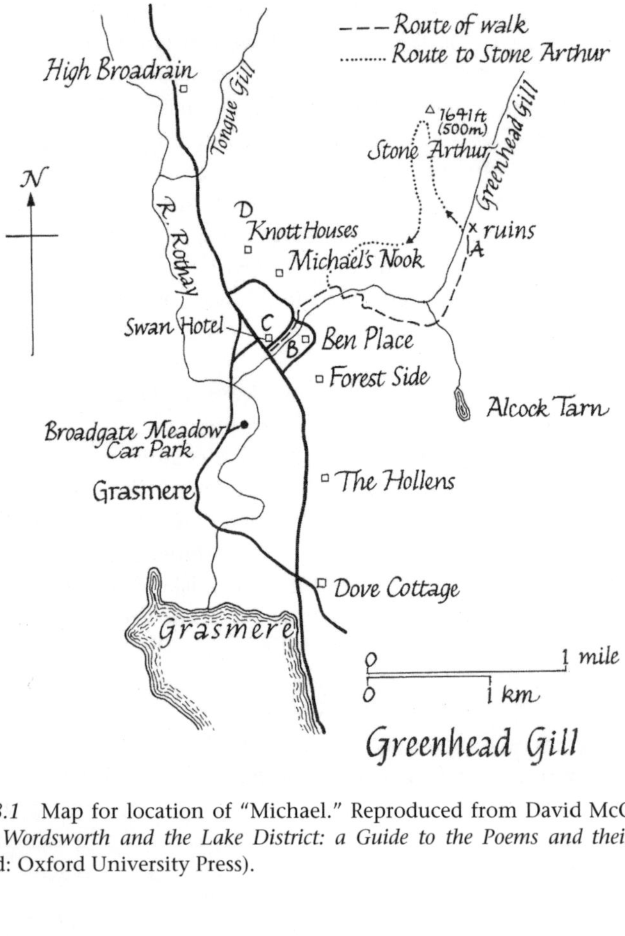

Figure 8.1 Map for location of "Michael." Reproduced from David McCracken (1984) *Wordsworth and the Lake District: a Guide to the Poems and their Places* (Oxford: Oxford University Press).

Figure 8.2 2007 literary field trip to Greenhead Ghyll in the Lake District. Photography by Polly Atkin.

shows students doing this on the 2007 literary field trip.[5] Of course this site also functions as the symbolic core of the published poem, returning us to the text. These alternative perspectives (compositional; biographical; geographical; historical) on the known text should begin to cause students to reevaluate their own prior knowledge: in Gadamer's terms, to ask the right questions. A return to the published work, in the context of its reception, reinvigorated by new contexts can now occur.

Emerging from this account, at least five different ways of working for the literary field trip can be identified, moving between a response to the meaning of the literary work of art and the past writing of the poem in place (the writer's compositional self-situating) as well as a present shared experience of that place by the reader. These include:

1. The reading of literature on the site to which it refers and / or where it was written.
2. A mediated visit to place immediately *after* textual analysis in the classroom.

3. An unmediated visit to place *followed by* textual analysis in the classroom.
4. A comparison of the actual, published and compositional locations of a text, centred on the manuscript as an object that is also a place, or the arrangement of poems in a published collection (working with the archives at The Jerwood Centre, the Wordsworth Trust).
5. Open creative engagement with a site.

Teaching Wordsworth in the Lake District

Finally, then, I want to give two practical examples of teaching Wordsworth in the Lakes, emerging from the activities outlined above and the underlying principles of interpretation and response that have been discussed. I have undertaken such teaching at graduate level.

i. Place-specific poetry (readings on site)

As we have seen, Wordsworth's poetry lends itself to being read on site because of the ways in which he explicitly links a particular text to a particular place (within the text itself and in explanatory notes). Furthermore, we can revisit a spot which we know was the same place that the poet came to write, and which is also represented in the poem. Actual place is thus bound up with imaginary space twice over. A number of Wordsworth's poems also make a direct address to an imagined future reader so that to read them aloud in such places is to literally inhabit the role of addressee. In doing so, we are, of course, fulfilling Wordsworthian expectations. Wordsworth's disgust with those unable to appreciate his work in his lifetime led him away from "local acclamation" of the Public towards the future validation over time of the People (1974: 84). There are numerous Wordsworth poems for which this kind of exercise can be undertaken in and around Grasmere. The one I want to focus on here is "The Brothers Parting" ("I only looked for pain and grief"), a poem read together by five students and myself on 14 May 2008.

John Wordsworth, a sailor, lived with William and Dorothy from January to September 1800, when he was home on leave, sharing with them the period of their first inhabitation of Grasmere. On 29 September he set off to walk from Grasmere over to Patterdale and thence to Penrith and back to his ship. Dorothy's Journal entry for 29 September 1800, reads: "Wm & I parted with him in sight of Ulswater. It was a fine day, showery but with sunshine & fine clouds – poor fellow my heart was right sad" (2002: 22–3). John was drowned five years after this parting moment (in 1805) and this was the last time that the brothers and sister saw each other as he descended from Grizedale tarn into Patterdale and they returned to Grasmere.

Later, in 1805, Dorothy also recorded the writing of "I only looked for pain and grief," in a letter to Lady Beaumont. In the letter she brings together the temporality of her own, John's and William's responses to the landscape and to each other through it:

> My sister and I accompanied him to the top of it [the pass to Patterdale] and parted from him near a Tarn under a part of Helvellyn – he had gone up on Saturday with a neighbour of ours to fish there, but he quitted his companion, and poured out his heart in some beautiful verses to the memory of our lost Brother, who used to go sometimes alone to that same Tarn; for the pleasure of angling in part, but still more, for his love of solitude and of the mountains. Near that very Tarn William and I bade him farewell the last time he was at Grasmere, when he went from us to take the command of the ship. We were in view of the head of Ulswater, and stood till we could see him no longer, watching him as he *hurried* down the stony mountain. Oh! my dear Friend, you will not wonder that we love that place. I have been twice to it since his death. The first time was agony, but it is now a different feeling – poor William was overcome on Saturday – and with floods of tears wrote those verses. (Wordsworth and Wordsworth 1967: I, 598–9)

In a highly "Wordsworthian" way, Dorothy's account creates multiple layers of charged response and return to place, alone and in company, as well as a sense that the writing of the poem *in that place* performs a vital transformative function not only for William but for her as well in relation to the loss of John.

On our literary field trip we read the poem on the pass between the mountains leading from Patterdale to Grasmere under the stone monument put up by The Wordsworth Society in 1881.[6] The monument is situated supposedly at the point where William and Dorothy parted from John as he returned to sea. We considered the authenticity or otherwise of the spot (was this the exact place?) but decided this did not really matter to us, since we were in any case walking the route from Patterdale back to Grasmere and asserting another kind of authenticity in doing so (following an ancient pass, as well as one much-trodden by the Wordsworths). The words on the stone (presumably the final stanza of the poem) were no longer readable. The wind had eaten them away, so that the epitaphic content of the poem was also physically embodied here.

When, with the final stanza, the poem turned to comment directly upon its own potential as a lasting epitaph, I, for one, felt a charge at knowing that by stopping there we were actualizing the meaning of the text:[7]

> Well, well, if ever verse of mine
> Have power to make his merits known,
> Then let a monumental Stone
> Stand here – a sacred Shrine;
> And to the few who come this way,
> Traveller or Shepherd, let it say,
> Long as these mighty rocks endure,
> Oh do not Thou too fondly brood,
> Although deserving of all good,
> On any earthly hope, however pure!
>
> (Wordsworth, W. 1984: 311)

What were we doing here? Were we just reconstructing a past moment, following in Wordsworth's footsteps on a "literary pilgrimage" and giving way to authorial reification? Was our interpretative model closer to Schleiermacher than Gadamer – or did it partake of both? As travellers in the present, we had our own lived experience (the easy chat and warmth of the path on the way up; the surprising cold of the point where the stone was situated just beneath the bleakness of Grizedale tarn, with the wind rushing up the valley; the sympathetic company; the shared reading; the anticipation of lunch). At the same time the literary text had both shaped and directed us (we had chosen the route in part in order to experience this reading) and we had participated in a reading which fulfilled one purpose of the text, allowing us to *become* the living focus of its meaning, the recipients of its message within our own lived experience.

ii. Interactive creative response

A more experimental kind of fieldwork activity to be undertaken might be described as an "open creative response," with the emphasis on individual sense and imaginative engagement with place rather than using the mediation of text. This kind of activity involves interaction in the field and then a return and shared feedback. This is a point where what might constitute a "literary" or a "cultural geography" field trip occupy similar ground. Staying with Wordsworth, and Grasmere, one might choose to run such an activity in, say, the churchyard at the centre of the village in which Wordsworth and his family are buried. Preparatory contextual material could be given here (or afterwards). It might include: Wordsworth's planting of the yew trees, his interest in epitaphs and examples of these, as well as the *Essays on Epitaphs*, the description in the letters of the Wordsworth children playing in the churchyard and the family's need to move house from the nearby vicarage (where they were living) after the deaths of two of the children in 1812, as well as larger historical information on the epitaphic mode in eighteenth-century literature and on Wordsworth's use of it. Students would then be taken to the churchyard with a series of activities to undertake, involving close observation and response to place. The tasks set (to be undertaken in any order) could include:

- walk round the churchyard in whatever way you like, recording your walk in any way you like (why did you choose this route?)
- during the time of your stay, pick up one object to bring back to the group (why did you choose this object?)
- select a gravestone; write a description of it/ of your reflections on it (why did you choose this grave?)
- listen for two minutes and record all the sounds that you hear
- look around you for two minutes and record continuously all that you see
- take one photograph to bring back to the group (why did you photograph this?)
- if you feel able, write a short poem/ list or paragraph summing up the "spirit" of this place.

This kind of activity encourages students to engage directly and individually with a particular place and allows room for a different kind of response, both in the field and on return to the group. It could be used to feed into a number of different activities, creative or critical, in the follow-up session.

What does the literary field trip allow, or create, that would not otherwise exist? I hope I have begun to show that where the meaning of the text is itself bound up with complex concerns about place and identity, responding to it on the spot need not result in a reductive authorial response but in a full experience of text within a unique context. The Lake District, as a "preserved" space (a National Park) is particularly suited for such activities. This is not to suggest, however, that a site which had been radically altered by time, and for which the original context no longer existed except in written form, would prove any less rewarding. Literature problematizes our relationship to place but it also significantly enriches it. The literary field trip allows for a two-way process, an enacted dialogue between text and world, between the past writer and the present reader, in which the reader (of landscape and word) becomes the experiential nexus.

Notes

1. The chapter draws upon two teaching experiences: an MA module entitled "On Location in the Lakes: Place, Space and Poetry" and an annual summer term field trip to the Lakes with MA and PhD students organized by myself and Simon Bainbridge as co-directors of the Wordsworth Centre, Lancaster University. The annual summer Wordsworth Conference of course also offers a similar experience.
2. For a sceptical reading against Bate, see Pinkney 1995.
3. It is interesting to note that when Bate reproduces Heaney's comment as I have given it above (on p. 88 of *Romantic Ecology*), he omits the final comment in the quotation after the colon.
4. I have discussed both of these issues in detail elsewhere. See forthcoming papers: "The Making of Meaning in Wordsworth's *Home at Grasmere*" and "The Mapping of Meaning in Wordsworth's 'Michael' " in *Studies in Romanticism*.
5. Photograph by Polly Atkin.
6. See Gill 1988: 242–3. Gill states that "by the second meeting of the Wordsworth society in Grasmere in 1881 it had been decided that some of Wordsworth's elegiac lines should be carved in the rock at the parting place, so as to bring together for hikers passing by the biographical fact, Wordsworth's poetry, and the mountain landscape itself" (243).
7. In fact the final "message" of the poem's conclusion is oddly out of tune with its overall mood and loving focus upon John. Thus, the truer "utterance" seems to be that of the brotherly relationship and the act of final separation rather than the negative sentiment of the end of the poem.

Works cited

Bate, Jonathan (1991) *Romantic Ecology: Wordsworth and the Environmental Tradition* (London and New York: Routledge).

Clifford, Nicholas and Gill Valentine (2003) "Getting Started in Geographical Research," in *Key Methods in Geography*, eds. Nicholas Clifford and Gill Valentine (London: Sage Publications).

Coleridge, Samuel Taylor (1957) *The Notebooks of Samuel Taylor Coleridge*, ed. Kathleen Coburn (London: Routledge & Kegan Paul).

Doel, Marcus A. (2003) "Analyzing Cultural Texts," in *Key Methods in Geography*, eds. Nicholas Clifford and Gill Valentine (London: Sage Publications).

Gadamer, Hans-Georg (2003) *Truth and Method*, 2nd edn., trans. and rev. by Joel Weinsheimer and Donald G. Marshall (London: Continuum).

Gill, Stephen (1998) *Wordsworth and the Victorians* (Oxford: Oxford University Press).

Hartman, Geoffrey (1970) "Wordsworth, Inscriptions, and Romantic Nature Poetry," in *Beyond Formalism: Literary Essays 1958–1970* (New Haven: Yale University Press).

Heaney, Seamus (1980) "A Sense of Place," in *Preoccupations: Selected Prose 1968–1978* (London and Boston: Faber and Faber).

Lounsbury, John F. and Frank T. Aldrich ([1979]1986) *Introduction to Geographic Field Methods and Techniques*, 2nd edn. (Columbus, OH: Charles E. Merrill).

McCracken, David (1984) *Wordsworth and the Lake District: a Guide to the Poems and Their Places* (Oxford: Oxford University Press).

Tony Pinkney (1995) "Naming Places: Wordsworth and the Possibilities of Eco-Criticism," in *News from Nowhere: Theory and Politics of Romanticism*, eds. Tony Pinkney, Keith Hanley and Fred Botting (Keele: Keele University Press).

Ricoeur, Paul (1991) "Writing as a Problem for Literary Criticism and Philosophical Hermeneutics," in *A Ricoeur Reader: Reflection and Imagination*, ed. Mario J. Valdés (Hemel Hempstead: Harvester Wheatsheaf).

Schleiermacher, Friedrich (1977) *Hermeneutics: The Handwritten Manuscripts*, ed. Heinz Kimmerle, trans. James Duke and Jack Forstman (Missoula, MT: Scholars Press).

Stoddard, Robert (1982) *Field Techniques and Research Methods in Geography* (Iowa: Kendal/Hunt Publishing Company).

Wordsworth, Dorothy (2002) *Dorothy Wordsworth: the Grasmere and Alfoxden Journals*, ed. Pamela Woof (Oxford: Oxford University Press).

—— and William Wordsworth (1967) *The Letters of William and Dorothy Wordsworth: The Early Years 1787–1805*, 2nd edn., ed. Ernest De Selincourt, rev. Chester L. Shaver (Oxford: Clarendon Press).

Wordsworth, William (1974) *The Prose Works of William Wordsworth*, ed. W. J. B. Owen and Jane Worthington Smyser, 3 vols. (Oxford: Clarendon Press).

—— (1984) *William Wordsworth: The Major Works*, ed. Stephen Gill (Oxford: Oxford University Press).

—— (1992) *Lyrical Ballads and Other Poems, 1797–1800*, eds. James Butler and Karen Green (Ithaca: Cornell University Press).

—— (1993) *The Fenwick Notes*, ed. Jared Curtis (Bristol: Bristol Classical Press).

9
Teaching Romanticism with ICT

Stephen C. Behrendt

This essay originated in a talk I gave several years ago at a conference in London that dealt with teaching British Romanticism. Because I am an American, I began my remarks by musing upon the anomaly of an American talking to colleagues from *Britain* about teaching British Romanticism to American students. My larger subject, though, was teaching today's students in what are, for the most part, *yesterday*'s classrooms. In reality, those of us who teach Romanticism – on both sides of the Atlantic – have much in common when it comes to pragmatic issues concerning what increasingly corporate-minded administrators are fond of calling the "delivery" of our courses to those "consumers" that most of us still call "students." This administrative-speak finds its unfortunate parallel in that variety of student-speak that identifies the goal of college as a "university degree," rather than anything that includes "education" or any related variant. Today's curriculum, it seems, is driven less by "what we can (or should) offer" than by "what students will take." We have all grown accustomed to walking into classrooms populated by students – at all levels and regardless of academic concentration – who have little sense of historical or cultural continuity with respect either to discrete subject matter (say, "Romanticism") or to national or international history (including cultural history, or the "history of ideas" tradition). Perhaps conditioned by a determinedly localizing and instant-gratification-oriented culture, students often have as little sense of what happened during a period that they are studying as they have of what preceded and followed it.

I mention this to frame my observations here about the evolving role of Information and Communications Technology (which I shall, abbreviate hereafter simply as "ICT") in the teaching of Romanticism in today's classrooms, and with today's students. I shall begin with those classrooms themselves, and with the pedagogical implications that devolve from their nature as both physical and technological spaces. First, the physical aspect, which comprises two interrelated parts: room size and class size. At my university, zealous administrators occasionally run in-house seminars for new faculty to help them learn how to "deliver" their courses through a pedagogical model that they engagingly – and with little visual imagination – call "front-loading." The term, which of course derives from a piece of construction equipment that can scoop up large quantities of inert material from one pile and dump them upon another, equally inert pile, must seem apt to these administrators, whose teaching technique of choice is the mass lecture, with or without ICT laid on. Thus we have at my university what is called the "Century Club," an administration-generated coterie that celebrates professors who regularly offer their courses in lectures of 100 or more – preferably *much* more – in very large lecture halls. Not surprisingly, the only numbers required for membership in this clique are impressive student enrollment numbers; student *evaluation* numbers are not considered – no doubt with good reason. At the other end of the spectrum are the small, oddly shaped, ill-lit and typically derelict rooms to which smaller classes (like seminars and discussion sections) often are relegated. Like the cavernous teaching space, the cupboard-like one – especially if it is physically and aesthetically problematic – inevitably impacts one's teaching.

Introducing technology into classes that meet in rooms that are questionable at best when it comes to size, shape and equipment raises issues of pedagogy, for *how* we teach our classes necessarily depends to a considerable extent upon purely physical considerations such as these. It is both disappointing and frustrating to enter a classroom or lecture hall with a technology-rich presentation prepared, only to discover that the resident equipment is unresponsive – or even gone missing. In such circumstances even the most veteran instructor must improvise, and improvising for conventional oral delivery a presentation that has been prepared for electronically-enhanced delivery means that a good deal gets lost in the translation. Students tend to be sympathetic to such technological breakdowns, but they still undermine both the instructor's performance (and the confidence with which the students view her or him) and the material being presented at that session.

Clearly, one of our principal challenges as twenty-first-century teachers of Romanticism is to gain some facility – if not actual expertise – with various resources available to us in the form of ICT. Because our students are increasingly "interactive" in orientation and experience, and like to experiment with technology and with electronic gadgets, we can engage them productively in alternative, interactive classroom procedures. Moreover, because they typically bring diverse backgrounds to their studies, discovering unsuspected connections among aspects of the subjects they study may both delight and energize them. I have not gotten so far as text-messaging my students (some of my colleagues have), but I do interact with them by email, and many of us now use online tools like the popular Blackboard program, which includes modules for online communication (email, but also discussion forums that can be individually defined and configured), record-keeping, grading and student tracking, as well as an Internet portal that permits us to post our own materials and link to those of our colleagues and indeed to the entire Internet. Furthermore, growing numbers of students produce electronic versions of their work, including multi-media productions that often exhibit remarkable technological sophistication. And they do impressive PowerPoint presentations in class, although many read their screen texts to us, word for word, unless we remind them not to, which may leave them speechless. In many respects, though, they are well ahead of us on the learning curve when it comes to these electronic resources. When it comes to research projects, it is increasingly apparent that asking them to approach research in traditional ways may no longer be the way to proceed, especially since, given some interesting alternative projects, many discover to their surprise that they actually *enjoy* research.

Let me, then, offer some concrete examples and suggestions about teaching Romanticism with ICT. I shall start with some of my own experiences, adding and embroidering to suggest additional or alternative ways to proceed with both specialized and non-specialist students.

I will begin with a fairly simple example. I have gradually moved away from assigning the traditional "term paper" or research-based course report, opting instead for guided projects that offer my students opportunities for more personally satisfying activities while also dramatically reducing the occurrence of plagiarism, which can be a major problem despite the increasing sophistication of plagiarism-detection services such as Turnitin. The Internet makes it easy for students to buy pre-written papers there, or to have them custom written. And since so much is freely available online, it is not particularly difficult, either, for a student to stitch together an essay simply by cutting and pasting from a broad variety of websites. Notoriety notwithstanding, many students do not know – and might not care if they did know – that much of what is on the web is largely unvetted and therefore often unreliable. What matters is that it is *there* for the taking.

Therefore I like to assign what I call research portfolios, for which students assemble an extensive collection of conventional and online materials. This done, they write about the sort of extended essay – or other variety of project, including (ideally) a multi-media one – that could be developed from those materials. I encourage students to invest their time more in hands-on *investigating* than in writing up results, since (I explain) much of what one "does" in English studies is, after all, research of one sort or another. The results have been dramatic. I get far better products – more consistently – than I ever did with conventional term paper assignments. Moreover, because students become far more engaged with the research process, the resulting portfolios tend to be both extensive and inventive. And the whole issue of plagiarism simply goes away.

These research portfolios most often explore literature and culture directly, but I permit *non*-English majors to identify issues directly relevant to their majors. In either case, the project must be both definable and defensible within the course parameters. After clearing their topics with me, students collect their research materials, which they annotate and submit to me along with several original documents. I stipulate that *no more than* 50 per cent of the portfolio contents may come from Internet sources; the others must be from conventional print (or other) sources. Students copy selectively from their sources and include these documents in their portfolios, each tagged with two bits of information: (1) a complete bibliographical citation, and (2) a note indicating why this piece of information has been selected for inclusion. The finished portfolio includes this entire set of research materials (it's not unusual to receive the project in a crate) and the other documents, including a complete table of contents. The central document, a cover letter, explains why the student selected her or his particular topic and then describes in some detail the full-blown project that she or he believes could be generated from the assembled materials. This letter also outlines difficulties the student encountered and how she or he dealt with those difficulties, and discusses surprises or discoveries that emerged. In a final document, a self-assessment, the student evaluates her or his performance and the value that she or he sees in the finished project.

As may be obvious from this example, I believe that providing hands-on opportunities to do some of the things we do as scholars is pedagogically important. So let me describe several other types of projects that can draw usefully upon electronic and technological resources as well as more traditional ones. One such project evolved from teaching Romantic poetry at the time when we were first beginning to interrogate the traditional canon and were supplementing commercial anthologies with home-made course packets. It occurred to me to have students examine the contemporary public reception of Romantic-era poetry by both canonical and non-canonical authors. To that end I assembled a list of *volumes* of poems by authors ranging from Coleridge, Byron, and Shelley to Robinson, Opie, and Hemans, and including authors whose names are only now becoming familiar again, all of which had been reviewed fairly widely in the contemporary periodical press.

Because we have an excellent microform collection of British periodicals at my university, I had students look up contemporary reviews of the volume of their choice, make a bibliographical record, summarize each review, prepare selective transcriptions of all or part of at least some of the reviews, and compose a brief descriptive and analytical essay about the nature and the substance of the reviews. The project accomplished several important things for the students. First, it got them to look carefully at those contemporary reviews, which was a revelation in its own right. Students not only read the reviews, which they had to locate on the microfilms, but they also – perhaps inevitably – browsed as well, often finding themselves hooked on other reviews, essays and articles in the periodicals they were searching. As more and more facsimiles of periodical literature are made accessible online, more of this research can be done on the Internet, although many sources must still be consulted in less easy-to-manipulate media like microforms.

Second, this reception project revealed to my students how very different "reviewing" was two centuries ago, both in its frequent nastiness and in its pseudo-intellectual moralism. Both these matters yielded lively class discussions about reviewing generally and about the ostensible "standards" or "criteria" upon which critical opinion was based. These discussions led us to examine also the politics of individual journals, on one hand, and the gendered nature of critical discourse, on the other. Third, the project helped students to situate their volumes – and their poets – within their contemporary culture in a more informed and more sophisticated fashion. Many students subsequently elaborated their projects, attaching various interdisciplinary materials, principally gathered from online sources, to elaborate the social and cultural contexts for the original volumes and their authors.

Another effective class project is an annotated edition, a project that works best when assigned to "task groups" of no more than four students. I provide each group with copies of a relatively short volume of poems by an author whose works are not available in any modern critical or annotated edition. Pre-1800 works can be accessed on line through *Eighteenth Century Collections Online* (*ECCO*); later ones may be in online archives like *Bartleby, Project Gutenberg*, or *Google Books*, or on websites maintained by institutions and individuals. I ask the students to prepare an "edition" as if for a textbook publisher. Students read the poems and decide what must be annotated – words, expressions, topical references, literary and other allusions, and so forth. After compiling their lists, they determine what sort of annotations are required, and they set about generating them, drawing upon both electronic and print-based resources. Because this work can be considerable, having a task group rather than only one student responsible both distributes the work and requires the students to negotiate task assignments. Once they complete their annotations, the students write a brief biographical and critical introduction to the poet in general and to the volume in particular, situating both within the contemporary culture. Some groups produce conventional paper editions, but more choose to create electronic ones, embedding annotations and other apparatus in text links. The advantage of the electronic versions is that they can be placed on a website, making them accessible to other scholars. These projects engage students in unusual (for them) and sophisticated research while helping them discover new ways of looking at texts and addressing textual and editorial issues and problems. And they yield products in which students take genuine pride of ownership after what most describe as a level of engagement atypical for English course assignments. Especially when the finished products are placed on the Internet, students recognize (because they frequently receive feedback) that their work is contributing in a meaningful fashion to scholarship. It is a powerful lesson.

Let me now describe another somewhat more ambitious project that involves ICT. Some ten years ago I convinced my university to acquire the *Edition Corvey*, a remarkable microfiche collection of nearly ten thousand separate *titles* of primarily Romantic-era belles-lettristic works in English, French and German. The approximately thirty-two hundred English works represent a valuable unfiltered picture of literary publication, especially in fiction, during the period from 1815 to the 1830s, with additional representation from as early as the 1790s. Colleagues at Sheffield Hallam University (Emma Clery in particular) had in the 1990s developed a project called "Adopt an Author" that also involved the *Edition Corvey*. In their project, each student studied an individual woman author represented in the Corvey collection and prepared supplementary materials that were mounted on the website at Sheffield Hallam that is now called CW^3. I have subsequently asked my own students to do something comparable.

I provide students with a selected list of novels by women and men in the Corvey collection not generally available in conventional print format. Students choose one novel – sight unseen and with no special guidance from me – and then read it on microfiche. Each student prepares a synopsis of the plot and then consults other resources – microform, electronic and print – to locate and transcribe in their entirety as many as possible of the novel's contemporary reviews. The student also prepares a bibliography of the author's works and a brief biographical statement about the author, working from research sources other than "standard" literary guides (from which these authors are generally absent). Each student prepares a copy of the synopsis for everyone in the course and briefly presents her or his novel (and its author) in class during the last several weeks of the course. The student gives me all these documents in electronic form, as separate files, and after lightly editing them for consistency of format I mount them on a website I maintain that is devoted to "Studies in Romanticism at the University of Nebraska." I copyright the materials in each student's name, which they like a great deal, not just because they get a "publication" out of their project but also – more immediately gratifying – because they see their name on the web where others can see it, too, literally worldwide. Each student also gives me a statement describing and evaluating the project itself, and including the student's thoughts about the personal, intellectual and technological challenges, triumphs, and defeats involved in the project; this statement does *not* go on the web.

When I assign this project I explain why issues like canonicity and periodicity are critical to Romantic studies today, and I stress how textual recovery projects have already dramatically affected how we see our field. I stress, too, the immediate and demonstrable impact of the individual projects, which will provide students and scholars everywhere with documentary records of works that they might not otherwise discover without reading each of them personally. In other words, I involve my students directly in the working community of Romantic scholars, and they generally invest their time and energy with genuine enthusiasm. By extraordinary serendipity, the first time I assigned this project one undergraduate non-major submitted his materials quite early in the term, and I quickly mounted them on the website, with his name and copyright mark on each document. The very next day a scholar in Australia emailed an inquiry about this student's research and asked to be put in touch with him. When I reported this to my class at our next meeting, the astonishment in the room was palpable. And they were hooked.

I cannot stress enough how effective activities like these are for modeling what we do as scholars and teachers. Our scientist colleagues have laboratories in which they work with students at all levels, often co-publishing with them the results of their more advanced work. We tend not to think of ourselves that way, I believe, and that strikes me as a mistake. It sells *us* short, it sells our *students* short, and it sells the inherent interest of our *materials* and our *scholarship* short. What students can learn from activities like those I have described about problem-solving and creative cultural archaeology can have far-reaching real-world applications for the field as well as immediately personal career relevance for individual students, regardless of their academic specialization.

Let me offer two more illustrations. I have now had students undertake a comparable project with volumes of non-canonical Romantic poetry, again posting the copyrighted products on the website. Instead of a plot synopsis, students in this case prepare descriptive and analytical essays about their volume, along with the bibliographical and biographical documents and transcriptions of reviews. In a seminar in Romantic-era women poets, graduate students prepared electronic editions of volumes of poetry, adding annotations and other supplementary materials. The difficulty with this project was that preparing the texts themselves was almost prohibitively time-consuming. We could not simply scan texts with OCR software because the original pages had too much "noise" on them – too many surface irregularities, inking problems, spotting, and the like – so students had to key in the texts. Doing so ate away at the time that we had budgeted both for supplementary research and for marking up the texts in XML; the texts were posted simply in HTML. Nevertheless, this project provided hands-on experience in preparing texts for electronic rendering and in wrestling with applied editorial procedures, furnishing these students with a "head start" in dealing with electronic and technological aspects of contemporary Romantic studies.

These illustrations are, of course, only part of the story, and I offer them as suggestions for activities that others might wish to adapt for their own needs. Instructors have an ever-expanding array of electronic resources, from hardware and software to online archives, bibliographies, text manipulation devices, and interactive websites, all of them variously geared to the needs of both the dedicated, advanced scholar/teacher in Romanticism and the average undergraduate student.

Sometimes the challenge is simply to find these resources and to work one's way through them, a process that can be both exhilarating and dizzying. In the remainder of this essay I shall survey some important and useful electronic resources for Romanticists, but I want first to say a bit about some resources that fall under the heading of "teaching aids." Here I am thinking about packages like the ubiquitous Microsoft PowerPoint presentation software, which becomes increasingly design-rich with each successive iteration, as well as about video-editing programs like Adobe Premiere and Macromedia Flash, and online sites like YouTube. While both students and their teachers can easily be carried away by the "special effects" such programs offer, it is no stretch to observe that not just our students but also our primary-school-age children are often more adept with this technology than many of us are. This is not all bad, since it can provide us with the (often unsettling) experience of having our students teach *us*. While it bothers me when things go awry, technologically, in a classroom, I have learned to look past my embarrassment and to observe that individual students delight in showing me how to make things right, and that the entire class is often de-mystified just a bit as the unstated barrier between "student/learner" and "professor/teacher" is bridged, however briefly. In these moments, too, we can enjoy a refreshingly productive community with our students, if we can just relax enough to do so. I have learned from students how to make animations work in otherwise plain presentations, for example, and how to achieve visual effects that students find particularly effective or engaging (and which I would not otherwise have suspected). In the process I have refamiliarized myself with the feelings of unease, incapacity and plain embarrassment that are the common lot of student learners. Humbling it is, but also instructive.

Let me turn, then, to some particular resources that instructors may find helpful in teaching an electronically-enhanced Romanticism. Primary among these are some basic research tools. Because most of us routinely require research projects of our students, whatever the course, it is helpful to have them work regularly with online bibliographical resources like the integrated catalogue of the British Library and the *English Short Title Catalogue*, available on the same site. Other national research libraries like the National Library of Ireland and, in the United States, the Library of Congress and the New York Public Library, offer splendid resources both for searching primary texts and for verifying bibliographical information. In Britain, another important resource is the Copac academic and national library catalogue, which gathers on a single website the catalogues of all the United Kingdom National

Libraries, a wide range of major university libraries, specialist collections such as the National Art Library (at the Victoria and Albert Museum), and the catalogue of Trinity College Dublin Library, in Ireland. Another portal site, LIBWEB, is a compilation of library servers worldwide that is updated daily and that presently includes over 7900 homepages from libraries in 146 countries.

Additional resources provide internet access to museums whose collections are more interdisciplinary and that include areas like history, archeology, art and culture generally. One of the most useful of these is the Virtual Library Museums Page, with links to an exciting array of museums, galleries and archives around the world. The British Museum's website is, of course, an invaluable starting point for research of all sorts. Another especially useful site, *BritishBattles.com*, documents British military history during the "long" Romantic period, with detailed information about battles fought by Britain and its Empire forces from the eighteenth century to the end of the nineteenth century, supplemented with illustrations and maps. Among the numerous chronologies, the best is called, simply, *Romantic Chronology*; concentrating on the "long" Romantic period, this site documents the eighteenth and nineteenth centuries, with cross-links to persons and events in history, literature and the arts, and to texts and other supplementary materials. Finally, no student – whatever her or his academic area – should be unaware of the vast resource called *The Voice of the Shuttle*. This sprawling website contains links not just to literature and the arts, but also to all areas of the Humanities, along with copious supplementary resources for research and study; despite the inevitable dead links and inexplicable omissions, the site is a goldmine of riches both for cursory surfing and for dedicated research.

Increasing numbers of primary texts are coming on line in electronic form, with sites serving as "clearing houses" and access portals. Some of these are maintained by individual scholars and teachers; these tend to be limited in scope and addressed to the particular interests of those who maintain the sites. Others are institutional; somewhat broader in scope and typically maintained by the institutions rather than by individuals, these are generally more stable and longer-lived. One particularly noteworthy site is *Romantic Circles*, based at the University of Maryland (USA) and boasting excellent scholarly electronic editions, peer-reviewed critical and theoretical essays ("Praxis"), reviews, a forum on pedagogy, and links to specialized chronologies, bibliographies, indexes and concordances. For Romantic-era women's poetry, the University of California, Davis, is building an electronic archive of full texts (*British Women Romantic Poets, 1789–1832*), especially by lesser-known poets whose lives and works are the subjects of recovery efforts among contemporary scholars. Alexander Street Press has published online textbase collections of Romantic-era poetry by Scottish and Irish women containing fully searchable texts and recent bio-critical essays on the authors. Jane Austen's Chawton House, restored as a working research library, sponsors a *Novels-On-Line* site that provides full texts, in several formats, of novels by eighteenth and early nineteenth-century women writers.

This is probably the place to mention, also, *British Fiction, 1800–1829: a Database of Production, Circulation & Reception*. Maintained at Cardiff University, this growing site boasts bibliographical records of upwards of 2000 works of fiction written by some 900 authors, along with diverse contemporary materials that include anecdotal records, circulating-library catalogues, newspaper advertisements, reviews, and subscription lists. It both supplements and supersedes contextual materials like the synopses and contemporary reviews of Romantic-era women's novels posted at Sheffield Hallam University's *CW*³ website, cited earlier.

Additional sites combine range of coverage with accessibility and, often, commercial sales pitches. At one end of the spectrum are sites like *FullBooks.com* and the *On Line Books Collection*; both provide links to full texts of books of all sorts. Such sites are only as reliable as those who create and maintain them, however; typically, they contain both links that have gone dormant and links that lead to commercial sites rather than actual texts, and so they can be problematic. On the other hand, they do provide texts which students can download and manipulate in various ways. At the other end of the spectrum are established and reliable sites like *Bartleby* and *Project Gutenberg*, the latter of which includes more than 17,000 texts in the public domain. Another important resource in this category is *Literature Online*, the site maintained by Chadwyck-Healey and available, by subscription only, in many research and public libraries; this virtual library contains over 350,000 literary texts together with full-text journals, author biographies and other critical and reference resources. Although it overlaps only the early end of the Romantic era, the *Eighteenth Century Collections Online* (*ECCO*), also a subscription-based service, provides access to a vast cache of eighteenth-century texts, in electronic form as PDF images, drawn from all disciplines. Finally, Google's digital library initiative, *Google Books*, is bringing online the collections of major public and academic research libraries in flexible, searchable formats. And for secondary scholarly materials, two essential websites are the comprehensive MLA International Bibliography and JSTOR: The Scholarly Journal Archive; the latter provides online access to full texts of scholarly articles and monographs.

Students and instructors should also be aware of websites maintained by professional organizations in Romanticism. In Britain, the principal organization is the British Association for Romantic Studies (BARS). Chief in North America are the North American Society for the Study of Romanticism (NASSR) and the International Conference on Romanticism (ICR). These sites provide links to other useful teaching and research sites and to conferences, symposia and lecture series to which both undergraduate and graduate students are invited and to which they may submit their work. Especially for graduate students, such sites offer a revealing picture of the scholarly community of Romantic studies.

There are of course many ways to incorporate resources like these in one's teaching. If the classroom is sufficiently equipped, for instance, one can create bookmarks in advance and then do real-time computer searches in class to pursue issues that arise in discussion. Or one can set up files of visual materials – paintings, sculpture, caricature art, architecture and the like – and then link to them in class to illustrate a lecture or discussion; this is sometimes less cumbersome (and more flexible) than preparing a PowerPoint presentation, for example. One can also ask students to prepare materials on their own and present them in class sessions, and – especially with smaller classes – also to modify them literally "on the fly" as discussion transpires. If multiple students have computer terminals or are using laptops in a wireless environment, it is possible to devote portions of class sessions to online searching by individual students who then share their findings with the group. Activities like these are especially helpful in teaching the historical and cultural contexts for literature, since online resources can provide fascinating insight into details of quotidian experiences, including fashions, daily life, and the appearances of people and places being studied. Such online activities typically facilitate a classroom spontaneity that can be exhilarating – when everything works; and when it fails to work, that failure can often be turned to advantage with an (at least partially) improvised discussion of what may be gained even from the dead-ends and misfires with which all scholars are familiar.

Confronted with the task of concluding this essay by some means short of simply stopping ("Connection Lost"), I'd like to point to three significant online journals for the study and teaching of Romanticism.

One of these I have already cited: *Romantic Circles*; perusing theoretical discussions, pedagogical models, and sample course materials available there will lead one to an abundance of valuable and timely secondary resources. The same is true for *Romanticism and Victorianism on the Net*, which publishes scholarship, pedagogy and theory, all of it timely as well. Finally, *Romantic Textualities* contributes to this rich mix a further layer in the form of its additional commitment to textual scholarship and editing, especially electronic. The tools and materials will continue to appear and evolve; no question. Now it is up to us to make the most of them.

Works cited

Alexander Street Press, http://www.alexanderstreetpress.com.
Bartleby, http://www.bartleby.com/.
British Association for Romantic Studies (BARS), http://www.bars.ac.uk/.
BritishBattles.com, http://www.britishbattles.com/
British Fiction, 1800–1829: a Database of Production, Circulation & Reception, http://www.british-fiction.cf.ac.uk/.
British Library, http://www.bl.uk/.
British Museum, http://www.britishmuseum.org/default.aspx.
British Women Romantic Poets, 1789–1832, http://digital.lib.ucdavis.edu/projects/bwrp/index.htm
Copac Academic and National Library Catalogue, http://copac.ac.uk/.
Edition Corvey, CW^3, http://www2.shu.ac.uk/corvey/CW3/.
Eighteenth Century Collections Online (*ECCO*), http://www.gale.cengage.com/DigitalCollections/products/ecco/index.htm.
English Short Title Catalogue, http://estc.bl.uk/.
FullBooks.com, http://www.fullbooks.com.
Google Books, http://books.google.com/.
International Conference on Romanticism (ICR), http://icr.byu.edu/.
JSTOR: The Scholarly Journal Archive, http://www.jstor.org/.
Library of Congress, http://catalog.loc.gov/.
LIBWEB, http://lists.webjunction.org/libweb/.
MLA International Bibliography, http://www.mla.org/bibliography.
National Library of Ireland, http://www.nli.ie/en/homepage.aspx.
New York Public Library, http://www.nypl.org/.
North American Society for the Study of Romanticism (NASSR), http://publish.uwo.ca/~ nassr/.
Novels-On-Line, Chawton House, http://www.chawton.org/library/novels.html.
On Line Books Collection, recently retitled "The Internet Public Library", http://www.ipl.org/div/books/.
Project Gutenberg, http://www.gutenberg.org/wiki/Main_Page/.
Romantic Chronology, http://english.ucsb.edu:591/rchrono/.
Romantic Circles, http://www.rc.umd.edu/.

Romantic Textualities, http://www.cf.ac.uk/encap/romtext/.
Romanticism and Victorianism on the Net, http://www.ron.umontreal.ca/.
"Studies in Romanticism at the University of Nebraska", http://www.unl.edu/Corvey/html/index.htm.
Virtual Library Museums Page, http://vlmp.museophile.com/.
The Voice of the Shuttle, http://vos.ucsb.edu/.

10
Close Reading Romanticism

Sarah Wootton

"At its most basic, English is about reading the lines of the text ... it's the lines themselves we are following, and everything which happens in this discipline has to begin happening there" (Barry 2003: 9).[1] While I do not yearn for what Elaine Showalter ironically refers to as the "sacred rite of the New Criticism" – nor, indeed, advocate what has often been viewed as a formalist denial of context – this essay will argue that teaching literature starts and ends with the close reading of the text (2003: 62).[2] In October 2003, an entire issue of the *Romantic Circles Praxis Series* was devoted to ways of teaching John Keats's "Ode on a Grecian Urn," an "exemplary text," according to Jack Stillinger (2003), that holds a central place in the history of close reading.[3] What emerges as a constant in this group of essays is how Keats's poetry helps students to consider literature from a variety of different perspectives. Moreover, while encompassing a wide range of theoretical approaches, the focus of this collection is firmly on the text itself, reinforcing the recent observation by Ben Knights and Jonathan Gibson that "'close reading' is coming back to centre stage" (2008: 23). Knights and Gibson also argue that theory and history need not be incompatible with close reading. As I hope to demonstrate in this essay, teaching Romanticism involves both an attention to the particularities of the text and a consideration of historical contexts.

I will now illustrate and explore some of these issues through an analysis of Keats's poem "La Belle Dame sans Merci." My primary aim when teaching this poem is to foster an awareness of what Michael Benton refers to as "literary 'double-takes,' where readers engage both in the swift interpreting of the words and in the reflective interpreting of their responses to the words" (1992: 65). One way in which I encourage students to engage critically with alternative viewpoints, and also to reflect on the *strangeness* of this tale, is to display a range of images relating to the poem. As well as showing students well-known images of the poem, by artists such as Waterhouse and Dicksee, I introduce more obscure visual renderings by Russell Flint, Meynell Rheam, Cadogan Cowper, and illustrations by Jessie Marion King and Robert Anning Bell. Combining familiar and less familiar images encourages students to consider various and often conflicting, visual interpretations of the poem, while also serving as a means of introducing and challenging influential readings of gender politics in the poem.[4] A by-product of viewing these images is that, despite the varying treatments of the source, the Belle Dame is depicted as a woman; the literalizing effect of the visual, in this instance, challenges the supernatural *othering* of the female figure, and thereby draws attention to the source of the vision, or "latest dream," in Keats's poem.[5]

Students invariably identify that, after being prompted by an external speaker for the opening three stanzas, this is the knight's narrative. What is often less clear is how many other speakers are present in the poem. Does the Belle Dame speak, for example, in the following lines?

> And sure in language strange she said –
> "I love thee true."
>
> (ll. 27–8)

The quotation marks imply that these are the Belle Dame's words, or that she is indirectly voiced by the knight. However, her language is described as "strange," indicating that what "she said" is in some way unfamiliar, and the inclusion of the qualifier "sure" serves to emphasize the knight's uncertainty. What precedes the Belle Dame's *line* not only undermines the knight's role as interpreter of the Belle Dame's words, actions and even her identity, but also makes us more attentive to the often overlooked speakers in stanza ten. Even if we accept that these speakers are, once again, indirectly voiced by the knight, it is the "pale kings and princes" who call this woman "La Belle Dame sans Merci" (ll. 37, 39).[6] The irony is not lost on students that the "language strange," which requires translating, is not in fact the Belle Dame's; foreignness is ascribed to her, and these words then frame the narrative.

Keats's poem is, essentially, a word-puzzle; a close examination of the text, in conjunction with visual aids, reveals a series of clues and riddles. The reader can search, futilely, for an answer, a conclusive version of events, which only serves to bring the knight back to the same point at which the poem began: his continued "loitering" in the final stanza indicates that he has made no progress whatsoever (ll. 2, 46). Alternatively, we can acknowledge the ambivalence of story-telling and, even, of language itself. In other words, the poem can be read as a commentary on the process of interpretation; despite the plentiful harvest, the protagonist is paralysed in a semantic wilderness that is unseasonably "withered" and "cold" (ll. 3, 47, 36, 44). Keats's knight represents every reader's worst nightmare: if we are not attentive to the subtle suggestiveness of verbal texture, or attempt to contain the complexity of the text, a premature closure – the death of creative thought – will prevail. "La Belle Dame sans Merci" therefore offers an excellent opportunity for students to consider the interpretative possibilities associated with Keats's Negative Capability as well as raising awareness about strategies of reading more generally.

Above all, I encourage students to look for what Barry refers to as "micro-patterns" (2003: 13). When teaching Samuel Taylor Coleridge's "The Rime of the Ancient Mariner," for instance, I divide students into small groups to discuss the differences between the 1798 and 1817 versions of the text; as a larger group, we then consider whether the later editorial additions, such as the marginal glosses, direct, or in any way enhance, a reading of the poem. We also concentrate on the blessing of the water snakes, which are previously described as "slimy things", as a potentially pivotal moment in the poem that may signal the beginning of the end of the mariner's spiritual drought.[7] The physical release from his penance, when the dead albatross falls into the sea, would seem to reinforce the moral at the end of the poem: "He prayeth well, who loveth well / Both man and bird and beast" (ll. 612–13). Focusing on the religious subtext of the poem can also lead students to reflect on the interiority of the mariner's experiences; relating back to the changing description of the water snakes, is the poem, I ask, more about perception than *actual* events?

Although this reading is compelling, primarily as an antidote to the perplexing ambiguity of the poem, I direct students to aspects of the poem that are resistant to such an interpretation. For example, as the mariner approaches the shore, he seeks salvation in the figure of the hermit: yet the hermit's faith falters when confronted with the mariner, just as the semblance of his piety is undermined by the "rotted old oak-stump" upon which he prays (l. 522). Furthermore, the mariner's victims initially appear to be chosen at random – "he stoppeth one of three" – but this is revised towards the end of the tale: "That moment that his face I see, / I know the man that must hear me: / To him my tale I teach" (ll. 2, 588–90). I invite students to consider the basis upon which the mariner makes his selection and the relevance of the wedding that frames the tale. We then move on to discuss the position of the implied reader who, by inference, has also become a "sadder and a wiser man" (l. 624). These are just a few of the intriguing issues that arise from a closer scrutiny of Coleridge's poem in the classroom.

Another Romantic author whose work benefits from this approach is Jane Austen. If, as Barry suggests, readers initially search for an "overall structural pattern" or "macro-pattern" upon which to base an interpretation, then *Sense and Sensibility* is an ideal novel to teach (2003: 11). The opposing characteristics of two sisters, Elinor and Marianne, facilitate a wider debate about the contemporary cult of sensibility. However, as above, I encourage students to look for the "micro-patterns" that may problematize any governing schema. Towards the end of the novel, for example, Austen gives us a rare glimpse into the thoughts of Mrs Dashwood:

> She now found that she had erred in relying on Elinor's representation of herself.... She found that she had been misled by the careful, the considerate attention of her daughter...[8]

The passage ostensibly relates to the recognition of Elinor's selfless conduct. Yet even while Mrs Dashwood is contemplating Elinor's virtues, she is painfully conscious, as the words "erred" and "misled" suggest, of the estrangement between her eldest daughter and herself. I invite students to consider whether this quotation affects their opinion of Elinor's relationship with her mother; and, more specifically, whether our perception of Mrs Dashwood's preferential treatment of Marianne has altered.

Once subjected to scrutiny, students are often eager to offer further instances where Elinor can be seen in an ambiguous light. The quotation below, for instance, follows an exchange in which Lucy Steele is nauseatingly effusive about Lady Middleton:

> Marianne was silent; it was impossible for her to say what she did not feel, however trivial the occasion; and upon Elinor therefore the whole task of telling lies when politeness required it, always fell. (104)

We are, once again, asked to consider the different dispositions of the sisters: Marianne highlights Lucy's obsequiousness by refusing to reply, while Elinor diplomatically, and somewhat heroically, manages a civil response. Elinor only resorts to falsehood when "required," yet there is a suggestion that the *model* sister is capable of what Marianne is not – deceit. The complicated syntax results, here as above, in the negative means overshadowing the positive outcome. The final clause implies that even Austen's most beloved heroines may be lessened or tainted by their supposedly well-meaning interventions.

Both of the examples above are aimed at highlighting the significance, and possible consequences, of maintaining social appearances, a theme that runs throughout Austen's fiction. Mrs Dashwood's telling comment about Elinor's "representation of herself" directs attention onto the prominence of roles in the novel. When approached from this perspective, it becomes increasingly apparent to students that Marianne reads, or more appropriately misreads, Willoughby as "the hero of a favourite story" (38), a character he seems, at first, ideally suited to play. Later, after his liaison with Colonel Brandon's ward is revealed, Willoughby finds his former mode of address inadequate; he is reduced to the "hackneyed metaphor[s]" that Marianne denounces earlier in the novel (276).[9] The purpose of the lengthy conversation Willoughby has with Elinor is not merely to expose him as a fraud, however. When he asks, "do you think me most a knave or a fool?" and refers to himself as a "hard-hearted rascal" and a "fine hardened villain" (270, 275, 276), Willoughby is reflecting, somewhat ironically, on the limitations of the roles that he has, until now, acted out.

Elinor's *interview* with Willoughby in chapter forty-four can be advantageously analysed in the classroom, especially when tracing the former's changing and ambivalent responses to the latter. Earlier in the novel, Elinor is drawn to what she perceives to be his candour; yet, paradoxically, her empathy with Willoughby increases after the details of his questionable conduct are known. Elinor meets Willoughby's unexpected appearance at Cleveland with a "look of horror," and matches his violent expressions with accusations of "wanton cruelty" and "irreparable injury" (269, 273). After scrutinizing the relevant sections of the text, students can reflect on the extent to which Elinor is "influenced" – to use Austen's term – by the very same language that personifies Marianne prior to her breakdown.[10] Elinor refers to the increasing "heroism" of Marianne after her illness, and is "everything by turns but tranquil" when realizing that Edward Ferrars remains unattached; restraint is, on this occasion, pointedly left to the propriety of the narrator (223, 308). While Elinor's gradual, and Marianne's more dramatic, changes in temperament suggest a rather tidy reading of the conclusion as extolling the virtues of a tempered romanticism, students are always keen to express their anxieties over the "confederacy" against Marianne, and point to the telling phrase in the line: "her [Marianne's] whole heart became, *in time*, as much devoted to her husband, as it had once been to Willoughby" (321, 322, *emphasis added*). Even more problematic is that in a novel primarily concerned with negotiating appearances, Elinor, the central protagonist, gives an *almost* faultless performance and, ultimately, profits from concealment.

Close analysis of this kind not only generates alternative, challenging readings of Romantic texts. When teaching Byron's *Manfred*, for instance, the cultural phenomenon of the Byronic hero emerges as a prominent topic. Brainstorming sessions in small groups are aimed at identifying which of Manfred's character traits might be considered typically Byronic – his singularity, "I disdained to mingle with / A herd" and self-proclaimed "bright intelligence," for example – alongside aspects of the poem that may detract from or complicate this perception: "Oh! I but prolonged my words, / Boasting these idle attributes."[11] A close analysis of the text reveals that the Byronic ego is often accompanied, and even undermined, by an unflinching self-scrutiny and agonizing awareness of mortality. After considering the extent to which Manfred is indebted to, and has subsequently influenced, other anti-heroes, students are encouraged to nominate possible Byronic heroes from literature and popular culture. This not only emphasizes the pervasiveness and durability of the Byronic hero, but also highlights the diverse ways in which a Romantic figure has evolved. Manfred provides the blue-print for the Byronic hero, yet he also remains an enigma; like the hero of Byron's *Lara*, he is "Distinct but strange" (Canto I, 231).

A vital consideration, when teaching *Manfred*, is form. One of Susan Wolfson's primary objectives in *Formal Charges* is to "make a case for the pleasures, intellectual and aesthetic, of attending to the complex charges of form in poetic writing" (1997: 1). With this in mind, I ask students to consider the following questions: what makes *Manfred* a dramatic poem; what, if anything, is dramatic about it; what differentiates this work from, say, the multiple monologues in *The Giaour*? In practical terms, could this dramatic poem – with acts, scenes, and settings – be staged; if not, why not? In an effort to address some of these issues, students prepare and act out the final two scenes of *Manfred*. In addition to the questions above, I ask students to consider whether the exchange between Manfred's dependants in Act Three, scene three performs a similar function to the subplots in Shakespeare's plays, while also comparing Manfred's celebrated speech on the "noble wreck in ruinous perfection" (III. iv. 28) with Hamlet's soliloquies (a notable antecedent of the Byronic hero). As well as tackling issues of form and performance, this exercise reinforces the fact that while Manfred's soliloquies give the audience access to his consciousness, he is not the only speaker. For example, performing Herman and Manuel's dialogue at the beginning of Act Three, scene three presents an alternative view of the protagonist's tortured introspection and intellectual superiority; compared unfavourably with his father, Manfred is shown to have abnegated his social responsibilities. Similarly, what Manfred presents as a freedom from constraint or creed, the Abbot describes as an "awful chaos," a nihilistic void (III. i. 164). The dramatic aspect of this poem means there is no one viewpoint; Manfred, in effect, competes with a host of alternative voices.

Thus far, I have discussed close reading in the context of classroom discussion and analysis. Is close reading in this way desirable when lecturing? For the last few years, I have given the first lecture, "Themes, Images, and Definitions," on a module entitled "Literature of the Romantic Period." As an introduction to this vast topic, I aim to provide some historical, social and cultural context, discuss the possibilities and problems that arise from attempting to define Romanticism, and consider the ways in which concepts of Romanticism have evolved. Attention to the details of the texts in this instance helps to avoid generalizations; this is particularly important when, for example, considering the work of Wordsworth, a self-confessed "worshipper of Nature."[12] In "Tintern Abbey," the process of reviving and reinterpreting formative experiences in nature is described as a "joy," a "sense sublime," but also as a "presence that disturbs" (ll. 95–6). Focusing on lines such as these illustrates how Wordsworth's reverence for nature, as the source of poetic inspiration, is often accompanied by feelings of fear, guilt and isolation.

Conversely, it is equally important to demonstrate those moments of "Abundant recompense" when the younger Wordsworth's trepidation is surpassed by a mature reflection on the scene (l. 89). The following lines from the opening stanza of "Tintern Abbey" provide an excellent opportunity for close reading as a group in the lecture:

> Once again I see
> These hedge-rows – hardly hedge-rows, little lines
> Of sportive wood run wild – these pastoral farms
> Green to the very door, and wreathes of smoke
> Sent up in silence from among the trees
> With some uncertain notice, as might seem,

Of vagrant dwellers in the houseless woods,
Or of some hermit's cave, where by his fire
The hermit sits alone.

(ll. 15–23)

Wordsworth here depicts what students readily identify as an archetypal rural idyll; and, once prompted, they begin to detect the artifice behind its construction – in the words "uncertain" and "seem," for example, and attempts to de-cultivate the enclosed land in the first subclause. The smoke is, of course, coming from the iron-furnaces on the banks of the river, but rather than encouraging students to think of the poet as merely in a state of denial – or manipulating the landscape to serve his own poetic ends – it can be more profitable to call attention to the Romantic themes of memory and loss. The passage above is illustrative of an elegiac tone and trope that pervades much of Wordsworth's work; the present self is mourning for what he imagines the past self to have experienced.

At this point in the lecture, I introduce the poetry of Charlotte Smith, with a particular emphasis on her seminal work *Beachy Head,* to generate a dialogue with a more widely-recognized poet.[13] Smith, also an "early worshipper at Nature's shrine," shares Wordsworth's love of "upland solitudes," which separates, and even exiles, them from the rest of mankind.[14] As in "Tintern Abbey," Smith depicts idyllic pastoral scenes: "his independent hut / Cover'd with heather, whence the slow white smoke / Of smouldering peat arises" (ll. 195–7). I also demonstrate how Smith's distinctive notes on herbs, weeds and wildflowers contribute to the prevailing effect of rustic simplicity.[15] Through analysing the Wordsworth passage above similar tensions in Smith's poetry emerge between the desire to preserve an uncultivated landscape and the lure of the picturesque: in *Beachy Head,* the "rudest scenes" are "*Almost* uncultured" (*emphasis added*), while the visual impression of a "rustic form" is created by "bowery shades" and a "sylvan seat" (ll. 347, 334, 585, 587, 597).[16] Happening upon "Ideal bowers of pleasure" is not unique to this Romantic poem, but Smith's treatment of *natural* artifice provides an illuminating parallel with Wordsworth (l. 559).

Smith's poetry, along with the work of other women poets of the period, has been read as part of "an alternative Romanticism that seeks not to transcend or to absorb nature but to contemplate and honor its irreducible alterity" (Curran 1993: xxviii). As well as outlining this gendered approach to Romantic poetry, I also present the possibility that an "alternative," yet comparable, tradition of self-investment may be found in Smith's feminized landscape:

> And I'll contrive a sylvan room
>   Against the time of summer heat,
> Where leaves, inwoven in Nature's loom,
>   Shall canopy our green retreat.
>
> (ll. 613–16)

These lines effectively create or, to use Smith's own loaded word, "contrive" the impression of nature as a dressed domestic interior. Close reading this passage raises a dual possibility: the above can be read as Smith's attempt to reclaim nature for the female poet; equally, it can be read as a different means of inhabiting and monopolizing the source of inspiration. Either way, examining Smith's poetry alongside Wordsworth's generates a productive friction between authors and texts, while also providing an opportunity for students to reflect on critical perceptions of Romanticism and wider debates about canonicity.

Close reading enables students and critics alike to examine the intricate nuances of Romantic texts, and explore the resonant interplay between texts and contexts. As Frank Lentricchia and Andrew DuBois comment, "The common ground, then, is a commitment to close attention to literary texture and what is embodied there" (2003: ix). This practice does not limit possible avenues of interpretation; on the contrary, it encourages students to recognize and analyse the "ambivalent magnetism" of Romantic texts (Benton 1992: 63). The works discussed above – and many more besides – invite and sustain the manifold readings that facilitate and foster the dynamic teaching of this period. Yet, as Wolfson (2003) confesses, after branching out into gender criticism, new historicism, textual scholarship and theory, "At the same time, I have to say, the core is still close-reading." In short, and without the need for hesitation or apology, close reading is both the cornerstone and the afterword of literary studies.

Notes

1. I would like to thank Professor Michael O'Neill for his generous encouragement and assistance with this essay.
2. The formalist criticism of the last decade or so has engaged with the possibilities and limitations of this approach as well as incorporating historical and

cultural context to a greater or lesser extent. In *Formal Charges: the Shaping of Poetry in British Romanticism*, Susan Wolfson outlines a method that involves the "intensive reading of poetic events within a context of questions about poetic form and formalist criticism" (1997: 1). See, amongst others, Cronin, Stabler and O'Neill.

3. With its rigorous concentration on irony, paradox, symbolism and ambiguity, Keats's poetry, especially the shorter narrative poems and Odes, was ideally suited to the New Criticism; these same poems were then subsequently at the forefront of the new historicist backlash against this movement. For example, "To Autumn," traditionally celebrated for its sensuousness and disinterested sensibility, has been re-read as resonant with allusions to the contemporary social and political climate. See, for instance, Roe (1995 and 1997).
4. See, for instance, Swann 1988.
5. Keats 1988: l. 35. All quotations from this edition.
6. Anne Mellor argues for the significance of these speakers in *English Romantic Irony* (1980: 93–4).
7. Coleridge 2000: L. 125. All quotations from this edition.
8. Austen 1995: 301. All quotations from this edition.
9. In chapter eighteen, Marianne declares "I detest jargon of every kind, and sometimes I have kept my feelings to myself, because I could find no language to describe them in but what was worn and hackneyed out of all sense and meaning" (Austen 1995: 85).
10. After Willougby's departure, we are told that "She [Elinor] felt that his influence over her mind was heightened by circumstances which ought not in reason to have weight.... But she felt that it was so, long, long before she could feel his influence less" (Austen 1995: 283).
11. Byron 1970: III. i. 121–2; II. ii. 96, 97–8. All quotations from this edition.
12. Wordsworth, "Lines Written a Few Miles above Tintern Abbey, on Revisiting the Banks of the Wye during a Tour, July 13, 1798" (Wordsworth 1985: l. 153). All quotations from this edition.
13. Kay K. Cook discusses similar ways of incorporating *recovered* women writers into existing courses (Cook 1997). See also Zimmerman 1997 in the same collection of essays.
14. Smith 1993: ll. 346, 228. All quotations from this edition. Social and emotional outcasts feature strongly in the work of Smith and Wordsworth; for example, the figure of the hermit appears in both "Tintern Abbey" and *Beachy Head*. Smith's ambivalent treatment of the hermit at the end of her poem, when his engagement with other human beings ultimately leads to his death, generates another parallel with the equally curious treatment of the hermit in Coleridge's "The Rime of the Ancient Mariner."
15. Smith's notes demand a dynamic practice of close reading in themselves. As Cook comments, "The reader must therefore work back and forth between two texts: the result is a reader-constructed version of the text that extends beyond the generic boundaries of poetry, prose, autobiography, and scientific writing" (1997: 99).
16. A similar tension between "The grace of young Simplicity" (Smith 1993: l. 96) and an effusive description of birds, which reaches a poetic climax with the peacock, is evident in "The Jay in Masquerade," a poem that appeared in *Beachy Head, Fables, and Other Poems* (1807).

Works cited

Austen, Jane (1995) *Sense and Sensibility*, ed. Ros Ballaster (London: Penguin).

Barry, Peter (2003) *English in Practice: In Pursuit of English Studies* (London: Arnold).

Behrendt, Stephen C. and Harriet Kramer Linkin, eds. (1997) *Approaches to Teaching British Women Poets of the Romantic Period* (New York: The Modern Language Association of America).

Benton, Michael (1992) *Secondary Worlds: Literature Teaching and the Visual Arts* (Buckingham: Open University Press).

Byron, Lord (1970) *Byron: Complete Poetical Works*, ed. Frederick Page, rev. edn. John Jump (Oxford: Oxford University Press).

Coleridge, Samuel Taylor (2000) *The Complete Poetical Works of Samuel Taylor Coleridge*, ed. Ernest Hartley Coleridge, Vol. 1 (Oxford: Clarendon Press).

Cook, Kay K. (1997) "The Aesthetics of Loss: Charlotte Smith's *The Emigrants* and *Beachy Head*," in *Approaches to Teaching British Women Poets of the Romantic Period*, ed. Stephen C. Behrendt and Harriet Kramer Linkin (New York: The Modern Language Association of America): 97–100.

Cronin, Richard (2000) *The Politics of Romantic Poetry: In Search of the Pure Commonwealth* (Basingstoke: Macmillan – now Palgrave Macmillan).

Keats, John (1988) *John Keats: the Complete Poems*, ed. John Barnard, 3rd edn. (London: Penguin).

Knights, Ben and Jonathan Gibson (2008) "Up Close: a Round Table On Close Reading," *English Subject Centre Newsletter*, 14: 21–3.

Lentricchia, Frank and Andrew DuBois, eds. (2003) *Close Reading: the Reader* (London: Duke University Press).

Mellor, Anne (1980) *English Romantic Irony* (London: Harvard University Press).

O'Neill, Michael (1997) *Romanticism and the Self-Conscious Poem* (Oxford: Clarendon Press).

O'Rourke, James, ed. (2003) *"Ode on a Grecian Urn": Hypercanonicity & Pedagogy, Romantic Circles Praxis Series*, http://www.rc.umd.edu/praxis/grecianurn/.

Roe, Nicholas (1997) *John Keats and the Culture of Dissent* (Oxford: Clarendon Press).

——, ed. (1995) *Keats and History* (Cambridge: Cambridge University Press).

Showalter, Elaine (2003) *Teaching Literature* (Oxford: Blackwell).

Smith, Charlotte (1993) *The Poems of Charlotte Smith*, ed. Stuart Curran (New York and Oxford: Oxford University Press).

Stabler, Jane (2002) *Byron, Poetics, and History* (Cambridge: Cambridge University Press).

Stillinger, Jack (2003) "Fifty-nine Ways of Reading 'Ode on a Grecian Urn,'" in *"Ode on a Grecian Urn": Hypercanonicity & Pedagogy, Romantic Circles Praxis Series*, http://www.rc.umd.edu/praxis/grecianurn/.

Swann, Karen (1988) "Harassing the Muse," in *Romanticism and Feminism*, ed. Anne K. Mellor (Indiana University Press): 81–92.

Wolfson, Susan (1997) *Formal Charges: the Shaping of Poetry in British Romanticism* (Stanford: Stanford University Press).

—— (2003) "The Know of Not to Know It: My Returns to Reading and Teaching Keats's 'Ode on a Grecian Urn"', in *"Ode on a*

Grecian Urn": Hypercanonicity & Pedagogy, Romantic Circles Praxis Series, http://www.rc.umd.edu/ praxis/grecianurn/.

Wordsworth, William (1985) *William Wordsworth: The Pedlar, Tintern Abbey and The Two-Part Prelude*, ed. Jonathan Wordsworth (Cambridge: Cambridge University Press).

Zimmerman, Sarah M. (1997) "Charlotte Smith's Lessons," in *Approaches to Teaching British Women Poets of the Romantic Period*, ed. Stephen C. Behrendt and Harriet Kramer Linkin (New York: The Modern Language Association of America): 121–8.

11
Theorizing Romanticism

Sue Chaplin

Overview: contexts of Romanticism and the challenge of "theory"

To speak of the "challenge of theory" in the context of Romanticism and, more specifically, in the context of teaching Romanticism is to raise a problem and call forth a justification: why would one endeavour to teach undergraduate Romanticism "theoretically"? Students at this level invariably find literary theory demanding. They also find Romanticism – of all of the "period" courses that they encounter on our degree – challenging, not least because the concept is so difficult to pin down. To combine elements of literary theory with an introduction to Romanticism in a compulsory first-year module delivered to over one hundred students in twelve weeks would seem to be asking for trouble logistically and pedagogically. Moreover, it raises difficulties that pertain to the very project of theorizing Romanticism. There remains some hostility within the arts and humanities towards "theory" and this is perhaps nowhere more apparent than in Romantic studies; as David Simpson puts it, "theory is one of those terms that has caused arguments in seminars and tantrums at dinner parties" and he goes on to highlight the relationship of "various constructions of Romanticism" to the persistence of this aversion within the Anglo-American academy (Simpson 1993: 1, 2). If we take Culler's broad account of "theory" as that which "critiques common sense" or "concepts taken as natural" (4) then it becomes clear that a certain construction of Romanticism has indeed worked against "theory" in defining and validating Romanticism in terms of passion against reason, nature over culture, experience over abstraction and so on. As Simpson puts it, "Romanticism has served literary criticism as an ally in its disciplinary habit of downplaying or denying the usefulness of theory" (2). This "disciplinary habit" can be approached in terms of McGann's conceptualization of the "Romantic Ideology": it functions to produce and validate "concepts taken as natural" which are then posited, like Romanticism itself, as somehow intrinsically resistant to "theory." To teach Romanticism(s) from a variety of theoretical perspectives that are themselves contested and that do not privilege "theory" itself as a paradigm encourages students at least to *begin* to think beyond the "disciplinary" habits of (not just Romantic) criticism.

In a first-year undergraduate module, however (and particularly one taught simultaneously to two cohorts: BA English and History and English), it is not possible to assume much, if any, advanced understanding of literary criticism and theory. Indeed, one of the main aims of this first-year module is to prepare students for further undergraduate study by introducing key critical and theoretical terms and concepts in a manner that does not divorce theory from critical practice. This final point is vital: for first years, the module *is* challenging and must be delivered in such a way as to ground students thoroughly in the key texts and contexts of the period before any theoretical analysis is offered. The module therefore is not "theory-led"; I do not deliver lectures on "Romanticism and Psychoanalysis" or "Romanticism and Poststructuralism" as one might in a third-year undergraduate or postgraduate module. Rather, the module is arranged around texts, themes and concepts that allow various theoretical readings of Romanticism to emerge gradually and accessibly. Accordingly, what I will present in this essay is a selection of points within the module at which Romanticism *can* be opened up to a degree of theoretical analysis without leaving students dazed and confused. This will entail a summary of four lectures (with references where appropriate to the accompanying seminars) and a discussion of the final three weeks of the module in which students are encouraged theoretically and critically to confront the question: "What is Romanticism?" The Appendix to the essay presents the entire lecture schedule so as to enable readers to assess the way in which the sessions discussed here fit in with the module curriculum as a whole.

Introductory session: defining "Romanticism"?

I begin the lecture series with a blatant attempt to problematize Romanticism as a critical concept and a literary period. In so doing, I gesture towards the final three weeks of the module in which we explore various twentieth and twenty-first century constructions and deconstructions of Romanticism and consider the extent to which they reproduce or contest what McGann and others have termed "the Romantic Ideology" (1981). For now, though, it is sufficient that students understand that Romanticism is at the very least a slippery notion, that it did not exist as a coherent concept in the era that we term "Romantic" and that the very idea of a clearly defined "Romantic period" is controversial amongst historians and critics. I offer the students three alternative historical constructions of the Romantic period and try to convey how each is implicated in and reflects certain post-Romantic political and cultural preferences: 1770–1850 (the lifespan of Wordsworth); 1785–1830 (the time-frame chosen by the Norton anthology of the period which is the module's set text); 1776–1832 (a period framed by the American revolution and the passage of the Reform Act in Britain). I introduce the class to some of the key works of the "Big Six" and explain that British Romanticism has tended to be defined canonically in terms of the work of these writers. This canonization of the "Big Six," I point out, has had important implications for the literary study of Romanticism: it excludes all of the women and most of the men who were writing in the period and it ignores or neglects those genres (most notably fiction and drama) that are not associated with these half-dozen writers. Without blinding the students with theoretical terminology at such an early stage, I do try to take this opportunity to refer them to recent attempts within, for example, Marxist, Postcolonial and Feminist theory to address these issues of exclusion, effacement and neglect.

Having possibly undermined the foundations of the entire module in the first half of the first lecture, I then try to formulate a definition (albeit, as the students will now appreciate, a necessarily provisional definition) of Romanticism. There are a number of undergraduate guides to Romanticism that are pertinent here: Roe (2005); Ruston (2007) and Day (1996). Ruston's guide is particularly useful in an interdisciplinary context and I recommend students to read the first chapter in advance of the session. I begin the lecture with Margaret Drabble's broad appraisal of the key cultural, political and aesthetic components of the European Romantic movement:

> a literary movement and profound shift in sensibility, which took place in Britain and throughout Europe roughly between 1770 and 1848. Intellectually it marked a violent reaction to the Enlightenment. Politically it was inspired by the revolutions in America and France. Emotionally it expressed an extreme assertion of the self and the value of individual experience together with a sense of the

> infinite and the transcendental. Socially it championed progressive causes. The stylistic keynote of Romanticism is intensity, and its watchword is "Imagination." (quoted in Day 1996: 1)

I discuss each element of Drabble's definition in turn, distributing extracts from primary texts to exemplify her points: Blake's *America: a Prophecy*; Shelley's "England in 1819"; Wordsworth's "Tintern Abbey"; Yearsley's "A Poem on the Inhumanity of the Slave Trade"; Keats' "Ode to a Nightingale." It must be borne in mind, though, that not all students will have a decent understanding of the contexts of Romanticism that Drabble's definition evokes – of the American and French revolutions, of the "Enlightenment" and "sensibility," or of the wider processes of urbanization and industrialization that shaped Romantic understandings of liberty, the individual and the imagination. This lecture aims to fill in those gaps in order that students can move on to an appreciation not only of the key tenets of Romanticism and its major texts, but also of "Romanticism" itself as a historically and conceptually contested category. To this end, a critical source that I find very useful in the introductory sessions (the lecture and the accompanying seminar) is Jerome McGann's "Rethinking Romanticism" (1992). The inclusion of this article in the introductory class is a little premature in some ways since it anticipates our more theoretically-advanced discussions in the final three weeks of the module. However, it does provide (combined with the more recent introductory guides cited above) an accessible overview of the literary and historical construction of "Romanticism" as a critical category. Given the module's theoretical approach to Romanticism, this is a key learning outcome even at this early stage since it discourages students from taking "Romanticism" as in some sense a *given*, as a concept the meaning of which is beyond question. The following quotation from Culler is useful here in emphasizing the importance of contesting what appear to be fixed categories of thought. It might also help overcome the students' own hostility towards theory, for there is no doubt such hostility exists!

> [Theory is] an attempt to show that what we take for granted as "common sense" is in fact a historical construction, a particular theory that has come to seem so natural to us that we don't even see it as a theory. As a critique of common sense and exploration of alternative conceptions, theory involves a questioning of the most basic premises or assumptions of literary study, the unsettling of anything that might have been taken for granted: What is meaning? What is

an author? What is it to read? What is the "I" or subject who writes, reads, or acts? How do texts relate to the circumstances in which they are produced? (4)

Lecture three: Romanticism, colonialism, slavery

Having explored the political contexts of early Romanticism in the second lecture, this session focuses upon the abolitionist struggles of the late-eighteenth and early-nineteenth centuries and considers from a variety of historical and theoretical perspectives the implication of Romanticism in the colonial and imperial projects of the period. First semester modules in modern European history (on the joint honours programme) and eighteenth-century literature (for single honours students) will have equipped the class with at least a basic understanding of the material practices of slavery and the ideologies of race and empire that shaped and supported them. The aim here is to introduce students to the diversity of racial, colonial and abolitionist discourses of the period and to more complex critical interpretations of Romanticism, colonialism and slavery. Students for the first ten minutes of the lecture are asked to consider, individually or in pairs, a variety of pro and anti-slavery texts that will include extracts from Edward Long's *History of Jamaica,* Blake's "The Little Black Boy," Wordsworth's "To Toussant L'Ouverture" and extracts from Hannah More's "Slavery: a Poem." Students are requested briefly to record their impressions of how at least one of these works conceptualizes and represents racial identity – African and European – in the context of slavery. These records will form the basis of our initial discussions in the subsequent seminar.

The following section of the lecture introduces students to theoretical approaches to race, colonialism and imperialism mainly through some of the work of Edward Said and Homi Bhabha: a key learning outcome here is that students emerge with a basic grounding in aspects of postcolonial theory and its relevance to an understanding of Romantic writings and their contexts. In practical pedagogic terms, my aim is at the very least to unravel the rather naïve understandings of race and culture that first-year students invariably bring with them into the seminar room. In relation to slavery, I have noticed in this and other modules that students tend to think in starkly oppositional terms, setting racist slave traders against enlightened, libertarian abolitionists and interpreting the abolitionist debate and Romantic writings on slavery according to this binary. In particular, they have only a tenuous grasp in my experience of the implication of national literatures *in* the projects of slavery and empire, whether or not a particular text appears to support an "abolitionist" position. Said's distinction between "imperialism" and "colonialism" is significant here, as is his insistence that neither can be understood purely in terms of material, political and economic practices of invasion, domination and acquisition:

> Neither imperialism nor colonialism is a simple act of accumulation and acquisition. Both are supported and perhaps even impelled by impressive ideological formations that include notions that certain territories and people require and beseech domination, as well as forms of knowledge affiliated with domination: the vocabulary of classic nineteenth-century imperial culture is plentiful with such words and concepts as "inferior" or "subject races," "subordinate peoples," "dependency," "expansion," and "authority." (8)

Students are encouraged to consider the extent to which even an apparently avowedly anti-slavery text of this period might be read as an expression of "forms of knowledge affiliated with domination" and are asked briefly at this point in the lecture to return to the extracts distributed at the outset with this perspective in mind.

The final section of the lecture further pursues the relation between culture, empire and slavery through some of the works of Southey, Yearsley, Cowper and the black poet Phyllis Wheatley. We end the lecture with a consideration of the following short poem by Wheatley:

> On Being Brought from Africa to America
>
> 'Twas mercy brought me from my pagan land,
> Taught my benighted soul to understand
> That there's a God – and there's a saviour too;
> Once I redemption neither sought nor knew.
> Some view our sable race with scornful eye –
> "Their colour is a diabolical dye."
> Remember, Christians, Negroes black as Cain
> May be refined, and join the angelic train.
>
> (12)

As an advanced exercise for seminar three students are asked to consider this poem from the perspective of Homi Bhabha's "Of Mimicry and Man: the Ambivalence of Colonial Discourse" and are directed in particular to the following quotation:

> Colonial mimicry is the desire for a reformed, recognisable Other, as *a subject of difference that is almost the same, but not quite*. Which is to say that the discourse of mimicry is constructed around an ambivalence; in order to be effective, mimicry must continually produce its slippage, its excess, its difference. The authority of that mode of colonial discourse that I have called mimicry is therefore stricken by an indeterminacy: mimicry emerges as the representation of a difference that is itself a process of disavowal. Mimicry is, thus, the sign of a double articulation; a complex strategy of reform, regulation and discipline, which "appropriates" the Other as it visualises power. Mimicry is also the sign of the inappropriate, however, a difference of recalcitrance which coheres the dominant strategic function of colonial power, intensifies surveillance, and poses an immanent threat to both "normalised" knowledges and disciplinary powers. (Bhabha, in Rice and Waugh 2001: 381)

This is a difficult passage, of course, and it is sufficient that students acquire a basic understanding here of what Bhabha means by "colonial mimicry" and how Wheatley's poem might be understood to "mimic" colonial conceptualizations of the Other. At the very least, it is important that students simply *look up* the terms in this passage that they are unlikely to understand, a step that in my experience students are bafflingly reluctant to take! With this in mind, students are encouraged to submit a glossary of key terms and concepts in respect of the above passage. This is not compulsory, but it is an important preparatory exercise for assignment two (see below).

Lecture four: poetic revolutions: reality, representation, imagination

The following extracts are distributed to students at the beginning of the fourth lecture and they are followed here by a summary of my opening remarks.

> First Extract:
>
> The muses wove, in the loom of Athena, a loose and changeable robe like that in which Falsehood captivated her admirers; with this they invested Truth and named her Fiction. She now went out again to conquer with more success: for when she demanded entrance of the

passions, they often mistook her for Falsehood, and delivered up their charge; but when she had once taken possession, she was soon disrobed by Reason, and shone out, in her original form, with native effulgence, and resistless dignity. (Johnson: 456)

Second Extract:

Words are too awful an instrument for good and evil to be trifled with: they hold above all other external powers a dominion over thoughts. If words be not (recurring to a metaphor before used) an incarnation of the thought but only a clothing for it, then surely they will prove an ill gift; such as one as those poisoned vestments, read of in the stories of superstitious times, which had the power to consume and alienate from his right mind the victim who put them on. Language, if it do not uphold, and feed, and leave in quiet, like the power of gravitation or the air we breathe, is a counter spirit, unremittingly and noiselessly at work to derange, to subvert, to lay waste, to vitiate and to dissolve. (Wordsworth 1974: 84)

Notes:

In the first extract, Samuel Johnson describes fiction as providing a useful "robe" for Truth. Underlying his musings on truth and fiction is what we call a "Mimetic" theory of art; as Johnson puts it elsewhere: "It is the greatest excellency of art to imitate Nature." In Johnson's view, art is capable of representing "Nature," or "Truth," in a manner that is beneficial to the human understanding. Note, though, that Johnson clearly perceives Truth to exist independently of art and to be superior to art. Fiction is fickle and arbitrary – after all, we *make it up* – but Truth is not. Truth is not contaminated by the fiction that clothes it; strip away the fiction and Truth appears in its pure "original form." Note also that Johnson makes his point here by fictionalizing the relation between truth and fiction: he offers us an allegory. Implicitly, the reader is encouraged to put Johnson's theory into practice, to peel away the fiction in order to reveal the truth about art and its uses. And if Johnson's theory is correct, then the "truth" of this allegory will not be compromised by the fact that it appears in the form of a fiction: the medium and the message – the "robe" and the "original form" of truth beneath – are distinct here. Or are they? We will return to this point later.

Turn now to the second extract. Wordsworth here addresses a similar point, but from quite a different perspective. Spare a few minutes to consider how Wordsworth expresses the relation between word and thought here and how it differs from Johnson's appraisal of the relation between truth and fiction.

By means of these extracts and the commentary I have summarized above, I aim at the beginning of lecture four to introduce students to Romantic theories of representation and the imagination and to certain twentieth-century interpretations of those theories. Abrams's *The Mirror and the Lamp*, for example, is the key critical text in terms of the mid-twentieth-century conceptualization of a Romantic shift from mimetic to expressive theories of art. I find these two extracts useful in introducing students not only to this argument, but to those wider concerns regarding knowledge and authentic speech that Romanticism inherits from the Enlightenment (and that twentieth-century literary theory arguably inherits from Romanticism). In this regard, William Keach's "Romanticism and Language" (Curran 1993: 95–119) provides an excellent account of the aesthetic and epistemological problematics of early Romanticism; it is a challenging essay for undergraduates, but, accompanied by other more introductory materials, it provides a sound opportunity for students to stretch their theoretical understanding of this topic.

The lecture moves on to introduce students to the central claims regarding poetic language, thought and feeling in Wordsworth's "Preface" to the *Lyrical Ballads* and Coleridge's *Biographia Literaria*: a key learning outcome here is that students come to appreciate the Romantic problematization of the relation between word and object, between what Coleridge terms the "arbitrary signs" of speech and the entities they represent (625). In the lecture and seminar, we assess the different responses of Wordsworth and Coleridge to this dilemma (for example, Wordsworth's conceptualization of the Imagination, Coleridge's valorization of "eternal language" and his theory of the Symbol) and in so doing the students begin to encounter a range of new theoretical perspectives. I take the opportunity here gently to introduce them to postructuralist readings of Romantic texts that emphasize precisely the arbitrary relation between signs and objects – "signifier," "signified." Chapter two of Day's *Romanticism* provides one of the best undergraduate introductions to postructuralist readings of Romanticism that I have come across and I usually distribute this chapter to students in advance of the seminar. Along with this, judiciously chosen and carefully annotated extracts from Hartman and de Man work well to expand students' theoretical understanding and, when used in conjunction with primary texts (such as Book Six of *The Prelude,* "Alastor," and "Dejection: an Ode"), their close-reading skills.

Lecture five: the Romantic sublime

This is not an easy topic to introduce to first-year students and with this in mind I recommend Philip Shaw's excellent critical guide to the sublime as compulsory reading (2006). It provides particularly insightful and accessible accounts of the Burkean and Kantian sublime which are invaluable here. Most importantly, though, I think it is vital from the outset to engage the students' imagination in this session. I tend to begin with a range of images of iconic mountain landscapes (Mount Blanc in particular) which the students are asked to describe in one word. The usual responses are: "majestic"; "awe-inspiring" (or, more usually in the student argot, "awesome"); "inhospitable"; "brutal"; "exhilarating"; and, occasionally, "sublime." We then turn to John Dennis's attempt to conceptualize the sublime in terms of the individual's experience of precisely this sort of landscape, either directly or through poetic representation. This final point is vital: the sublime can emerge for Dennis as an *effect of poetic language*. This relates Dennis back to the philosophical tradition of ancient Greece (to Longinus, in particular) and forward to the Romantic poets for whom the connection between objects, experience and speech is a key concern. Students have already considered this point in lecture four and here we return to Book Six of the *Prelude* to consider in particular the "crisis" in thought and speech that befalls the poet crossing Simplon Pass and how that "crisis" might be related to the Romantic conceptualization of the Sublime. I must stress again that this is not a "theory-led" session and our main focus remains the text and its contemporary contexts. Nevertheless, we do touch upon a variety of theoretical interpretations of the *Prelude* that have identified in this crisis (which occurs elsewhere in this poem and in Wordsworth's other works) an anxiety concerning the poetic "self" and its relation to the world. We examine Thomas Weiskel's (1976) and Neil Hertz's (1985) psychoanalytic readings of the Wordsworthian sublime in terms of oedipal conflict and "blockage." We end with a consideration of the two critical works that students will be required to read for the accompanying seminar, Anne K. Mellor's *Romanticism and Gender* (1993) and John Pipkin's "The Material Sublime of the Women Poets" (1998). These pieces offer different feminist readings of the Romantic sublime and can also be used productively to introduce students to feminist contestations of the Romantic canon.

First assessment: week eight

No lectures or seminars take place during week 8. Students should be working on their first assignment (a 1500-word essay) and to this end they are invited to attend personal tutorials with me during the lecture and seminar slots. Below is a sample of essay questions from the module. It is stressed to students that they must demonstrate an understanding not only of primary materials, but of criticism and theory.

- To what extent was Romanticism a revolutionary movement?
- Discuss the importance of colonialism and imperialism to an understanding of Romanticism.
- Discuss the importance of one or more of the following to Romantic-era writing:

  Imagination
  Language
  Symbol
  The Sublime

- Discuss the relation between Romanticism and the environment with particular reference to "eco-criticism."
- Discuss the relationship between the Gothic and Romanticism.

Lectures 9, 10 and 11: rethinking Romanticism

The final three weeks of this module do have a high theoretical content. The lectures and seminars are designed to interrogate the concept of "Romanticism" from the perspective of mid-to-late twentieth century developments in literary theory and criticism. In lecture nine, we examine the conceptualization of Romanticism that emerges out of the work of, for example, M. H. Abrams and Réné Wellek, before addressing the various challenges to that paradigm that have emerged over the last four decades. As an introduction for undergraduates, I recommend David Simpson's "Romanticism, Criticism and Theory" (1993), Jerome McGann's "Rethinking Romanticism' (1992), and Mellor's 'Romanticism, Difference and the Aesthetic" (1999). Simpson's essay provides a lucid and accessible overview of theoretical developments in Romanticism studies in the late twentieth century whilst McGann and Mellor revisit their earlier works (*The Romantic Ideology* and *Romanticism and Gender*, both compulsory reading for students) and place them within fresh critical contexts. For more advanced reading, students might be referred to chapter nine of Paul Hamilton's *Metaromanticism: Aesthetics, Literature, Theory* (2003), "The Romanticism of Contemporary Ideology", or chapter one of Leon Chai's *Romantic Theory: Forms of Reflexivity in the Revolutionary Era* (2006), "The Triumph of Theory."

Second assessment: week twelve

Students are required to produce a 1500-word critical analysis of one piece of theory or criticism which also demonstrates a good understanding of at least two primary texts. Students must also supplement their analysis with a glossary of key critical and theoretical terms. To this end, students are required to attend an individual tutorial before which they must submit a plan of their analysis. If they do not do this, they are not allowed to submit their second assignment. Students choose from a variety of texts which consist either of individual essays or extracts from longer works. A sample of set texts is given below.

Extract from M. H Abrams *The Mirror and the Lamp.*
Paul de Man, "The Rhetoric of Temporality."
Geoffrey Hartman, "Romanticism and Anti-Self-Consciousness."
Extracts from Jerome McGann, *The Romantic Ideology: a Critical Investigation.*
Extracts from James Chandler, *England in 1819: the Politics of Literary Culture and the case of Romantic Historicism.*
Extracts from Anne K. Mellor *Romanticism and Gender.*

Conclusion

I said at the outset that the question, "What is Romanticism?" is theoretical as well as literary and historical. In conclusion, I would go further: I would say that the question "What is Romanticism?" is primarily a question in and for theory. Indeed, it is possibly the inaugurating question of literary theory. As Jean Luc Nancy and Phillipe Lacoue-Labarthe contend, the emergence of Romanticism marks "the inauguration of the theoretical project in literature . . . the theoretical institutionalisation of literary genre" (1988: 6). To teach Romanticism theoretically therefore is not purely a matter of introducing students to various theoretical ways of reading texts, but to place *literary theory and criticism itself* within the interdisciplinary contexts of Romanticism. What we have come to term "theory" and "criticism" (and along with that what we understand by "literature" and even "identity") is implicated in what we have come to term "Romanticism." At the very least, this provides a lively point of departure and return for the module: "We are all 'Romantics': Discuss."

Appendix

Lecture One: Introducing Romanticism
Lecture Two: Revolutionary Romanticism
Lecture Three: Romanticism, Colonialism, Slavery
Lecture Four: Poetic Revolutions: Reality, Representation, Imagination
Lecture Five: The Romantic Sublime
Lecture Six: Romanticism and the Environment: "Eco-Criticism"
Lecture Seven: Romanticism and the Gothic
Week Eight: Assignment Preparation (see above)
Lecture Nine: Critical Perspectives: Abrams to De Man
Lecture Ten: Critical Perspectives: The Romantic Ideology: Marxism and New Historicism
Lecture Eleven: Critical Perspectives: The Gender of "Romanticism": Feminist Interrogations.
Week Twelve: Assignment Preparation (see above)

Works cited

Abrams M. H. (1953) *The Mirror and the Lamp: Romantic Theory and the Critical Tradition* (New York: Norton).
Bhabha, Homi (2001) "Of Mimicry and Man: the Ambivalence of Colonial Discourse," in *Modern Literary Theory*, ed. Philip Rice and Patricia Waugh (London: Hodder Arnold): 380–6.
Bloom, Harold, ed. (1970) *Romanticism and Consciousness: Essays in Criticism* (New York: Norton).
Chai, Leon (2006) *Romantic Theory: Forms of Reflexivity in the Revolutionary Era* (Baltimore: Johns Hopkins University Press).
Chandler, James (1998) *England in 1819: the Politics of Literary Culture and the Case of Romantic Historicism* (Chicago: University of Chicago Press).
Coleridge, Samuel Taylor (1956) *Collected Letters of Samuel Taylor Coleridge*, ed. Leslie Griggs (Oxford: Clarendon Press).
Culler, Jonathon (1997) *Literary Theory: a Very Short Introduction* (Oxford: Oxford University Press).
Day, Aidan (1996) *Romanticism* (London: Routledge).
De Man, Paul (1983) *Blindness and Insight: Essays in the Rhetoric of Contemporary Criticism* (Minnesota: University of Minnesota Press).

—— (1984) *The Rhetoric of Romanticism* (New York: Columbia University Press).
Derrida, Jacques (1987) *The Truth in Painting* (Chicago: Chicago University Press).
Greenblatt, Stephen, M. H. Abrams, Jack Stillinger, and Deirdre Shauna Lynch, eds. (2005) *The Norton Anthology of English Literature: the Romantic Period* (New York: Norton).
Hamilton, Paul (2003) *Metaromanticism: Aesthetics, Literature, Theory* (Chicago: University of Chicago Press).
Hartman, Geoffrey (1970) *Beyond Formalism* (New Haven: Yale University Press).
Hertz, Neil (1985) *The End of the Line: Essays on Psychoanalysis and the Sublime* (New York: Columbia University Press).
Johnson, Samuel (1825) *The Complete Works of Samuel Johnson*, ed. R. Lynam (London: Dove Press).
Keach, William (1993) "Romanticism and Language" in *The Cambridge Companion to British Romanticism*, ed. Stuart Curran (Cambridge: Cambridge University Press): 95–119.
McGann, Jerome (1981) *The Romantic Ideology: a Critical Investigation* (Chicago: Chicago University Press).
—— (1992) "Rethinking Romanticism," *English Literary History*, 59: 735–54.
Mellor, Anne K. (1993) *Romanticism and Gender* (London: Routledge).
—— "Romanticism, Difference and the Aesthetic," *Pacific Coast Philology*, 34.2: 127–41.
Nancy, Jean-Luc and Philippe Lacoue-Labarthe (1988) *The Literary Absolute: the Theory of Literature in German Romanticism* (Albany: State University of New York Press).
Pipkin, John G. (1998) "The Material Sublime of the Women Poets," *Studies in English Literature, 1500–1900*, 38.4: 597–619.
Poems of Phillis Wheatley (1969) (Bedford, MA: Applewood Books).
Roe, Nicholas (2005) *Romanticism: an Oxford Guide* (Oxford: Oxford University Press).
Ruston, Sharon (2007) *Romanticism* (London: Continuum).
Said, Edward (1994) *Culture and Imperialism* (London: Random House).
Shaw, Philip (2006) *The Sublime* (London: Routledge).
Silverman, Hugh and Gary E. Aylesworth, eds. (1990) *The Textual Sublime: Deconstruction and its Differences* (Albany: State University of New York Press).
Simpson, David (1993) "Romanticism, Criticism and Theory," in *The Cambridge Companion to British Romanticism*, ed. Stuart Curran (Cambridge: Cambridge University Press): 1–24.
Weiskel, Thomas (1976) *The Romantic Sublime: Studies in the Structure and Psychology of Transcendence* (Baltimore: Johns Hopkins University Press).
Wordsworth, William (1974) *The Prose Works of William Wordsworth*, ed. W. J. B. Owen and Jane Smyser (Oxford: Clarendon Press).

Further reading

Clark, David L. and Donald C. Goellnicht, eds. (1995) *New Romanticisms: Theory and Critical Practice* (Toronto: Toronto University Press).
Favret, Mary A. and Nicola J. Watson, eds. (1994) *At the Limits of Romanticism: Essays in Cultural, Feminist and Materialist Criticism* (Bloomington: Indiana University Press).

Fay, Elizabeth A. (1998) *Romanticism: a Feminist Introduction* (Oxford: Blackwell).
Ferguson, Frances (1992) *Solitude and the Sublime: Romanticism and the Aesthetics of Individuation* (London: Routledge).
Fulford, Tim and Peter J. Kitson, eds. (1998) *Romanticism and Colonialism: Writing and Empire, 1780–1830* (Cambridge: Cambridge University Press).
Gamer, Michael (2006) *Romanticism and the Gothic: Genre, Reception and Canon Formation* (Cambridge: Cambridge University Press).
Haywood, Ian (2006) *Bloody Romanticism: Spectacular Violence and the Politics of Representation, 1776–1832* (Basingstoke: Palgrave Macmillan).
Labbe, Jacqueline M. (1998) *Romantic Visualities: Landscape, Gender and Romanticism* (Basingstoke: Palgrave – now Palgrave Macmillan).
McCann, Andrew (2002) *Cultural Politics in the 1790s: Literature, Radicalism and the Public Sphere* (Basingstoke: Palgrave – now Palgrave Macmillan).
McKusick, James C. (2000) *Green Writing: Romanticism and Ecology* (New York: St. Martin's Press – now Palgrave Macmillan).
Makdisi, Saree (1998) *Romantic Imperialism: Universal Empire and the Culture of Modernity* (Cambridge: Cambridge University Press).
Moller, Lis and Marie-Louise Svane, eds. (2001) *Romanticism in Theory* (Aarhus: Aarhus University Press).
Pinkney, Tony, ed. (1995) *News from Nowhere: Theory and Politics of Romanticism* (Edinburgh: Edinburgh University Press).
Rajan, Tilottama and Julia M. Wright (2006) *Romanticism, History and the Possibilities of Genre* (Cambridge: Cambridge University Press).
Thomas, Helen (2004) *Romanticism and Slave Narratives* (Cambridge: Cambridge University Press).
Whale, John C. and Stephen Copley, eds. (1992) *Beyond Romanticism: New Approaches to Texts and Contexts, 1780–1832* (London: Routledge).

12
Postgraduate Study of Romanticism in the UK, US and Canada: Posting and Positing a Twenty-First Century Romanticism

Harriet Kramer Linkin

Introduction: surveying Romanticism

In 1991 *College English* published the results of a survey I conducted in 1990 that sought to ascertain the Romantic canon that US higher education instructors established in the classroom through the authors they assigned. Not surprisingly, the big six male poets ruled the day: Keats, Coleridge, Wordsworth, Shelley, Byron and Blake, in that order. The big six similarly dominated the available teaching texts most instructors used, either the fifth edition of the *Norton Anthology of English Literature* (1986) or the first edition of David Perkins' *English Romantic Poets* (1967), anthologies that would later be revised to include more expansive sets of Romantic-era authors (and could not yet be supplemented by the largesse of the internet or the many canon-busting anthologies published by the turn of the twentieth century). Even so, the survey revealed that a significant percentage of the 239 instructors (from 164 institutions) who participated in the survey assigned many non-canonical writers, including Mary Shelley (56 per cent), Dorothy Wordsworth (49 per cent), Hazlitt (41 per cent), Charles Lamb (32 per cent), De Quincey (31 per cent), Austen (29 per cent), Wollstonecraft (29 per cent), Godwin (24 per cent), and Scott (21 per cent).[1] At the time I proposed surveying the field again in another twenty years to see what developments might ensue. Sharon Ruston's 2006 survey of ninety-seven UK higher education instructors (from sixty-six institutions) for the English Subject Centre's "Teaching Romanticism" conference provides an excellent preview ("Survey Results" 2006).[2] The big six still rule, albeit in a slightly different order of popularity – Coleridge, Wordsworth, Shelley, Keats, Byron and Blake – but are situated amongst numerous peers: Wollstonecraft (44 per cent), Burke (39 per cent), Austen (38 per cent), Mary Shelley (37 per cent), Clare (35 per cent), Smith (34 per cent), Barbauld (31 per cent), Godwin (29 per cent), Paine (28 per cent), Dorothy Wordsworth (27 per cent), Landon (25 per cent), Hemans (23 per cent), Robinson (22 per cent), Scott (22 per cent) and dozens more.[3]

More telling than the relative percentages is the larger shift in the way instructors now conceptualize Romanticism as a pedagogical field: while the big six occupy crucial positions in curricular representations of the Romantic-era community, they are presented as participants in a contemporary culture that not only includes once-marginalized "others" of various identity categories (gender, race, nation, ethnicity, class, sexuality) but also genres beyond poetry (fiction, drama, autobiography, travel writing, essays, conduct books) and topics beyond the literary (history, science, philosophy, politics, religion, art). For this essay I surveyed 240 institutions in the UK (77), the US (130), and Canada (33) with postgraduate programmes in literature and learned that postgraduate courses which focus exclusively on the poetry of the big six stand as the rare exception rather than the rule. Postgraduate instructors tend to design modules which implicitly build on or explicitly interrogate some a priori understanding of the role of the big six in a once-canonical Romanticism (even when course descriptions stipulate that no prior knowledge of the field is necessary). What follows explores the current state of postgraduate study in Romanticism from two perspectives: (1) how instructors and institutions configure Romanticism in the modules or syllabi they post to the world, and (2) how students are reconfiguring Romanticism through the doctoral dissertations they complete.

Overview of UK/US/CA pathways/courses in Romanticism: what instructors say

First and foremost, the study of Romanticism is not only alive and well but thriving, despite the understandable concerns voiced by many Romanticists that the field would be eclipsed or colonized by expansions in neighbouring fields, namely the long eighteenth century (1660–1832) and the long nineteenth century (1789–1914). Such concerns led William Galperin and Susan Wolfson to propose redefining Romanticism as the Romantic Century (1750–1850) in 1997 to encourage more specific employment listings for specialists in Romanticism and to discourage the notion that Romanticism functioned as little more than "the end-point of the eighteenth century (in which it is by definition marginal or ancillary) or as the adolescence of the nineteenth century." While their intervention may not have produced more employment listings, or deflected the incorporation of Romanticism into institutional constructions of eighteenth-century studies and nineteenth-century studies, their redefinition of Romanticism as a Romantic Century provided an elegant solution to the still vexing issue of conflating the historical period with an ideology or aesthetic. Romanticism – the period, the concept, the century – is not only holding its own but occupying significant space in the postgraduate curriculum of at least 65 per cent (or 156) of the 240 programmes surveyed. Upwards of 200 institutions list a catalogue course in Romanticism, or a larger umbrella course that specifies or allows for a topic in Romanticism, but catalogues only provide a generalized image of a potential curriculum. More importantly, a minimum of 156 programmes have scheduled one or more modules or classes in Romanticism during the past two-year cycle (2006–08): 60 per cent (or 46) of the 77 in the UK, 70 per cent (or 92) of the 130 in the US, and 54 per cent (or 18) of the 33 in Canada.[4] Given the fact that most of these classes are optional rather than required, the plenitude of curricular offerings for postgraduate study of Romanticism is remarkable. Equally remarkable is the range of courses available to students, who not only find women writers, autobiography or gothic literature in Romanticism, but find Romanticism through courses on women writers, autobiography and gothic literature, one of the more felicitous consequences of expanding the canon in Romanticism.

Romanticism in the UK: modules, pathways, masters

In the UK the increasing popularity of themed degrees or pathways seems to have had a beneficial impact on the study of Romanticism.[5] Nearly half (22) of the 46 programmes that regularly offer modules in Romanticism provide a good twenty-four options that enable students to complete a named MA or MA pathway in Romanticism (seven), an MA or MA pathway in eighteenth-century studies that specifically includes Romanticism (nine), or an MA or MA pathway in nineteenth-century studies that specifically includes Romanticism (eight):

MA in Romanticism (7)
MA in Romantic Formations (University of Leeds)
MA in Romantic and Sentimental Literature, 1770–1830 (University of York)

MA in Pan-Romanticisms (University of Warwick)
MLitt in Romantic Studies (University of St Andrews)
MA in English Literature: Romanticism (University of Bristol)
MSc in English Literature: Romanticism (University of Edinburgh)
MA in English Studies: Romantic Literature (Sheffield Hallam University)

MA in Eighteenth-Century Studies that includes Romanticism (9)
MLitt in Enlightenment, Romanticism and Nation (University of Glasgow)
MA in Writing and Society 1700–1820 (Queen Mary, University of London)
MA in Eighteenth-Century Studies (King's College, University of London)
MA in Eighteenth-Century Art, Literature, Identity (University of Plymouth)
MA in Eighteenth-Century Studies: Text, Culture and Society (University of Sheffield)
MA in Eighteenth-Century Studies (University of Southampton)
MA in Eighteenth Century Studies 1750–1850 (University of York)
MPhil in English: Eighteenth-Century and Romantic Studies (University of Cambridge)
MA in English: The Enlightenment to Romanticism (University of Exeter)

MA in Nineteenth-Century Studies that includes Romanticism (8)
MA in Romantic and Victorian Literature (Lancaster University)
MA in Nineteenth-Century Studies (University of Sheffield)
MA in Nineteenth Century Literature and Culture (University of Sussex)
MA in English: Romantic and Victorian Literary Studies (University of Durham)
MSt in English: 1780–1900 (University of Oxford)
MA in English: Nineteenth Century Literature and Culture (Oxford Brookes University)
MA in English Literature: The Long 19th Century (University of Nottingham)
MLitt in English Studies: The "Long" Nineteenth Century (University of Dundee)

The other twenty-four postgraduate programmes offer multiple modules in Romanticism to complete MA degrees in fields such as English Studies, Literary Studies, Literature and Material Culture, Gothic Studies,

Women's Writing, Children's Literature or Victorian Studies.[6] Although the particular components (and emphases) of the themed degrees continually change (the 2007–08 MA in Renaissance and Romantic Literature at the University of Liverpool became the 2008–09 MA in Renaissance and Eighteenth-Century Literature), a closer look at the current modular structure of the three MA degrees focused exclusively on Romanticism in 2008 – at the University of Leeds, the University of York and the University of Warwick – provides a wealth of information on how Romanticism is being construed and taught at the postgraduate level in the UK.

Perhaps the most comprehensive MA in Romanticism currently runs at the University of Leeds, whose MA in Romantic Formations offers a series of modules that seem to capture nearly every critical and curricular development in Romanticism over the past twenty years. The core module on "Romantic Identities: Literary Constructions of the Self, 1789–1821" asks students to investigate Romantic modes of self-construction by reading canonical poetic texts against other literary representations of the self (autobiography, letters, travel writing, diaries, the novel), and to question the dominance of a male Romantic sublime by reading the work of women writers and male essayists. Beyond the core (and a required research methods module to prepare for the completion of a dissertation), students select three additional modules among the following (not all of which are offered at once): (a) "Nation and Empire in British Romantic Writing," which looks at Romanticism, nationalism and imperialism via representations of national and racial "others" in the work of canonical figures, slave narratives, abolitionist poetry and travel writing; (b) "American Revolutions: Representing America from Independence to *The Last of the Mohicans*," which explores the representation of America and Americans (including Native Americans) on both sides of the Atlantic; (c) "Irish Writing in an Age of Revolution," which considers ideas about nationhood, representations of the Celtic past, Irish Catholicism, the Anglo-Irish Ascendency, and uses of Gothic and oriental imagery in work by Irish writers; (d) "Women Writing Revolution," which examines the ways women writers responded to the French Revolution; (e) "Gender and Romanticism," which looks at the formation and contestation of gender identities (masculinities, femininities, "queer" sexualities) in canonical and lesser-known popular texts (gothic literature, the novel, narrative poetry and social theory) by men and women; (f) "Sensibility and Society 1744–1811," which traces the development of sensibility, sympathy and sentiment as key terms in the literary and philosophical discussion of gender, virtue, conduct, commerce, nationhood and community; (g) "Critical Theory: from Enlightenment to Modernity," which queries the extent to which current theoretical concerns with history, subjectivity, ideology, writing, gender, terror, race and cultural identity begin in the Enlightenment; or (h) "Blake: Word and Vision," the only course to focus on one of the big six, and the most controversial one at that.

While the curriculum at Leeds intentionally integrates the more canonical with the less canonical to present the Romantic era as a historical period of literary and cultural diversity, the MA in Romantic and Sentimental Literature, 1770–1830 at the University of York calls equally intentional attention to the ideological divide that reified Romanticism as a Romantic aesthetic within a Romantic half-century:

> The Romantic movement has traditionally been seen to dominate the aesthetic and literary output of the late eighteenth and early nineteenth centuries, but recent critical and historical scholarship has emphasized the range and diversity of contemporary literary forms and styles of writing which cannot comfortably be treated as though they were part of that movement. By setting Romantic and Sentimental writings alongside each other the MA offers students an opportunity to find their own paths through the literary and cultural history of the period. (MA in Romantic and Sentimental Literature 1770–1830)

In the required core module, students begin to find their path by reading major Romantic writers against key Sentimental – or Anti-Sentimental – writers. Beyond the core, students take another three modules that might focus on contemporary politics, print culture, women writers, theatrical performance, aesthetic representations of identity, or orientalism, as follows: (a) "James Gillray, Richard Lee, and the Great Propaganda War of 1795," which compares and contrasts the radical plebeian versus pro-government propaganda published in 1795 (especially caricature-art); (b) Popular Romanticism," which considers how ideas of "the popular" and "the people" affected the production of Romantic-era literature for a growing reading audience; (c) "Femininity and Literary Culture: English Women Writers and the Politics of the 1790s," which explores how women writers responded to the French Revolution; (d) "Romantic Confessions and Poetic Personae, 1790–1830," which examines the construction of literary identity and authorial personae in a variety of confessional texts and forms (from Rousseau to Landon); (e) "Romantic Performances," which focuses on dramatic forms and theatrical performances in late Georgian London to consider, among other things, the intersection of theatre, nationhood and gender; and (e) "British Orientalisms in the Long Eighteenth Century," which explores writings about "the East." Additional modules available from the Centre for Eighteenth Century Studies cover a broader interdisciplinary terrain to investigate "Eighteenth-century British Perceptions of the South Pacific," "Changing Faces of British Anti-Slavery," "Gendering the Exotic and Exoticising Gender," "Women and Politics in Britain, *c.*1760–1850," "Radical Identities in Britain in the Age of Romanticism, *c.*1819–50," or "British Country Houses and their Families, 1680–1880."

The interdisciplinary options available at York are brought to the forefront of the MA in Pan-Romanticism at the University of Warwick, which presents Romanticism as a transnational phenomenon that shapes the literature, art and history of England, Germany, France and Italy. The core module, "Introduction to Pan-Romanticisms," is team-taught by faculty from all four national literatures who spend four weeks on British Romanticism (Burke, Wollstonecraft, Smith, Robinson, W. Wordsworth, Coleridge, Scott, Keats, Hemans, Byron, Jones, Landon and P. B. Shelley) and six weeks on European Romanticism (Novalis, F. Schlegel, A. Schlegel, de Stael, Chateaubriand, Stendhal, Hugo, Manzoni, Leopardi and Verri). In addition to the core and a required research module, students complete another two modules, one of which must be outside the English and Comparative Literature department. Some of the options include (a) "Rivalries and Couplings in British Romantic Literature," which highlights the literary and social interaction of canonical and lesser known authors in intriguing pairings; (b) "The Lure of Italy," which considers the impact of Italy on German and French writers in connection with travel literature, the grand tour, art, architecture and archaeology, fictional representation and political consciousness; (c) "German Romanticism," which works through drama, prose, and verse; (d) "Reason and Revolution in 18th-century France," which takes up a set of politically-charged themes (religious difference, class, gender, the individual) in various works; (e) "Exhibitions and Audiences in Georgian London," which explores the emergence of an exhibition culture and English style of painting during the long eighteenth century; (f) "Consumption and Culture in 18th-Century Britain," which examines the development of a consumer society in the long eighteenth century; (g) "Politics and Opinion in Hanoverian Britain," which looks at eighteenth-century political culture; and (g) "Romantic Elegy," a close study of the elegiac poetry of Gray, Smith, Coleridge, W. Wordsworth, Clare, P. B. Shelley, Hemans and Tennyson.

Although each one of the MA programmes outlined above presents Romanticism or the Romantic period within a particular framework, all three share a set of assumptions about the discipline that seems to be representative of postgraduate instruction in Romanticism throughout the UK. At the UK institutions surveyed for this essay, the modules that study Romanticism claim to present a truly expansive field of writers, genres and topics that address, among many other things, the Romantic poetry and poetics of the once exclusive big six.

Romanticism in the US: treading the transatlantic

Two significant differences between postgraduate instruction in the UK and graduate instruction in the US should be noted at the outset: first, on average graduate students in the US are required to complete more taught courses in MA programs (10–12 classes) or PhD programs (8–15) than postgraduate students in the UK, who spend a comparatively greater amount of time conducting independent research (with supervision). Second, very few graduate programmes in the US offer themed MA degrees, and perhaps a handful offer a pathway in an area that includes Romanticism (such as Nineteenth-Century Studies or Gothic Studies). Thus unlike the discussion of postgraduate study of Romanticism in the UK above, which provides detailed information on three specific MA programmes that strive to exemplify twenty-first-century Romanticism, this section's overview of graduate study of Romanticism in the US seeks to identify larger trends evidenced in an analysis of 151 course descriptions that were posted online by the ninety-two institutions that offered graduate courses in Romanticism during the past two years.

Although one wants to bear in mind Blake's caveat on the dangers of generalizing, the 151 courses sorted fairly easily into one of four basic categories that either (1) highlighted a specific *genre* within the Romantic period, such as poetry, the novel, or drama; (2) sought to cover all or part of a historical *period* (variously defined as early/first generation, later/second generation/the Regency, or the Romantic period 1770–1830, etc.); (3) took a *thematic* approach that focused on a specific issue for the Romantic-era community; or (4) concentrated an entire course on one or more *authors* (Austen, Wordsworth, Keats, Blake, Byron, Wordsworth-Coleridge, Wordsworth-Keats, Wordsworth-Blake-Byron) (see Table 12.1).

The 151 courses also sorted fairly easily (or perhaps uneasily) into four groupings that denote the range of canonical/marginalized authors each course delineated within its field of study. Courses either focused

Table 12.1 Primary US categories: genre, period, theme, author

Genre: 27%	*Period: 28%*	*Theme: 34%*	*Author: 11%*
16 Poetry	4 Early	26 History	13 Single
21 Novel	6 Late	14 Theory	4 Multiple
3 Drama	32 Full	5 Print	
		3 Green	
		4 Unique	
40 Total	42 Total	52 Total	17 Total

Table 12.2 Range of authors included: canonical to marginalized

Big Six: 6%	*Big Six Plus: 18%*	*Expanded: 67%*	*Women: 9%*
4 Genre	5 Genre	26 Genre	5 Genre
5 Period	8 Period	27 Period	2 Period
	2 Theme	49 Theme	1 Theme
	12 Authors		5 Authors
9 Total	27 Total	102 Total	13 Total

(1) exclusively on the *big six* (or five) male poets; (2) primarily on the *big six plus* a few additional figures (poetic precursors, European poets, women writers, essayists) who contextualized the work of the big six; (3) entirely on an *expanded canon* or community that elevated the once-marginalized (based on authorial identity or literary genre) to canonical status or questioned the concept of canonicity; or (4) exclusively on *women writers* (see Table 12.2).

Further sorting revealed the following distribution within each of the four major fields (see Table 12.3).

Like all classification schema, these groupings and charts condense a multitude of important particularities that complicate the project of compartmentalizing 151 multiform Romanticism courses into discrete categories and subcategories. Ultimately all the courses fit into the period category, given their nominal concern with Romantic-era themes, authors and genres, but the subcategories enable a few specific observations about graduate study of Romanticism in the US.

First, only 2 per cent or four of the 151 graduate courses on Romanticism tracked in the US focus on the poetry of the big six, thus bearing out the assertion in the second paragraph of this essay that "postgraduate courses which focus exclusively on the poetry of the big six stand

Table 12.3 Primary US categories in terms of authors included

	Big Six: 6%	*Big Six Plus: 18%*	*Expanded: 67%*	*Women: 9%*
Genre	4 Poetry	5 Poetry	3 Poetry 20 Novel 3 Drama	4 Poetry 1 Novel
Period	3 Early 2 Entire	2 Late 6 Entire	1 Early 4 Late 22 Entire	2 Entire
Theme		1 Theory 1 Unique	25 History 13 Theory 5 Print 3 Green 3 Unique	1 History
Author		8 Single 4 Multiple		5 Single
151 Total	9 Total	27 Total	102 Total	13 Total

as the rare exception rather than the rule." At the same time, it seems somewhat surprising that courses focused exclusively on the big six combined with courses focused primarily on the big six (with a few additional writers such as Mary Shelley or Dorothy Wordsworth) constitute nearly a quarter of the 151 courses (24 per cent or 36 total), a percentage potentially skewed through the inclusion of the twelve author courses dedicated to the big six (plus). Second, courses dedicated to the study of Romantic-era poetry (10 per cent or 16), once the premier genre of the age and subject of instruction, now stand a clear second to courses dedicated to the study of the once-marginalized Romantic-era novel (14 per cent or 21), to courses that examine the period as comprised by multiple genres and literary forms (24 per cent or 37), and to courses that take a thematic approach to the politics and history of the age (34 per cent or 52). Among other things the specific distribution of the sixteen poetry courses points to the ongoing contestation of the canonical/marginal, with four courses devoted to the big six, five courses primarily on the big six (plus), three courses that designate a field of active male and female poets (the big six in tandem with Smith, Barbauld, Baillie, Hemans, Opie, or Barbauld, Burns, Clare, Scott, Williams, Yearsley, or Barbauld, Clare, Hemans, Landon), and four courses that posit an alternate tradition of women poets (Smith, Barbauld, Robinson, Tighe, Hemans, Landon and more, often extending into the Victorian period). Third, courses that present the Romantic period as an expansive community of diverse writers or take a thematic approach to the period as an expansive community of diverse writers not only predominate in US classrooms (60 per cent or 89) but teach the field as a multi-genre, multi-identity, multi-topic course, as evidenced by the following representative description:

> *English Romantic Literature*: As we all know, the end of the Eighteenth Century and the beginning of the Nineteenth Century in Great Britain was a time of tremendous dislocations – social, economic, and philosophic. We will consider the emergence of Romanticism as a response to these dislocations, focusing especially on such general topics as Romanticism and Revolution; Romanticism and Gender; Romanticism and the Gothic; Romanticism, Slavery, and Colonialism; and Romantic Canons. In addition to key works by the six canonical Romantic poets, we'll be reading poetry by Charlotte Smith, Anna Barbauld, Dorothy Wordsworth, Felicia Hemans, and Hannah More. There will also be novels by William Godwin (*Caleb Williams*), Jane Austen (*Emma*), Mary Shelley (*Frankenstein*) and Charlotte Dacre (*Zofloya, or The Moor*); slave narratives by Equiano and Mary Prince; the melodrama, *Obi; or Three Finger'd Jack*; and Wollstonecraft's *Vindication of the Rights of Woman.* ("Graduate Course Descriptions" 2008)

In classrooms across the US, graduate instruction in Romanticism offers students access to a host of literary forms (poetry, novels, plays, autobiographies, essays, criticism, treatises, pamphlets, broadsides, histories, travel literature, conduct books, children's literature), a prodigious cast of writers (dozens of men and women from England, Scotland, Ireland, India, Africa, America, Germany, Italy and France whose names would fill this page), and a broad range of historical, political, cultural and aesthetic concerns (gender, race, class, sexuality, subjectivity, nationalism, imperialism, colonialism, slavery, feeling, sensibility, aesthetics, architecture, landscape, history, science, form, authorship, the public sphere).

Finally, although one doesn't want to say too much about the relative popularity of some thematic approaches over others, seventeen programmes offered new courses in "Transatlantic Romanticism," a topic of great interest in the US: perhaps no wonder, given the opportunity for instructors to situate "America" within British Romanticism for US students who generally prefer American literature over British literature. But more relevant than the relevance factor, courses titled "Transatlantic Romanticism, 1798–1867," "the Romantic Atlantic," "Black Romanticism," "Transatlantic Literature: Romanticism and Science," or "Archives of Transatlantic Revolution and Empire, 1750–1850" signal the emergence of a nomenclature (like "the Romantic Century") that neatly captures twenty-first century Romanticism's concern with history, culture and politics, evidenced in this instance in courses that trace the circulation and reception of ideas, texts, images and bodies back and forth across an Atlantic that spans continents and centuries.

Romanticism in Canada: confirming conjunctions

The twenty-six postgraduate courses taught at eighteen Canadian institutions during the period surveyed not only confirm the emphasis on Romantic diversity and cultural history evidenced in UK and US classrooms but may provide the greatest composite national challenge to the canon that once was: not a single course focuses on the big six (or the big six plus) and even the most narrowly focused courses draw upon an expansive community of canonical and non-canonical Romantic-era writers (including author-centered courses such as "The Addicts and Addictions of Thomas De Quincey," "Jane Austen and the 'Silly' Novel," and "Austen and Scott"). A commitment to interrogating canonicity manifests in pointed course titles like "~~Romantic~~ Literature in the Age of Public Opinion," which promises to "'defamiliarize' the Romantic and provide a sociological matrix for reading literary texts of this and subsequent periods" (Queen's University), or in the sheer number of course titles – no less than thirteen of the twenty-six – that deploy the conjunction "and" to foreground or complicate connections between "Romanticism and its Others,"[7] including "Romanticism and Empire," "Romanticism and India," "Romanticism and its Critics," "Romanticism and the Rise of Consumerism," "Romanticism and Genre," "The Tale of Terror and Other Popular Genres: Romantic Poetry and the Marketplace," and "Women and Men in the Romantic Period." Even courses that might seem to take the conventional two-generation approach to a relatively contained Romantic period of thirty-five years' duration transform that approach and period into something radically new, as in "Revolution and Enlightenment: Literature and Thought 1790–1825," which reconstitutes and repopulates the first generation as "the revolutionary period (Blake, Godwin, Wollstonecraft, Fenwick, Hays)" and the second generation as the revolution's "second wave in the Regency period, which we will study not through Scott and Austen but through

Table 12.4 Primary categories in Canada: genre, period, theme, author

Genre: 23%	*Period*: 19%	*Theme*: 46%	*Author*: 12%
4 Poetry	1 Early	6 History	3 Multiple
2 Novel	1 Late	3 Theory	
0 Drama	3 Full	3 Print Culture	
6 Total	5 Total	12 Total	3 Total

the survival of radicalism in the work of Mary Shelley, Percy Shelley, and Godwin once again" (University of Western Ontario). Equally telling, courses that study Romantic-era poetry (four of the twenty-six) consistently position that once-sublime genre as a site of contentious forces, as in "Romantic Revolutions" (University of Alberta), which declares "during the age of Revolution and Romanticism, poetry underwent a radical revolution as a field of struggle and medium of communication between contending social forces and political ideologies."

Akin to the US, Canadian postgraduate programmes rarely offer themed MA degrees or pathways in literary fields, thus furthering the distinctiveness of UK programmes in Romanticism and making direct comparison between Canada and the UK untenable. But a sort of the twenty-six Canadian postgraduate courses in Romanticism into the categories used in the preceding section intriguingly corroborates trends witnessed in the US distribution (see Table 12.4).

Despite the comparatively smaller number of courses to chart, settling these twenty-six courses into distinctive categories proved far more difficult than the 151 US courses: for instance the two courses on the novel take a decidedly cultural approach; the three "author" courses examine the novel (as well as culture); and all of the period courses implement a cultural (and often thematic) approach. In Canada postgraduate study of Romanticism may well be a study of ~~Romanticism~~.

Overview of dissertations in Romanticism: what students do

This concluding section offers an all-too-brief brief look at doctoral dissertations completed in 2007 (compared to 1997 and 1987) to see how postgraduate students are reconfiguring Romanticism in their research. That postgraduate students demonstrate a strong interest in pursuing studies in Romanticism seems clear from two indices: first, 14 per cent (or 67) of the 457 students who applied for postgraduate awards from the Arts and Humanities Research Council sought funding for projects in the Nineteenth Century: Romantics/Mid-late Nineteenth-Century category, the second largest category after 1945–Present (Table 1a). Second, 14 per cent (or 50) of the 345 English Literature dissertations listed in the 2007 *Dissertation Abstracts International* index focused on Romantic-era literature. That figure is significantly greater than 1997, when 8 per cent (or 61) of the 728 dissertations listed in *DAI* focused on Romantic-era literature, or 1987, when only 7 per cent (or 35) of the 497 dissertations did.

In 1987 most dissertations focused squarely on one or more of the big six or Austen: 32 of the 35 listed in *DAI* address Wordsworth (13), Blake (5), Keats (3), Shelley (2), a combination that included Coleridge but not Byron (6), and Austen (3). Interestingly, two of the twenty-nine on the big six take a feminist approach (Wordsworth's debt to women poets and Keats's representation of the female). The other three indicate the major changes to come: two focus on gothic literature and one explores women novelists of the 1790s as revolutionary. The dissertations completed by 1997 reflect the impact of those changes in no uncertain terms. Although the big six continue to get attention as individuals – Byron (four), Blake (three), Wordsworth (three), Shelley (one) – and in combinations that include Coleridge and Keats (three), less than a quarter (14) of the sixty-one studies focus on them. Four dissertations look at male and female poets in tandem, one champions Leigh Hunt, fourteen focus exclusively on women writers (poets and novelists), ten examine the novel (gothic, historical, national, political, revolutionary), three redeem the drama, two consider print culture (the anthology, the book), and fourteen pursue critical or thematic concerns that register the impact of cultural studies through work on slavery, race, science, politics, subjectivity, the public sphere and tourism.

In 2007 the *DAI* registered a single dissertation on one of the big six: Keats. The only other dissertation among the fifty focused entirely on one of the big six examined biographical information available for "William and Catherine Blake" (an inclusion that says a great deal). Elsewhere the big six figure as participants in an expansive community of Romantic-era writers (25 of 48), and single author studies focus on "Pagan" Taylor, Robinson, Shelley, Owenson and Scott. While women writers (ten) and gender matters (eight) continue to hold prominent places in the collective imagination, 90 per cent of the dissertations completed in 2007 approached Romantic-era writings (literary and non-literary) through the lens of cultural studies to contemplate representation vis-a-vis a wide array of discourses and discursive strategies, including medicine (diagnosis), science (chemistry, empiricism, discovery), anatomy (anorexia, the breast), fashion, sympathy, revolution, reform, empire, colonialism, the transatlantic, national identity (Scotland), religion (Islam, Methodism, Catholicism), literacy, cartography, photography, historiography, print sociology (annotations, footnotes) and more. Also notable were a series of dissertations (seven) that viewed work in the Romantic period as the beginning of a cultural, critical or aesthetic phenomenon extending across the nineteenth century and sometimes into the twentieth century. These 2007 dissertations not only reflect the current emphases of postgraduate instruction in Romanticism in the UK, US and Canada but signal its future as the authors of these studies take up their own academic posts and continue constructing twenty-first century Romanticism.

Notes

1. An additional twenty-eight authors were assigned by less than 20 per cent of the respondents (555).
2. Four of the ninety-seven participants came from non-UK higher education institutions (Asian University of Bangladesh, Cottonwood High School, Telemark University College of Norway, and the University of Nebraska in the US).
3. Ruston invited respondents to identify how much attention is given to specific authors; respondents could tick "mention briefly," "consider one poem or short extract of," "dedicate one seminar or lecture to the work of" and "not taught." The percentages listed here do not include respondents who ticked "mention briefly" ("Survey Results" 2006).
4. These statistics are only as reliable as the information published on university websites in the UK, US and Canada.
5. See Smith 2007.
6. More programmes offer MA degrees or pathways in eighteenth- and nineteenth-century studies, but only those programmes offering modules in Romanticism were listed above.
7. "Romanticism and its Others" was the title of the 1997 North American Society for the Study of Romanticism conference at McMaster University, which "sought to address the question of alterity and Romanticism, i.e., the others 'within' and 'without' what is called 'Romanticism'," October 2008).

Works Cited

Arts and Humanities Research Council (2007) "Competition Overview 2007", http://www.ahrc.ac.uk/FundedResearch/Documents/pg_statistical_overview_2007.xls.

Galperin, William and Susan Wolfson (1997) "The Romantic Century," North American Society for the Study of Romanticism Conference, McMaster University, October 1997, *Romantic Circles*, http://www.rc.umd.edu/features/crisis/crisisa.html.

"Graduate Course Descriptions" (2008) University of Maryland Department of English, http://www.englweb.umd.edu/courses/GradSpring2008.doc.

Linkin, Harriet Kramer (1991), "The Current Canon in British Romantics Studies," *College English*, 53: 548–70.

MA in Romantic and Sentimental Literature, 1770–1830, Centre for Eighteenth-Century Studies, University of York, http://www.york.ac.uk/inst/cecs/gsp/romantic.htm.

Perkins, David, ed. (1967) *English Romantic Poets* (New York: Harcourt Brace Jovanovich).

"Romanticism and its Others" (1997) North American Society for the Study of Romanticism conference at McMaster University, http://www.humanities.mcmaster.ca/~ hccrs/research/NASSR.HTM.

Smith, Samantha (2007) "The Taught MA in English," Report Series: 15, *English Subject Centre*, http://www.english.heacademy.ac.uk/archive/publications/reports/taughtma.pdf.

"Survey Results: Teaching Romanticism Questionnaire" (2006) *BARS Website*, http://www.bars.ac.uk/teaching/survey/surveyresults.php.

13
Teaching Romanticism in Japan

Steve Clark and Masashi Suzuki

I

Simon May, in *Atomic Sushi* (2006), describes his induction as a visiting academic teaching Romantic philosophy in Japan in the following way:

> Judging by their brassiness and in the case of many of the undergraduates, their indolence, my students at Tokyo had specific frontal lobe problems of their own. Their deference was restricted to my first meeting with them – when I was duly bowed to and addressed as sensei (teacher)... thereafter they were bold, informal and to the point. They came and went from my lectures when they felt like it, nodded off when they were tired or bored, asked direct and usually excellent questions, left their mobile phones on, and giggled, whispered and flirted during the classes as students do everywhere. The tone was set at the beginning of the academic year when they all introduced themselves. Without a hint of shyness they all stood up and began to speak. Their interest seemed to coalesce around the grimmer German philosophers. (May 2006: 59–60)

His area of expertise may not exactly be British Romanticism but close enough for a few initial comparisons to be made. The model of instruction is knowledge transmission from a proven specialist (Oxford "doctorate in philosophy" (10)) convinced that he is deserving of "deference" from students instantly disparaged for "specific frontal lobe problems" (a gibe at the doctrine of *nihonjihron*, Japanese specialness). Their subjects of interest – Hegel, Kierkegaard, Heidegger, Novalis – seem legitimate enough; yet the student who has "decided to learn German, French and English," so as to read "all philosophy in the original" is deemed self-evidently worthy of derision. The language of the formalized ritual of self-introduction is not specified, but would almost certainly have been Japanese, which May himself does not understand (hence the equivocation of "seemed to coalesce"); if all he presumably recognizes is the proper names of the "grimmer German philosophers," how he can ascertain that there is no "hint of shyness," or indeed other characteristics such as "brassiness"? The "indolence" may be attributed to a degree of burn-out through undergoing the arduous entrance examination process, combined with the lack of relevance of class-credits to future employment. (Even entrance to graduate school is not based on undergraduate evaluation, but on a separate test procedure.) If they "nodded off when they were tired or bored," this may be a result of long commuting times, and the number and length of classes (and how would British students cope with one-hundred-minute stints of tuition in a second language?).

Even the highest echelons of Japanese education have acquired a dubious reputation. Alex Kerr in *Dogs and Demons* (2001) again fulminates against Todai:

> Tokyo University (Todai), the very pinnacle of the elite, is an academic shambles by European or American standards. Todai graduates make few important contributions to world scholarship or technology; they go straight into government ministries, where they proceed to collect bribes, lend money to gangsters, falsify medical records, and cook up schemes to destroy rivers and seacoasts – with hardly a dissenting voice from their colleagues or professors. Few important schools in advanced countries can be said to have contributed so little of social value. (Kerr 2001: 300)

Yet if Todai graduates are deemed culpable for the collapse of the bubble economy, they must also be accorded credit for the post-war policies that established Japan as one of the most powerful economies in the world in the first place. This quotation forms part of a broader jeremiad about the state of contemporary Japan, but the specific criticism is frequently repeated: the education system is designed to suppress, if not wholly eradicate, any possibility of a "dissenting voice." It would therefore seem inevitably inimical to originality, spontaneity and creativity, indeed any kind of characteristic that might be loosely associated with Romanticism and its pedagogic inheritance running from Mill and Arnold into contemporary secondary and tertiary education in Britain.

Two simultaneous and contradictory charges appear to be made. It is difficult to see how higher education can be, on the one hand, a sinister state-controlled conspiracy and, on the other, a flagrant "shambles." There is a greater degree of centralized control over the curriculum, evident in periodic eruption of rows over textbooks concerning the history of Japan's relation with its Asian neighbours. Equally, however, there is a tradition of the autonomy of the *sensei* in structuring his or her classes: this means that, in comparison to Britain, there is very little coordination within a department over the range of topics taught, or standardization of marking procedures (hence the degree of scepticism with which grades are often viewed, even by the students themselves). If there is a tradition of large-group lecturing, there has also been the emergence of new technologies of distance learning, open courseware and web-based interactivity, for example in Kaz Oishi's site at the Open University of Japan (Oishi).

In many ways, Japan may be regarded as an introspective, even xenophobic, culture, but this must be weighed against the long-standing practice of importing foreign expertise (such as May) originally as part of a process of nation-building and technology transfer dating from the late-nineteenth century onwards. In literary scholarship, William Empson is perhaps the best-known example, but the tradition is long and often distinguished, as George Hughes has documented. With regard to the tragi-comic situation of the contemporary neophyte teacher, appointments are initially made based on elite academic qualifications, but in the majority of institutions, the classes will necessarily be focused on a fairly diffuse concept of language and culture: all students in Japanese higher education are obliged to continue studying English so, in brute practical terms, that is where the money is. (It would not be unusual for a new appointee, with no previous training in ELT, to be immediately confronting classes of sixty or more understandably disaffected students.)

The introduction of the JET scheme to employ native-speakers at secondary school level, has produced a veritable plethora of teaching memoirs, the best of which is perhaps Will Ferguson's *Hokkaido Highway Blues*. Throughout the genre, there is an oddly pre-emptive defensive antagonism: despite insisting on the "absurdly large salary" (7), doubts about one's own professional status and competence as a foreign interloper are redirected onto the educational context as a whole: "what with the shouts and screams and flirting squeals and the play-fights and the constant treks to the bathrooms. And that's just the teachers, the students are even worse" (Ferguson 1998: 91).

This essay will attempt to locate and define the special circumstances surrounding the reception of Romanticism in Japan. This includes most obviously a pedagogy involving two languages; and the assimilation of British texts as part of an indigenous Romantic tradition. It will perhaps be helpful at this point to have a more historical overview of the development Japan's university system, before returning to the issue of the present and future status of Romantic studies within it.

II

The practice of teaching English Romanticism in Japan has been closely related to the ways it was received and transformed through translations in magazines or anthologies, lectures given at the Imperial Universities and other major institutions, and so on, in the periods of Meiji (1868–1912), Taisho (1912–1926) and the early Showa (1926–1930s). The history of the reception of English Romantic Literature in Japan is deeply concerned not only with university curricula, but also with the passions and emotions represented in Romantic poetry which were immediately congenial to Japanese people; its medievalism and lyrical celebration of nature were particularly appealing. Romanticism in Japan is by no means an exclusively academic phenomenon.

In the early Meiji period such poets as Shimazaki Toson (1872–1943), Kitamura Tokoku (1868–1894) and Togawa Shukotsu (1871–1939) translated English Romantic poets like William Wordsworth, and such eminent scholars of English Literature as Natsume Soseki (1867–1916), also a famous novelist, and Ueda Bin (1874–1916), a critic, poet and translator as well, were influenced by Romantic literature. Through translation they tried to not only to understand Western culture, but also to incorporate it as an integral part of Japanese literature.

Bungaku-Kai (*Literary World*, 1893–1898) was a literary magazine started by Shimazaki Toson, a novelist and poet, Kitamura Tokoku, a passionate poet, critic and translator, Ueda Bin, and others in 1893; *Bungaku-Kai* was the first to introduce English Literature, especially English Romantic literature, into Japan. In this magazine, Kitamura Tokoku discussed Lord Byron's *Manfred* and Wolfgang von Goethe's *Faust*, and wrote a dramatic poem *Horai-Kyoku* (*Music of Horai*, 1891), which showed the strong influence of Byron and Goethe. Shimazaki Toson's *Wakana-Shu* (*Collection of Young Greens*, 1897) was his first collection of fifty-one Romantic lyrics on love, youth, nature and wandering, comparable to the aesthetic of *Lyrical Ballads*, in their use of plain everyday words.

Then came the "Shirakaba"(White Birch) school of Japanese Literature in the Taisho period, a name given to a group of young literati, mostly graduates of Gakushu-In University, which was characterized by its anti-naturalism and worship of individualism. Yanagi Muneyoshi (Soetsu) (1889–1961) in particular was instrumental in introducing William Blake in their magazine *Shirakaba*. He wrote *Iriamu bureiku: kare no shogai to seisaku oyobi sono shiso* (*William Blake: His Life, Works and Thought*, 1914) at the age of twenty-five and became one of the great precursors of Blake studies in Japan.

Natsume Soseki read English at Tokyo Imperial University and, like others of his generation, also studied abroad. After two years of study-stay in London, he became a lecturer of English at his *alma mater* in 1903, but he turned down the professorship and entered the Asahi Newspaper Company in 1907. As early as 1893, he made an influential speech on "English Poets' Concepts of Nature," indebted to Victorian critics such as Edmund Gosse (1849–1928) and Leslie Stephen (1832–1904). He suggested that "Pope didn't reveal his inner feelings, though very much affected by the natural world imbued with spirit," and esteemed highly Wordsworth as a poet who "had an excellent rapport with nature and even identified himself with her." This line of argument was also used in one of his representative works *Bungaku-Hyoron* (*Literary Essays*, 1909): the fifth chapter of the book proposes that though Pope had occasions to let his powerful feelings overflow, the burden of the age of prose meant that he could not help but write poems loaded, indeed burdened, with primarily intellectual appeal.

With the rise of the "Shirakaba," the English Romantic movement was singled out from other areas of English Literature to become part of the mainstream to be studied at universities. In the early Showa period, eminent Professors of English at the Imperial Universities such as Saito Takeshi at Tokyo, Ueda Bin at Kyoto and Doi Kochi at Tohoku were all deeply involved in the translation, teaching and critical appreciation of English Romantic literature.[1]

Even from this brief summary, it would seem reasonable to assume that during the first period of the reception of English Literature in Japan, Romantic literature was the most highly valued in the universities, and therefore also exerted an enormous influence on subsequent literary movements in Japan. Since many professors of the Imperial Universities were specialists in English Romantic literature, it was natural that their students should choose the Romantics for the subjects of the theses; their formal lectures were also characterized by their preferences. This is an interesting reversal of what was happening at Cambridge

University and other major institutions in England and America because of the increasing impact of the anti-Romantic bias of Leavisite and New Criticism from the 1930s to the 1960s. The popularity of Romantic topics can be confirmed by glancing at some of the representative titles of graduate theses and lectures at Tokyo, Kyoto and Tohoku Imperial Universities in those days, details of which were carried in *Eigo-Seinen* (*The Rising Generation*), a literary magazine on English literature started in 1898. According to volume thirty-three (1898), of all the graduate theses to be submitted at Tokyo Imperial University in 1898, four out of twenty-three were on Wordsworth and Keats, one on Coleridge, Cowper and Scott; in 1906 (volume thirty five), of all twenty-three graduate students, six chose Romantics for their theses. In 1930 (volume sixty-three), at Kyoto Imperial University, among twenty-seven graduate theses, three were on Shelley, two on Wordsworth, and one on James Thomson. In the same year, at Tohoku Imperial University, two of seven graduates chose the Romantics for their theses.

It should also be noted here that Francis Turner Palgrave's *The Golden Treasury of English Songs and Lyrics* (1861), known for its partiality for Romantic poets rather than earlier generations of poets, was used for the standard textbook in the Imperial Universities, until at least the 1970s.[2]

The reaction against Romanticism that has emerged over the past twenty years is not the result of modernist or post-modernist aesthetics or new historicist critique, but comes from a challenge to the validity of the discipline of literary studies as a whole. The fact that must be faced now as a fait accompli is that a large number of "departments of English" are gone. In some national universities (especially ex-Imperial Universities), however, they still carry on teaching English Literature on a small scale, whereas in some private universities, "English" is divided into "Culture" (as in "British Culture," "European Culture" or "Comparative Culture"), and "English Literature." Students in Japan as in other parts of the world nowadays seem to prefer "culture" to "literature." The big problem, therefore, is how to get as many students as possible interested in English Literature, before even beginning to consider specializing in the Romantic period. Decreasing numbers are working on the Romantics for their graduate theses.

The number of students who major in English has been drastically reduced, and even these are less concerned with reading books than with viewing films or pictures; they do not necessarily have a strong inclination to enjoy any particular Romantic author, so intensive or close reading of any particular text (poem, novel, play or whatever genre) is difficult to do in the classroom. And the traditional format of lectures, unless they are dealing with contemporary or trendy issues like ecology or visual arts, or unless they are perceived as overstepping the bounds of old academic fields, is unlikely to be welcomed by students. At Kyoto University, for example, "Modern European Culture and Its Representation" is taught through ninety-minute lectures which focus on the microscope and its cultural impact and critical heritage in England. A detailed syllabus of the course (a series of thirteen to fifteen lectures in one semester) with the (tentative) title of each lecture is given beforehand, and printed materials (handouts) are distributed each time. The success (or otherwise) of the class can usually be gauged from the enthusiasm students show during a brief discussion or questions and answers done at the end of the lecture. The strength of this approach is that it combines literary and cultural contexts with the history of science and development of a wider spectrum of interpretative communities.

Larger period anthologies such as the Norton or Duncan Wu's Blackwell collections are of limited use in a Japanese context, not only for reasons of simple length, and assumptions of cultural familiarity but also for their deeply-ingrained models of implied teleology. It is much more convenient for the individual *sensei* to select and circulate short texts for intensive study over the customary thirteen to fifteen week semester. The immediate problem, if teaching in English, is how to structure the customary ninety to 100 minute duration of classes. There are a range of options to break this up, including visual materials, student presentations and class discussion. Rather than strive for comprehensive coverage, sharp and restrictive focus tends to generate a more positive response, while also facilitating interdisciplinary and cross-cultural juxtapositions. At undergraduate level, it is often preferable to approach Romantic texts as part of a more widely-ranging thematic focus such as gender and poetry, nation and empire, or introduction to narrative theory. Representative topics at graduate level, for example, would be a comparative study of Wordsworth and the Chinese poet Li Po (701–62), or cinematic narratology in recent dramatizations of Austen. Reading speeds are undeniably slower, but there is also a Confucian-derived tradition of close and thorough exegesis, which is eminently compatible with New Critical and deconstructive modes of close analysis. What Japanese students know, they usually know well.

For example, at Kyoto University, a post-graduate course offers "An Intensive Reading of Romantic Poems" over a thirteen to fifteen-week semester. This is a class designed to give practice in the understanding and discussion of Romantic poetry. In 2008, for example, Byron's *The Vision of Judgment*, was particularly chosen for the class (the selection is usually made by teachers but sometimes by students) because it will help students to gain more knowledge of the nuanced relation between politics and satire in the Romantic period. Individual students are allotted several stanzas of the poem for each class; they are required to consult the *OED* very closely before the class, to give grammatical explanations of each word or phrase and detailed interpretations of the poem, and finally to translate it into Japanese. To translate the poem into Japanese is mandatory because it is one of the most useful ways for us to know whether they understand it. Some parts of the poem are very difficult to render into Japanese, so what is asked of them is a literal, not literary, translation. Past and present criticisms on the poem and its historical background are also discussed from time to time during the class. To develop an appreciation of the poem and to give a good presentation in the class, students should expect to delve more deeply into the tradition of satire and the social, political and religious contexts of the poem.

Several study groups of Romantic Literature of about ten to thirty membership are scattered throughout Japan from Hokkaido, the northern part of Japan to Kyushu and Okinawa, the southern part of Japan, and each has its own long tradition. They hold regular meetings a few times a year, and pursue and discuss "hot" Romantic issues. Many of the younger scholars (newcomers) have jobs concentrating on English language teaching rather than their academic specialisms, but they are committed to injecting much-needed vitality into their groups.

The Japan Association of English Romanticism was founded in 1975; it is one of the largest literary societies in Japan with a membership of about 400, and so comparable in scale to that of the British Association of Romantic Studies (BARS). JAER holds a two-day conference in autumn every year, which is a very good occasion for students of Romantic literature to get to know each other and to gain incentive and inspiration from presentations. Younger academics of JAER are much more likely to have studied abroad and continue to be international in focus and keen on establishing connections with overseas universities.

By way of conclusion it would be no exaggeration to say that Romantic studies in Japan is doing as well as or perhaps even better than other literary periods. Recent priorities, however, have stressed English language teaching at the expense of more traditional literary scholarship; from the point of view of most university administrations, the preferred area of research interests is in fact TEFL (TESL), applied linguistics, or related areas. Minami Ryuta notes "the ways in which literature has been removed from English classrooms in Japanese secondary education" (146) over the past decade, with the predictable knock-on effect of far fewer students choosing to specialize in the subject at degree level. It is crucial for the future of Romantic studies that literary texts should remain central materials for teaching English as a second language in Japan, but here, as elsewhere, scholars whose qualifications were gained through intensive academic study must adapt their pedagogic techniques to new circumstances.

III

Considering the present and future condition of Romantic studies in Japan, one might begin by querying the validity of the traditional British division between language and literature teaching; being a professional teacher in Japan inevitably involves acquiring at least minimal competence in the former, before such issues as best practice in the teaching of Romanticism can be embarked upon. As Saito Yoshifumi remarks, both Japanese and foreign "scholar teachers [who] identify more closely with their specialisation than with their profession" (195) should break the habit of thinking of themselves as "specialists disguised as humble English teachers" (198). From a bureaucratic viewpoint, the initial question to be posed would be whether teaching any kind of literature at all distracts from more quantifiable goals and outcomes. The latter position is that adopted by the somewhat Orwellian-sounding MEXT (Ministry of Education, Culture, Sports, Science and Technology) in their action plan to cultivate "Japanese with English abilities" (MEXT 2003).

A few general points may be helpful. In Japan the study of foreign literature is inevitably subsequent to initial language training, although traditionally textbooks have used it as a resource. With recent changes, there has been a reversion to a more overtly utilitarian model of pragmatic use: the cultural capital invested in familiarity with the literary canon of a foreign culture has sharply diminished. More generally, studies of how English literature has functioned in a colonial context in India and elsewhere have amply demonstrated its complicity, if not taintedness, as a commodity: to be handled with care, if at all. As Miyoshi Masao puts it, whenever European or American culture is imported, "There is only the old acceptance of the authority of the West – even when a Western critic questions the authority of the West" (Miyoshi 1993: 285).

Japanese students usually possess impressive formal grammatical knowledge; perhaps to be expected given the generally-acknowledged excellence of teaching of mathematics and science. There has been much less emphasis on oral performance, partly a result of larger classes in school, allowing little if any question-answer dialogue, but also because of the nature of the minutely-defined syllabus, where listening-speaking skills have traditionally been subordinated to exercises in formal comprehension. So English literature of any kind will be encountered relatively late, usually with extremely variable degrees of supporting context. At Tokyo University, students do an eclectic range of area studies for years one to two based on the North American system of self-contained modules; then choose a specialization for years three to four. They will have limited chronological or sequential grasp of literary periodization, but this has also become increasingly true in British higher education, with the increasing appeal of cultural studies courses of various kinds siphoning off a considerable percentage of the potential student base.

The split between research interests and pedagogic practice in Japan is far more pronounced than in British universities; the core teaching of most academics remains in the general area of language and culture rather than specifically literature, let alone concentration on a single period such as Romanticism. (Though even in Britain one is unlikely often to teach one's research specialism; arguably it is not even desirable to.) As Yoshihara Yukari insists, there is a "structural problem" of academics with "backgrounds in English linguistics or literature" being "pressured to teach practical English without using English literature or theories of linguistics" (10).

With regard to academic career trajectories, the previously dominant pattern would have been to study for an MA over two to three years, which would have been sufficient to get a job, particularly for graduates at the major universities. With the inexorable demographic decrease in the overall numbers of students and economic problems over the last ten to fifteen years, the competitiveness of the job market means graduates are expected at the very least to have studied for a period abroad, preferably completing a doctorate (although there is now increasing pressure from MEXT to produce greater numbers of home-grown PhDs). It should be noted, however, that this places younger Japanese academics in a position of strength with regard to their Anglophone counterparts, because of their comparatively full assimilation of the European tradition (often in multiple languages) whereas Western critics will almost certainly have little (if any) familiarity with the Japanese or Asian contexts. (How many will have even passing acquaintance with the work of a Nobel laureate such as Oe Kenzaburo (awarded

1994), whose writing continuously refers to and adapts Blake, particularly in the magnificent *O Rouse up Young Men of the New Age* (1983; trans. 2002)?)

Characterizations of Japan as a culture of simulation and depthlessness are familiar enough, engaging in an eclectic pick-and-mix of cultural products from the global supermarket, with little or no concern for origin or genealogy. Post-Meiji Restoration, there is undeniably a disconcerting simultaneity to various forms of cultural reception: romantic art, literature and philosophy are assimilated alongside *fin de siècle* and modernist modes, Blake imported beside van Gogh. Yet there is also a striking global synchronicity: as Ian Buruma points out, Dada cafés opened in Tokyo almost simultaneously with their European counterparts in Berlin, Zurich and Paris (Buruma 2003).

Larger-scale narratives based on European culture therefore have no necessary relevance in a Japanese context: there is no inevitable developmental sequence of Enlightenment, Romanticism, Modernism. (Similarly in China, *The Prelude* was first translated less than 10 years ago, and hence has been received as a post-post-modernist text.) The "Big Six" poets of the traditional Romantic canon are a purely retrospective construct (as St Clair amply demonstrates in *Reading Nation*), Scott and Byron were the only figures of European prominence, and in the home market Campbell and Moore were hugely more influential poets in their time than Wordsworth, Keats or Shelley. One might make the case that in terms of simple availability, Blake's prophecies as much as Smart's *Jubilate Agno* should be read as texts of the modern period.

Any parallels discerned between Japanese culture and European Romanticism are likely to be deceptive. A psychologically-complex and temporally-extended female-authored novel (Murasaki Shikibu's *Tale of Genji, c.*1008) occupies the position of first classic text (a bit like having Proust in the position of Homer). Writers such as Matsuo Basho (1644–94), who appear to celebrate nature in a manner compatible with European conventions are underpinned by different aesthetic-political conventions (exclusion from court; complex intertextual relations with classical Chinese texts). Shinto may seem broadly compatible with various strands of European idealist philosophy, but serves primarily as a popular religious cult with few (if any) consistent tenets, rather than the product of a systematic aesthetics.

Indirect mercantile contacts between Europe and Japan date back to the Silk Road; the Portuguese arrived in 1543; the Englishman William Adams visited in 1600 and served as translator and envoy. In 1636, however, Europeans were driven out (with the exception of small Dutch enclave in Nagasaki) through the policy of *sakoku*, instituted because Christianity was seen as potentially subversive. Japan makes a curtain call in *Gulliver's Travels*, where the country is seen as fabulously mythical as Brobdingnag; and subsequently crops up in a few extremely scattered references to "bright Japan" (Blake, *Jerusalem* 24: 47). The relationship between Japanese culture and European Romanticism is a retrospective construct, inevitably mediated by the mid/late nineteenth-century vogue for *Japonisme* in both European high art and popular consumer culture.

With regard to the future of Romantic period studies in Japan, one might close with both general and localized points. Creative translation, whether of literary texts or academic approaches, need not necessarily imply secondary and inferior imitation. From an Italian perspective, Chaucer is the translator of Boccaccio, Wyatt of Petrarch; and from a German one, perhaps now Coleridge of Goethe with the newly authenticated version of *Faustus*. There is no point of seeking to return to an originary meaning, even if it were possible. In a Japanese context, Romanticism (like Enlightenment) is likely to mean / include modernity within itself, having been imported both as a means of definition of Meiji modernization and a critical reaction to that process. The open, and perhaps unresolvable, question remains of whether Japanese study of European Romanticism is better regarded as teleologically derived from the European tradition, or as a completely different phenomenon that must be understood on its own culturally specific terms.

On the level of pedagogic practice, in Japan there is no equivalent to the Arnoldian-Leavisite tradition of moral transformation, whereby Romanticism is seen as a resource towards individual emancipation (though in Continental Europe its inheritance might equally plausibly regarded as one of reaction). As recent studies of canon-formation and national identity have amply demonstrated, Romanticism undeniably moves back before going forward; in a Japanese context, however, the move over the past twenty years to political-historical interrogation of Romanticism as an ideological concept becomes secondary, if not specious. An initial case must be made for studying literary texts at all, before initiating any counter-movement of demystification of the traditional Romantic canon. In Japan, romanticism necessarily means something different, whether for better or for worse: the form which that difference is likely to assume over the coming decades remains open to continuous negotiation and debate.

Notes

1. Teaching staff at Tokyo Imperial University in the 1930s also included Ichikawa Sanki, a philologist, Saito Takeshi and Sawamura Torajiro, and William Empson, then known primarily as a poet, who was a lecturer at Tokyo Bunri Daigaku (Tokyo College of Literature and Science) in Japan from 1931–4.
2. The lecture list at the department of English in Kyoto Imperial University in 1933 shows that *The Golden Treasury* was still used. See volume 69 of *The Rising Generation*, 1933: 31.

Works Cited

Araki, Masazumi, Lim Chee Seng, Ryuta Minami and Yukari Yoshihara, eds. (2007) *English Studies in Asia* (Kuala Lumpa: Silverfish Books).

Buruma, Ian (2003) *Inventing Japan 1853–1964* (New York: Modern Library Chronicles).

Coleridge, Samuel Taylor (2007) *Faustus: From The German of Goethe*, ed. Frederick Burwick and James C. McCusick (Oxford: Oxford University Press).

Doi, Kochi (1977) *Doi Kochi Chosaku Shu* [*The Selected Works of Kochi Doi*], 5 vols. (Tokyo: Iwanami-Shoten).

Eigo-Seinen [*The Rising Generation*].

Ferguson, Will (1998) *Hokkaido Highway Blues: Hitchhiking Japan* (New York: Soho Press).

Hughes, George (2002) *Hearn no wadachi no naka de* (Kenkyusha: Tokyo).

Kerr, Alex (2001) *Dogs and Demons: Tales from the Dark Side of Japan* (New York: Hill and Wang).

Kuriyagawa, Hakuson (1929) *Bungaku-Ron* [*Essays on Literature*], Vol. 2, in *Kuriyagawa Hakuson Zenshu* [*The Collected Works of Hakuson Kuriyagawa*], 6 vols. (Tokyo: Kaizo-sha).

May, Simon (2006) *Atomic Sushi* (Alma Books: Richmond).

MEXT, Ministry of Education, Culture, Sports, Science and Technology (2003) "Japanese with English abilities", www.mext.go.jp/english/topics/03072801.htm.

Minami, Ryuta (2007) "No Literature Please, We're Japanese" in Araki et al., pp. 145–65.

Miyoshi, Masao (1993) "The Invention of English Literature in Japan," in *Japan in the World*, ed. Masao Miyoshi and H. D. Harootunian (Atlanta: Duke University Press): 271–87.

Natsume, Soseki (1975) *Bungaku-Hyoron* [*Literary Essays*], Vol. 10, in *The Collected Works of Soseki Natsume*, 17 vols. (Tokyo: Iwanami-shoten).

Oe, Kenzuburo (1983; trans. 2002) *O Rouse Up Young Men of the New Age* (London: Atlantic Books).

Oishi, Kaz, "Introduction to English Romanticism", Open University of Japan, www.campus.u-air.ac.jp/gaikokugo/romanticism/index.html.

Saito, Takeshi (1975–77) *Saito Takeshi Chosaku Shu* [*The Selected Works of Takeshi Saito*], 8 vols. (Tokyo: Kenku-sha).

Saito, Yoshifumi (2007) "English Studies at the Crossroads in Japan" in Araki et al., pp. 191–8.

Shincho Dictionary of Japanese Literature (1996) (Tokyo: Shincho-sha).

St Clair, William (2004) *The Reading Nation in the Romantic Period* (Cambridge: Cambridge University Press).

Suzuki, Zenzo (1970) "Soseki's View of Pope," *Bungei-Kenkyu* [*Studies in Literaturwissenschaft*] (Tohoku University), 65: 34–43.

—— (2007) "tempora mutantur, nos et mutamur in illis," *Annual Bulletin of the Johnson Society*, 31: 4–6.

Ueda, Bin (1978–81) *Teihon Ueda Bin Zenshu* [*The Complete Works of Bin Ueda*], 10 vols. (Tokyo: Kyoiku-Shuppan Centre).

Yoshihara, Yukari (2007) "The Past, the Present and the Future of the Project, 'English Studies in Asia,' " in Araki et al., pp. 9–23

Guide to Further Reading

Approaches to teaching

Approaches to Teaching World Literature
This MLA series contains a number of volumes that address Romantic-period texts and authors, including Austen, Blake, Byron, Coleridge, *Faust, Frankenstein*, Keats, Rousseau, Percy Bysshe Shelley, women poets, and Wordsworth.

Romantic Circles
http://www.rc.umd.edu/
The excellent *Romantic Circles* website has a section devoted to "Pedagogies," edited by Ron Broglio, Laura Mandell, and Tilar Mazzeo. This includes a new peer-reviewed online journal, *Romantic Pedagogy Commons*, which is dedicated to teaching.

Powell, Anna and Andrew Smith, eds. (2006) *Teaching the Gothic*, Teaching the New English Series (Basingstoke: Palgrave Macmillan).

General anthologies

Black, Joseph, et al., eds. (2006) *The Broadview Anthology of British Literature: Age of Romanticism* (Ontario: Broadview)

Damrosch, David, Susan Wolfson and Peter Manning, eds. (2006) *The Longman Anthology of British Literature: the Romantics and Their Contemporaries*, 3rd edn. (New York: Longman)

McGann, Jerome, ed. (1993) *The New Oxford Book of Romantic Period Verse* (Oxford and New York: Oxford University Press)

Mellor, Anne and Richard Matlak, eds. (1996) *British Literature: 1780–1830* (Fort Worth: Harcourt Brace)

O'Neill, Michael and Charles Mahoney, eds. (2007) *Romantic Poetry: an Annotated Anthology* (Oxford: Blackwell)

Stillinger, Jack and Deidre Lynch, eds. (2006) *The Norton Anthology of English Literature: the Romantic Period*, 8th edn. (New York: W. W. Norton)

Wordsworth, J. and J., eds. (2005) *New Penguin Book of Romantic Poetry* (Harmondsworth: Penguin)

Wu, Duncan, ed. (2005) *Romanticism: an Anthology*, 3rd edn. (Oxford: Blackwell)

Specialized anthologies

Ashfield, Andrew, ed. (1995) *Romantic Women Poets 1770–1838: an Anthology* (Manchester: Manchester University Press)

Baines, Paul and Edward Burns, eds. (2000) *Five Romantic Plays, 1768–1821* (Oxford: Oxford University Press)

Bohls, Elizabeth A. and Ian Duncan, eds. (2005) *Travel Writing 1700–1830* (Oxford: Oxford University Press)
Breen, Jennifer, ed. (1992) *Women Romantic Poets 1785–1832: an Anthology* (London: Dent)
—— ed. (1996) *Women Romantics, 1785–1832: Writing in Prose* (London: Dent)
Butler, Marilyn (1984) *Burke, Paine, Godwin, and the Revolution Controversy* (Cambridge: Cambridge University Press)
Cox, Jeffrey and Michael Gamer, eds. (2003) *Broadview Anthology of Romantic Drama* (Ontario: Broadview)
Ferber, Michael (ed.) (2005) *European Romantic Poetry* (New York: Pearson Longman)
Hampsher-Monk, Iain, ed. (2005) *The Impact of the French Revolution* (Cambridge: Cambridge University Press)
Jones, Vivien (1990) *Women in the Eighteenth Century: Constructions of Femininity* (London and New York: Routledge)
Jump, Harriet Devine, ed. (1997) *Women's Writing of the Romantic Period 1789–1836: an Anthology* (Edinburgh: Edinburgh University Press)
Keen, Paul, ed. (2004) *Revolutions in Romantic Literature: an Anthology of Print Culture, 1780–1832* (Ontario: Broadview)
Leader, Zachary and Ian Haywood, eds. (1998) *Romantic Period Writings, 1798–1832: an Anthology* (London: Routledge)
Newman, Lance, et al., eds. (2006) *Transatlantic Romanticism: an Anthology of British, American, and Canadian Literature, 1767–1867* (New York: Pearson)
Nichols, Ashton, ed. (2003) *Romantic Natural Histories* (Boston: Houghton Mifflin)
Scrivener, Michael, ed. (1992) *Poetry and Reform: Periodical Verse from the English Democratic Press, 1792–1824* (Wayne State University Press)
Weber, A. S., ed. (1999) *Nineteenth-Century Science* (Ontario: Broadview)
Wright, Julia, ed., (2008) *Irish Literature 1750–1900: an Anthology* (Oxford: Blackwell)
Wu, Duncan, ed. (1998) *Romantic Women Poets: an Anthology* (Oxford: Blackwell)

Student guides

Chantler, Ashley and David Higgins, eds. (2009) *Studying English Literature* (London: Continuum)
Day, Aidan (1995) *Romanticism*, New Critical Idiom Series (London and New York: Routledge)
Everest, Kelvin (1990) *English Romantic Poetry: an Introduction to the Literary Scene* (Milton Keynes: Open University Press)
Furniss, Tom and Michael Bath (1996) *Reading Poetry: an Introduction* (Harlow: Longman)
Heath, Duncan (2005) *Introducing Romanticism* (Cambridge: Icon Books)
Jarvis, Robin (2004) *The Romantic Period: the Intellectual and Cultural Context of English Literature, 1789–1830* (Harlow: Longman)
O'Flynn, Paul (2000) *How to Study Romantic Poetry* (Basingstoke: Palgrave – now Palgrave Macmillan)
Ruston, Sharon (2007) *Romanticism* (London: Continuum)

Stabler, Jane (2002) *From Burke to Byron, Barbauld to Baillie, 1790–1830* (Basingstoke: Palgrave Macmillan)

Companions and readers

Bainbridge, Simon, ed. (2007) *Romanticism: a Sourcebook* (Basingstoke: Palgrave Macmillan)

Breckman, Warren, ed. (2008) *European Romanticism: a Brief History with Documents* (Boston and New York: Bedford / St. Martin's – now Palgrave Macmillan)

Chandler, James and Maureen N. McLane, eds. (2008) *The Cambridge Companion to British Romantic Poetry* (Cambridge: Cambridge University Press)

Clery, Emma and Robert Miles, eds. (2000) *Gothic Documents: a Sourcebook, 1700–1820* (Manchester: Manchester University Press)

Curran, Stuart, ed. (1993) *The Cambridge Companion to British Romanticism* (Cambridge: Cambridge University Press)

Ferber, Michael, ed. (2005) *A Companion to European Romanticism* (Oxford: Blackwell)

Keymer, Thomas and Jon Mee, eds. (2004) *The Cambridge Companion to English Literature 1740-1830* (Cambridge: Cambridge University Press)

McCalman, Iain, ed. (2001) *An Oxford Companion to the Romantic Age* (Oxford: Oxford University Press)

Maxwell, Richard and Katie Trumpener, eds. (2008) *The Cambridge Companion to Fiction in the Romantic Period* (Cambridge: Cambridge University Press)

Porter, Roy and Mikuláş Teich, eds. (1988) *Romanticism in National Context* (Cambridge: Cambridge University Press)

Punter, David, ed. (2000) *The Blackwell Companion to the Gothic* (Oxford: Blackwell)

Roe, Nicholas, ed. (2005) *Romanticism: an Oxford Guide* (Oxford: Oxford University Press)

Wu, Duncan, ed. (1999) *A Companion to Romanticism*, 2nd edn. (Oxford: Blackwell)

Major studies

Abrams, M. H. (1953) *The Mirror and the Lamp: Romantic Theory and the Critical Tradition* (Oxford: Oxford University Press)

——. (1971) *Natural Supernaturalism* (New York: Norton)

Bewell, Alan (2000) *Romanticism and Colonial Disease* (Baltimore: Johns Hopkins University Press)

Butler, Marilyn (1981) *Romantics, Rebels, and Reactionaries: English Literature and its Background, 1760–1830*, repr. edn. (Oxford: Opus)

Chandler, James (1998) *England in 1819: the Politics of Literary Culture and the Case of Romantic Historicism* (Chicago: Chicago University Press)

Cronin, Richard (2000) *The Politics of Romantic Poetry: In Search of the Pure Commonwealth* (Basingstoke: Palgrave – now Palgrave Macmillan)

Curran, Stuart (1986) *Poetic Form and British Romanticism* (New York: Oxford University Press)

Kelly, Gary (1989) *English Fiction of the Romantic Period, 1789–1830* (Harlow: Longman)

Kitson, Peter J. (2007) *Romantic Literature, Race, and Colonial Encounter* (Basingstoke: Palgrave Macmillan)

Leask, Nigel (2008) *British Romantic Writers and the East: Anxieties of Empire*, 2nd edn. (Cambridge: Cambridge University Press)

McGann, Jerome (1983) *The Romantic Ideology: a Critical Investigation* (Chicago: Chicago University Press)

Mellor, Anne K. (1993) *Romanticism and Gender* (London: Routledge)

Newlyn, Lucy (2000) *Reading, Writing, and Romanticism: the Anxiety of Reception* (Oxford: Oxford University Press)

Ross, Marlon B. (1989) *The Contours of Masculine Desire: Romanticism and the Rise of Women's Poetry* (New York: Oxford University Press)

Thompson, E. P. (2002) *The Making of the English Working Class*, new edn. (Harmondsworth: Penguin)

Wolfson, Susan (1999) *Formal Charges: the Shaping of Poetry in British Romanticism* (California: Stanford University Press)

Web resources

The Age of George III
http://www.historyhome.co.uk/
Gives information on the period of King George III's reign (1760–1820), including the ministries that ran the country, events in Ireland and America, India, France and Britain.

The Bluestocking Archive
http://www.faculty.umb.edu/elizabeth_fay/archive2.html
Maintained by Elizabeth Fay, this website contains works by and about the Bluestockings.

C19: The Nineteenth-Century Index
http://c19index.chadwyck.com/marketing/index.jsp
This subscription database is an invaluable bibliographical source for teaching and research in the nineteenth century.

The Corvey Project
http://www.shu.ac.uk/schools/cs/corvey/
Hosted by Sheffield Hallam University, which has a microfiche collection of rare and unique works from the Corvey library in Germany. The website contains a searchable database, *Corvey Women Writers on the Web: an Electronic Guide to Literature, 1796–1834* and also publishes the journal *CW*^{3}.

Dictionary of Sensibility
http://www.engl.virginia.edu/enec981/dictionary/intro.html
The list of terms associated with sensibility on this website is particularly useful.

A Digital Resource for the Act of Union (1800)
http://www.actofunion.ac.uk/

A virtual Library with a searchable collection of pamphlets, newspapers, parliamentary papers and manuscript material contemporary with the 1800 Act of Union between Ireland and Britain.

Eighteenth-Century Collections Online
http://www.gale.com/EighteenthCentury/
A digitization project that your library may have subscribed to, which claims to have digitized "every significant English-language and foreign-language title printed in Great Britain during the eighteenth century." While there definitely are omissions this is an incredible resource, making many rare books, pamphlets, plays and collections of poems available online.

Literature Compass
http://www.literature-compass.com
If your library subscribes to this journal, you will be able to read the articles published in the Romanticism section, currently edited by Elizabeth Fay and Sue Chaplin. If not, you are able to pay to view single articles.

Literature Encyclopaedia
http://www.litencyc.com/index.php
Articles written on primary texts, critical accounts and authors. The Romantic period is well served with some good, short introductions to works.

Romantic Chronology
http://english.ucsb.edu:591/rchrono/
A densely detailed chronology of the period.

Romanticism and Victorianism on the Net
http://www.ron.umontreal.ca/
An refereed electronic journal devoted to British Nineteenth-Century Literature. The journal, which began publication as *Romanticism on the Net* in February 1996, is published four times a year. It expanded its scope in August 2007 to include Victorian literature.

Romantic Textualities
http://www.cf.ac.uk/encap/romtext/
A journal previously called *Cardiff Corvey: Reading the Romantic Text* (1997–2005). Over the years, the journal's activities have extended to include surveys of Romantic-era print culture made by the international scholarly community.

Index